Object-Oriented I/O Using C++ IOSTREAMS

CAMERON HUGHES
THOMAS HAMILTON
TRACEY HUGHES

John Wiley & Sons, Inc.

New York • *Chichester* • *Brisbane* • *Toronto* • *Singapore*

Publisher: *Katherine Schowalter*
Editor: *Tim Ryan*
Managing Editor: *Robert S. Aronds*
Text Design & Composition: *North Market Street Graphics, Dave Erb*

Designations used by companies to distinguish their products are often claimed as trademarks. In all instances where John Wiley & Sons, Inc. is aware of a claim, the product names appear in initial capital or all capital letters. Readers, however, should contact the appropriate companies for more complete information regarding trademarks and registration.

This text is printed on acid-free paper.

This publication is designed to provide accurate and authoritative information in regard to the subject matter covered. It is sold with the understanding that the publisher is not engaged in rendering legal, accounting, or other professional service. If legal advice or other expert assistance is required, the services of a competent professional person should be sought.

Library of Congress Cataloging-in-Publication Data:

Hughes, Cameron, 1960–
    Object-oriented I/O using C++ IOSTREAMS / Cameron Hughes, Thomas
Hamilton, Tracey Hughes.
        p.   cm.
    Includes index.
    ISBN 0-471-11809-5 (paper : acid-free paper)
    1. Object-oriented programming (Computer science)   2. C++
(Computer program language)   3. Computer input-output equipment.
I. Hamilton, Thomas.   II. Hughes, Tracey.   III. Title.
QA76.64.H84   1995
005.7'11—dc20   95-933
                                                                CIP

Printed in the United States of America
10 9 8 7 6 5 4 3 2 1

This book is dedicated to Lael, Cherub, and Rahamel,
and all those who participate in our annual science fair.

Contents

Chapter 3   *The IOSTREAM Class Hierarchy*

Preface

Writing I/O routines and programming I/O devices represent a substantial chunk of any programmer's time. I/O processing plays an important role in virtually all software. Without I/O devices and the routines that drive them, the computer would be of very little use—if any at all. Because I/O programming is a fundamental requirement for most programs large or small, it makes sense to aim for efficiency, reusability, and appropriateness.

The routines and programs must be efficient. Some system performance is measured solely by I/O performance. With today's emphasis on networks, GUIs, and I/O-intensive multimedia applications, efficiency is a basic requirement. The I/O routines should be reusable. The cost of software development demands reusable components. The pace in which new technology is introduced will simply not allow the programmer to constantly reinvent the wheel. In general, once I/O functionality has been tested and debugged, it should find its way into a library, where, if designed properly, it will be used over. Finally, I/O programming must be appropriate for the devices and data involved. For example, using buffered techniques can increase efficiency with some devices, and bring processing to a halt with others. Techniques for panning on a VGA graphics adapter may not translate when programming the IBM 8514.

Object-oriented programming using C++ IOSTREAMS, as the title of this book suggests, focuses primarily on two things:

- *Object-oriented input/output programming techniques*
- *C++ IOSTREAMS*

When C++ IOSTREAMS are used in conjunction with object-oriented programming techniques, the goals of efficiency, reusability, and appropriateness are readily achieved. The reader is expected to have a fundamental understanding of the C++ language and basic programming techniques. No previous understanding of C++ IOSTREAMS is assumed.

This book brings I/O programming into the world of *object orientation*. We endeavor to include the systems programmer's paradigm as well as the application programmer's paradigm. We explore a wide spectrum of I/O devices and techniques from communication port programming to device contexts and presentation spaces.

We introduce the *object-oriented stream* as more than just a programming convenience. We expose the fundamental workings of the IOSTREAM family of classes. The examples in this book have all been tested. We show examples of the IOSTREAM classes in the Windows and OS/2 environments. We give hints on how the IOSTREAM classes can be connected to the new multimedia operating systems. Most of the examples in Chapters 1 through 6 can run in any environment, with only minor modification needed. We have worked to stay as close to the latest ANSI C++ draft as possible. Where the ANSI draft was not clear, we sided with an intersection of the most popular implementations of the IOSTREAM classses.

C++ is an evolution of the C language, which adds object-oriented capability to C's rich, expressive power. The IOSTREAM classes are an evolution of the standard stream concept, which also add object capabilities to standard I/O library. The IOSTREAMS can be extended and specialized to encapsulate the new multimedia streams. We hope that this book will remedy the remarkable absence of material on such a vital aspect of C++ programming.

We would also like to say that we make no warranties that the programs contained in this book are free of error, or are consistent with any particular standard of merchantability, or that they will meet your requirement for any particular application. They should not be relied on for solving a problem whose incorrect solution could result in injury to a person or loss of property. The authors and publishers disclaim all liability for direct or consequential damages resulting from your use of the programs.

Acknowledgments

We would like to give special thanks to Carol, and Belinda, our book agents, Bernard David, Tim Ryan and Bob Aronds.

CHAPTER 1

Introduction: History and Concept of Streams

As our mental eye penetrates into smaller and smaller distances and shorter and shorter times, we find nature behaving so entirely differently from what we observe in visible and palpable bodies of our surrounding that no model shaped after our large scale experiences can ever be "true."

ERWIN SHRODINGER—*CAUSALITY AND WAVE MECHANICS*

Most good ideas in the computer industry are the result of gradual evolution; they are born through the efforts and insights of many individuals and organizations. The concept of *streams* is no exception. The *Input/Output Stream* is a collection of routines, data structures, and techniques that allow the programmer to address input/output in an efficient and generic fashion.

The stream concept has been a long time in the making. The seeds for its beginning can be seen in the advancements made in the evolution from second-generation languages; for example, assembly language, to third-generation languages, such as FORTRAN, COBOL, BASIC, C, and Pascal. Third-generation languages have made genuine attempts to have a simple set of generic commands or functions deal with all I/O devices connected to a system (Figure 1.1). For instance, in the Pascal language, **write(Filename,Output)** may send output to a console, printer, or mass storage file. This contrasts to the techniques used in assembly language to address I/O. To send output to the console, printer, or mass storage device, the second-generation assembly programmer needs to know port addresses, interleave information, memory configurations, interrupt locations, and hardware device names with an entire entourage of byte-swapping, data-conversion, and rapid memory-transfer techniques.

1

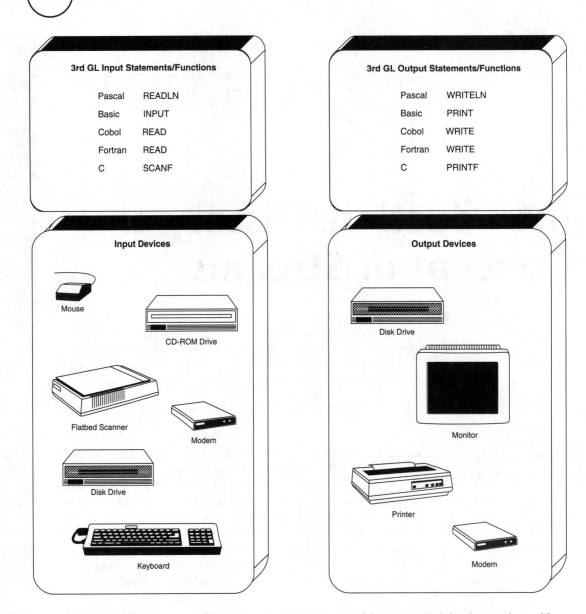

Figure 1.1   *Third-generation input and output statements and functions, and the devices they address.*

The stream concept took another large step forward during the advancement of operating systems from second generation to fourth generation. From the gains made in the design of IBM's DOS/VSE operating system that included LIOCS (Logical I/O Control System), to the pipe, filter, and text-translation concepts that were ultimately included in the UNIX operating system, the concept of the data stream and I/O Stream was born.

In industry, the C language, standard C library I/O routines, and the UNIX operating system implement the most visible application of the stream concept of input and output. UNIX was developed at Bell Laboratories in the 1970s largely through the efforts of Ken Thompson and Dennis Ritchie. The C and C++ languages were also developed at Bell Laboratories. Both languages were ultimately designed to run in the UNIX environment. Streams and the UNIX operating system philosophies are tightly coupled. The idea that all I/O should be to and from files, and that even devices are special kinds of files, is a major theme in the UNIX environment.

The concept of streams is closely tied to the notion of *device independence*. When a program or a routine is device-independent, the program or routine can run with little or no modification if there is a change in the device or the devices that the program or routine accesses. For example, if a routine has been designed to send output to the console and it is later decided that the output should go to a printer, the programming logic behind a device-independent routine will not have to be modified to accomplish the latter.

With device-independence, the programmer is not concerned with the details of the particular device that is accessed. Device-independence has been heralded as the ultimate goal in program portability and program reusability. Table 1.1 contrasts the concept of device-independence with device-dependence. We will discuss device-independence in more detail later. For now, let it suffice to say that where I/O is concerned, the closer we move to programs that are device-independent, the closer we move to the concept of streams.

Using the concept of streams, the programmer sees data coming into a system or data going out of a system as a stream of bytes. Ideally, this stream is not seen as coming from or going to any particular device. Rather, it is seen as a stream coming and going to a generic device that is capable of receiving or sending bytes (Figure 1.2). Although the generic I/O data stream is a powerful programming concept, it is not always the most efficient for a given job. However, no modern I/O library can be considered complete unless it supports the concept of streams.

Table 1.1   Contrast of Device-Independence and Device-Dependence Concepts

Device Dependence	*Device Independence*
Specific hardware	Portable across classes of hardware
Specific address	Uses handles and indirection
Expect specific resolutions	Can scale resolutions
Specific knowledge of underlying structure of hardware components	Access hardware high-level system API's
Program code tied to specific device names	Program code tied to IOSTREAMS

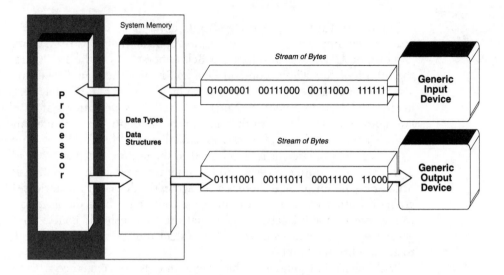

Figure 1.2   *Generic sequence of bytes going into or coming from input and output devices connected to a computer.*

Standard C IOSTREAMS

There are at least four good reasons for the C++ programmer to be proficient with the C **stdio** library:

1. Many C++ programs will coexist with C programs. The C programs will necessarily make calls to **stdio**.
2. There are many C libraries with tested and debugged code that can be linked into a C++ application.
3. There will be C I/O routines that must be converted to C++ IOSTREAMS.
4. The **stdio** library is a subset of C++ I/O capabilities.[1]

The C++ IOSTREAMS can work in conjunction with C **stdio** functions. The primary I/O functions in the C standard library are declared in the header file **stdio.h**. The implementation of these functions can be found in the C standard library. The **stdio** functions make up almost one-third of the standard C library. The following section presents a brief overview of the basic components of the C **stdio** library.

stdio Data Structures and Header Files

The **FILE** structure, or object, should be treated as a black box. Its internal structure normally contains a file descriptor and buffering information. **EOF** is a negative integral constant expression that is returned by several functions to indicate either an error has occurred, or the end of the file.

The global variable **errno**, while not part of the **stdio** library, can be set by some **stdio** library functions to indicate an error has occurred.

Preassigned Streams

There are three preassigned streams: **stdio**, **stdout**, and **stderr**. Some implementations include a **stdprn** and a **stdaux**. Before a program's main function is called, these streams will be opened. The streams **stdio**, **stdout**, and **stderr** are pointers to a **FILE** data structure. They are associated respectively to the standard input, standard output, and standard error. The keyboard is used as the input device, and the console is used for both standard output and error. Many functions use these streams implicitly, but each has a complementary explicit version. In the C **stdio**, it is not necessary to open or close these streams.

File Access Functions

File access functions allow for the opening, closing, reopening, and flushing of files associated with a stream.

```
Prototype: int fclose (FILE * stream);
```

DESCRIPTION The **fclose( )** function closes the file associated with the *stream*. Any buffered input is discarded, and any buffered output is written before the file is closed. The **fclose( )** function returns zero on success, and **EOF** on failure.

```
Prototype: int fflush (FILE * stream);
```

DESCRIPTION The **fflush( )** function writes all pending output in its buffered output *stream* to its destination device. The call of *fflush* (void (0)) flushes all open output streams.

```
Prototype: FILE * fopen (const char * filename, const char * mode);
```

DESCRIPTION The **fopen( )** function opens a file whose name is the string pointed to by *filename*. The string *mode* specifies the access mode of the stream on the file. The **fopen( )** function returns a pointer to the **FILE** object controlling the stream, or *null pointer,* on failure. In some implementations, additional access mode information can be included after the standard ANSI mode characters. In other implementations, an additional function, such as _fsopen, is supplied to permit opening files in a shared mode. Table 1.2 is a list of the ANSI standard open file modes.

```
Prototype: FILE * freopen (const char * filename, const char * mode,
          FILE * stream);
```

DESCRIPTION The function **freopen( )** opens a file whose name is the string pointed to by *filename*. The string *mode* specifies the access mode of the stream on the file.

Table 1.2   ANSI Standard Open File Modes and Their Meanings

Mode	Meanings
r	Open a text file for reading.
w	Truncate file to a length of zero, or create a text file for writing.
a	Append: Open or create a text file for writing at EOF.
rb	Open binary file for reading.
wb	Truncate a file to a length of zero, or create a binary file for writing.
ab	Append: Open or create a binary file for writing at EOF.
r+	Open a text file for updating (reading and writing).
w+	Truncate a file to a length of zero, or create a text file for updating.
a+	Append: Open or create a text file for update writing at EOF.
r + b or rb+	Open a binary file for updating (reading and writing).
w + b or wb+	Truncate a file to a length of zero, or create a binary file for updating.
a + b or ab+	Append: Open or create a binary file for updating, writing at EOF.

It then closes the supplied stream and associates a file with it. The **freopen( )** function returns the supplied stream on success, and a null pointer on failure.

Buffering Functions

The buffering modes are _IOFBUF,_IOLBUF, and _IONBUF, for *fully buffered, line-buffered,* and *not buffered.* Fully buffered means that data is stored within the stream until it becomes full, and is then transmitted as a block to or from the operating system. Line-buffered means that data is stored as a block until a new line is entered into the stream. Not buffered means data is transferred from a source or to a destination as soon as possible. Default stream buffering is implementation defined. Two functions, **setbuf( )** and **setvbuf( )**, are the means used to override these defaults.

```
Prototype: int setvbuf (FILE * stream, char * s, int mode, size_t size);
```

DESCRIPTION The **setvbuf( )** function is used to redefine and/or specify a programmer-defined buffer for the stream's use. If *s* is a null pointer, then **setvbuf( )** will allocate its own buffer; otherwise, the supplied buffer is used and assumed to be valid. If a buffer is supplied, its size is passed through to the fourth parameter, *size*. The buffer mode supplied by the third parameter will be _IOFBUF,_IOLBFU, or _IONBUF. This function must be used only after a stream has been associated with a file and before any other operation is done on the stream. If the **setvbuf( )** function is successful, it will return a zero. If *mode* is an invalid value or the **setvbuf( )** function fails, it will return a nonzero.

```
Prototype: void setbuf (FILE * stream, char * s);
```

DESCRIPTION The **setbuf( )** function is shorthand for **setvbuf( )**, with two behaviors. When the specified buffer is a null pointer, then _IONBUF is used for the buffering mode. Otherwise, the buffer mode is _IOFBUF, and the buffer size is defined by the macro BUFSIZE (which will be at least 256).

Direct Input/Output Functions

Direct input and output functions are patterned after UNIX system calls. In fact, their interface is exactly the same if *FILE* * is replaced with a file descriptor.

```
Prototype: size_t fread (void * ptr, size_t size, size_t count, FILE
           *stream);
```

DESCRIPTION The **fread( )** function reads *count* data elements of a specified size into the array pointed to by *ptr* from the stream specified by **stream*. The **fread( )** function returns the number of elements successfully read, which may be less than *count* if **EOF** or read error is found. If *size* or *count* is zero, then the **fread( )** function will return zero and the contents of *ptr*. The state of the stream will be unchanged.

```
Prototype: size_t fwrite (const void * ptr, size_t size, size_t count,
           FILE * stream);
```

DESCRIPTION The **fwrite( )** function writes *count* data elements of *size* length from the supplied array, *ptr*, into the specified stream. The **fwrite( )** function returns the number of elements written to the stream. If a write error occurs, the value returned will be less than *count.*

Getting and Positioning the File Pointer

The indicator is a count of bytes from the file's start to where in the file the next character is read from or written to. With the exception of the **rewind( )** function, these functions will reset the error state of the stream if successful.

```
Prototype: int fgetpos (FILE * stream, fpos_t * pos);
```

DESCRIPTION The **fgetpos( )** function will store the current value of the file position indicator for the specified stream in the object pointed to by *pos*. This value, sometimes called a *magic cookie*, is used by **fsetpos( )**. The **fgetpos( )** function returns zero on success, and a nonzero value upon failure. The **fgetpos( )** function stores an implementation-defined value in the global variable *errno* if an error occurs.

```
Prototype: int fseek (FILE * stream, long int offset, int whence);
```

DESCRIPTION The function **fseek( )** repositions the stream's file position indicator, according to the given byte offset condition on the last parameter *whence*. Binary streams may use any value for offset, but text streams should use a value obtained from a previous call to the **ftell( )**. The **fseek( )** function returns zero on success, and a nonzero value on failure.

```
Prototype: int fsetpos (FILE * stream, const fpos_t * pos);
```

DESCRIPTION The **fsetpos( )** function repositions the file indicator for the stream according to the value obtained from the call to **fgetpos( )** on the same stream. The value is stored in the object pointed to by **pos**. The function **fgetpos( )** returns zero on success, and nonzero upon failure. The **fsetpos( )** function stores an implementation-defined positive value in the global variable **errno** if an error occurs.

```
Prototype: long int ftell(FILE * stream);
```

DESCRIPTION The **ftell( )** function returns the current value of the file position indicator for the stream. If the stream is binary, the value will be the number of bytes from the beginning of the file. If the stream is text, the value is usable only by **fseek( )**. If the **ftell( )** function fails, it will return −1L and store an implementation-defined positive value in **errno**.

```
Prototype: void rewind(FILE * stream);
```

DESCRIPTION The **rewind( )** function sets the file position pointer for the stream to the beginning of the file. The **rewind( )** function returns no value and will not reset the error state of the stream.

Character Input and Output

There are several functions that perform text and character input and output. They are designed to read and write text streams on a character-by-character basis. Their actual implementation is optimized to transfer their data as quickly as possible, but they can be viewed as wrappers around the functions **fgetc( )** and **fputc( )**.

```
Prototype: int fgetc(FILE * stream);
```

DESCRIPTION The **fgetc( )** function gets the next single character from the specified input stream specified by **stream**. It obtains it as an unsigned **char** converted to an **int**. If **stream** is at the end of file, or a read error occurs, then the **fgetc( )** function will return **EOF**.

```
Prototype: char *fgets(char *s, int n, FILE *stream);
```

DESCRIPTION The **fgets( )** function gets a string, at the most, one less than **n** number of characters from the stream specified by **stream** and stores it in the supplied buffer **s**. The newline character is read and retained. The string is appended with a null character. The **fgets( )** function returns a pointer to the supplied buffer if successful, and returns a null pointer on failure.

```
Prototype: int fputc (int c, FILE * stream);
```

DESCRIPTION The **fputc( )** function writes a single character (which will be converted from an integer to an unsigned **char**) to the output stream specified by **stream** at the position designated by the file position indicator. If the file cannot position a file indicator or the stream access mode is appended, the single character will be appended to the stream. The **fputc( )** function returns the character if successful, and **EOF** on failure.

```
Prototype: int fputs(const char * s, FILE * stream);
```

DESCRIPTION The **fputs( )** function writes the string **s** to the specified output **stream**. The terminating null character is not transmitted. The **fputs( )** function returns **EOF** on failure, and a nonnegative value otherwise.

```
Prototype: int getc (FILE * stream);
```

DESCRIPTION The macro **getc( )** is an implementation of **fgetc( )**. It is important that the specified argument does not have any side effects, since the stream parameter may be evaluated more than once. For example:

```
int char = 0;
/* Get and count all pending characters for standard input */
while (getc (++char ? stdin : stdin) != EOF);
```

The value of **char**, if there are 10 remaining characters, will not necessarily be 10.

The **getc( )** returns the next character from **stream** if successful. If the stream is at the end of file, or an error occurs, **getc( )** will return **EOF**.

```
Prototype: int getchar(void);
```

DESCRIPTION The **getchar( )** function is equivalent to **fgetc (stdin)( )**. It is one of the implicit input calls on the preassigned standard input stream. This function returns the next character from **stdin**. If the stream is at the end of file, or an error occurs, the **getchar( )** function will return **EOF**.

```
Prototype: char * gets (char * s);
```

DESCRIPTION The **gets( )** function reads characters from **stdin** into a byte array pointed to by **s** until a new line or **EOF** is read. The new line character is discarded, and the null character is placed after the last character in the array. The **gets( )** function returns **s** if successful. If an error occurs or no characters have been read, a null pointer will be returned.

```
Prototype: int putc (int c, FILE * stream);
```

DESCRIPTION The **putc( )** function is implemented as a macro. It sends **c** to the **FILE** ***stream**. It is essentially equivalent to **fputc( )**. Both arguments should have no side effects, since **stream** may be evaluated more than once. The **putc( )** function will return the character written if successful, and **EOF** on failure.

```
Prototype: int puts(const char * s);
```

DESCRIPTION The **puts( )** function writes the string specified by *s* to **stdout**, and adds a \N to the output. The termination null character is not written to the **stdout**. The **puts( )** function returns a nonnegative value on success, or **EOF** if a write error occurs.

```
Prototype: int ungetc (int c, FILE * stream);
```

DESCRIPTION The **ungetc( )** function is used to push back characters specified by *c* into an input stream specified by **stream**. It guarantees that only one character will be successfully pushed back (because it may be unbuffered or its buffer may be full). The **ungetc( )** function returns the pushed-back character after conversion, or **EOF** on failure.

Formatting Functions

The formatted input and output functions of **stdio** are meant as a means of transferring data between systems. Binary representation of data is very platform-specific, while text data is more general. A standard means of translating binary data to a text format bridges this platform specificity.

Conversion routines exist in the **stdlib** library to translate integral and floating point values to and from strings. However, using such functions as **atof( )** to build a string for output is not as intuitive as specifying one line of output with one line of code.

Variable Arguments

Some languages have specific functions that permit a variable number of arguments. The C language supplies a means to define any function to have this ability. This is done through the **stdarg** library. The language defines ellipse declaration that indicates to a compiler that a variable number of arguments will be accepted by a function. The ellipse and **va_list** object (a pointer to *char*) can be viewed as equivalents. Just the latter requires the programmer to set up the block of variable parameters properly.

Format Specifiers

The format string contains plain characters and one format specifier for each of the following arguments. A specifier's form is:

```
% [flags] [width] [.prec] [h|1] type_specifier
```

The format string is a mini-language, where flags, width, and precision are used to justify output. The size modifiers ([h|1]) and type specification are used to describe how a parameter is translated. Only the type specifier is mandatory.

The primary caveat of format specifiers is that the input language differs from the output, though they look extremely similar. Output parameters are passed by value, while input is received by address. It is the programmer's responsibility to ensure that each format specifier has a target parameter. Extra target parameters will be ignored, but insufficient targets will probably result in a program crash.

Formatted Input/Output to Files

Text can be formatted for input or output under the control of a format string and retrieved or sent to a stream associated with a file.

```
Prototype: int fprintf (FILE * stream, const char * format, ...);
```

DESCRIPTION The **fprintf( )** function writes to an output stream specified by ***stream*** under the control of the format string specified by ***format*** (which are the format specifiers). The **fprintf( )** function returns when the end of the format string is reached. If there are insufficient arguments for the format string, the behavior of this function is unpredictable. If there are too many arguments for the format string, remaining arguments will be ignored. The **fprintf( )** function returns the number of characters converted, or a negative value on failure.

```
Prototype: int fscanf (FILE * stream, const char * format, ...);
```

DESCRIPTION The **fscanf( )** function reads data from the input stream specified by ***stream*** under control of the format string specified by ***format*** that determines the allowable input sequences and how they will be converted before assignment. If there are insufficient arguments for the format string, the behavior of this function is unpredictable. If there are too many arguments for the format string, remaining arguments will be ignored. The **fscanf( )** function returns the number of target parameters successfully filled, or **EOF** on failure.

```
Prototype:int printf (const char * format, ...);
```

DESCRIPTION The **printf( )** function is essentially equivalent to **fprintf( )** (stdout, *format, ...*). This function sends its output to the **stdout**. The **printf( )** function returns the number of characters sent to the **stdout** if successful, or a negative value on failure.

```
Prototype: int scanf (const char * format, ...);
```

DESCRIPTION The **scanf( )** function is essentially equivalent to **fscanf( )** (stdin, *format, ...*). The **scanf( )** function receives its input from **stdin**. The **scanf( )** function returns the number of input characters processed, or **EOF** on failure.

```
Prototype: vfprintf (FILE * stream, const char * format, va_list arg);
```

DESCRIPTION The **vfprintf( )** function is essentially equivalent to **fprintf( )**, where the programmer uses the **stdarg** library to convert a function ellipse declaration into a **va_list** object.

For example:

```
external portable_foo (const char * format, va_list args);
void foo (const char * format, ...)
{
   va_list  args;
   va_start (args, format);
   portable_foo (format, args);
   va_end (args);
}
```

As the example suggests, using **va_list** for exported functions is guaranteed to be portable, while the ellipse declaration is not. The **vfprintf( )** function will return the number of characters transmitted if successful, or a negative value on failure.

```
Prototype: int vprintf (const char * format, va_list arg);
```

DESCRIPTION The **vprintf( )** function is essentially equivalent to **printf( )** (**stdout**, *format, arg*). The **vprintf( )** function will return the number of characters transmitted or a negative value on failure.

Formatted Input/Output to Programmer-Defined Buffers

Formatted text can also be sent to a buffer instead of a stream.

```
Prototype: int sprintf (char * s, const char * format, ...);
```

DESCRIPTION The **sprintf( )** function is similar to **fprintf( )**, except the translated output is copied to the specified buffer **s** and not a stream. If **s** and *format* overlap, then the function's behavior is undefined. The **sprintf( )** function returns the number of characters (not counting the null character) copied into the supplied buffer.

```
Prototype: int sscanf (char * s, const char * format, ...);
```

DESCRIPTION The **sscanf( )** function is similar to **fscanf( )**, except that the supplied buffer **s** is the source instead of an input stream. Reading the null character from **s** is equivalent to reaching the end of file. If **s** and *format* overlap, then the function's behavior is undefined. The **sscanf( )** function returns the number of target parameters successfully filled, or **EOF** on failure.

```
Prototype: int vsprintf (char * s, const char * format, va_list arg);
```

DESCRIPTION The function **vsprintf( )** is essentially equivalent to **sprintf( )**. The variable argument list is replaced by *arg*. If **s** and *format* overlap, then the function's behavior is undefined. The **vsprintf( )** function returns the number of characters written to the array, absent the terminating null character if successful.

Error Handling Functions

Error handling functions checks or clears error or end-of-file indicators. They can also associate an error message with the error number stored in the ERRNO global variable.

```
Prototype: void clearerr (FILE * stream);
```

DESCRIPTION The **clearerr( )** function clears the stream's, specified by **stream**, end-of-file and error indicators. This function has no return value.

```
Prototype: int feof (FILE * stream);
```

DESCRIPTION The **feof( )** function checks end-of-file indicator, specified by **stream**, and returns a nonzero value if it is set.

```
Prototype: int ferror (FILE * stream);
```

DESCRIPTION The **ferror( )** function checks the stream's, specified by **stream**, error indicator, and returns a nonzero value if it is set.

```
Prototype: void perror (const char * s);
```

DESCRIPTION The **perror( )** function writes an implementation-defined error message mapped from the global variable **errno** to the standard error stream. If **s** is not a null pointer and does not point to a null character, it will be sent (followed with a colon and a space) before the mapped error message. The **perror( )** function has no return value.

File Operation Functions

The file operation functions can make a file inaccessible by the existing file name and accessible by a new file name. Temporary binary files can be removed or unique file names can be created in the current working directory.

```
Prototype: int remove (const char * filename);
```

DESCRIPTION The **remove( )** function makes the specified file, **filename**, inaccessible. If the file is open, the behavior of the function is undefined. The **remove( )** function returns zero on success, and a nonzero on failure.

```
Prototype: int rename (const char * old, const char * new);
```

DESCRIPTION The **rename( )** function makes the existing file, **old**, inaccessible by the **old** filename but accessible by the **new** filename. If a file exists with the **new** filename before the function is called, then its behavior is undefined. The **rename( )** function returns zero on success, and a nonzero value on failure.

```
Prototype: FILE * tmpfile (void);
```

DESCRIPTION The **tmpfile( )** function creates a temporary binary file that will be removed on closing it, or at program termination. What happens to this file following an abnormal program termination is implementation-defined. The **tmpfile( )** function returns a pointer to the temporary stream on success, and a null pointer on failure.

```
Prototype: char * tmpname (char * s);
```

DESCRIPTION The **tmpname( )** function generates a valid filename that is unique in the current working directory. The **tmpname( )** function can be called up to **TMP_MAX** times, after which its behavior is implementation-defined. If *s* is a null pointer, then a pointer to a static object containing the temporary name is returned. Otherwise, the static object is copied into the supplied buffer and a pointer to it is returned.

These functions represent some commonly used functions from the **stdio** library. These functions can, and in many installations do, coexist with the IOSTREAM classes. For more details on these functions and their implementations, refer to *The Standard C Library* by P.J. Plauger. These functions are used to implement the nonobject-oriented stream, and allow the programmer to achieve a high degree of device-independence. Device-independence is a challenge that presents itself constantly as new types of peripherals are added to the computer's environment. Normally, when a new device is added, a certain amount of device-dependent I/O code is written until the properties and characteristics of that new device are properly understood and generalized. When this happens, we can move from the device-dependent I/O routines to device-independent I/O routines.

The Advantages of IOSTREAMS over Traditional C Input/Output

Some languages have keyword commands to handle input and output. In the Pascal language, **read( )** and **readln( )** accept integer and string input and assign it to a variable. **write( )** and **writeln( )** output the contents of a variable to the designated output file. Files can be prepared for input and output with the **rewrite( )** or **reset( )** commands, respectively. The C++ language has no such keywords as part of its language. The C++ language has a library of functions that manage input and output. A library is a collection of predefined functions/classes that can be used in a program. When a program is compiled into an executable program, the linker searches for the object file where the function/class is located, and links that file to the executable code.

One advantage of using a library is that as new devices are developed, libraries or functions can be easily added to or even created by the programmer to handle input and output, instead of appending these libraries and functions to the language structure. For example, a library can be created to handle input and output for NTSC cards (video capture boards), sound cards, or virtual reality systems. Instead of adding keywords to the language, a programmer can create groups of functions, place them in a library, and thus extend the capabilities of the language. A programmer also has the flexibility of redefining already existing functions.

There are two facilities that manage the input and output, the standard input and output facility (**stdio**), which is nonobject-oriented, and the IOSTREAMS facility that is object-oriented. The standard input/output facility is a collection of functions. These functions are subroutines that have a number of C statements and that perform one task. The function has a data type, and this data type is returned to be used or discarded. The function has a unique name and may have an argument list. Table 1.3 lists the **stdio** functions in alphabetical order.

The IOSTREAMS are a collection of classes that handle input and output. A class is similar to a structure (record), with a private part and a public part. The private part contains the variables used by the class. The public part contains the services or member functions that operate on data. When an object is declared of a class type, a message is sent to activate a behavior (task)—in this case, an input or output task. The message is passed to the object, and the object selects the correct behavior to be performed. This is called a *single interface, multiple implementations.* Here lies the essential difference between the standard I/O and IOSTREAMS; the standard I/O is function-based, and IOSTREAMS are class-based.

To use these libraries, the preprocessor directives must be included in the program. When the source code is compiled, the preprocessor directive instructs the compiler to include these declarations in the program. The preprocessor **#include <stdio.h>** is included when using the standard I/O facility, and the **#include <iostream.h>** preprocessor when using IOSTREAMS.

Standard input/output contains several groups of functions. These functions can be categorized as formatted input and output functions, and error handling functions. Table 1.4 is a list of the standard I/O function names by category. There are six **printf( )** function derivatives, three **scanf( )** function derivatives, six **get( )** function derivatives, and five **puts( )** function derivatives.

Table 1.3   Standard Input and Output Functions Listed in Alphabetical Order

Standard Input/Output Functions					
fflush	fputc	fwrite	putc	sscanf	vsprintf
fgetc	fputs	getchar	putchar	sprintf	
fgets	freadf	gets	puts	vfprintf	
fprintf	fscanf	printf	scanf	vprintf	

Table 1.4   Standard Input and Output Functions Listed by Type

Standard Input Functions	Standard Output Functions	
fgetc	fflush	vfprintf
fgets	fprintf	vprintf
fread	fputc	vsprintf
fscanf	fputs	
fwrite	printf	
getchar	putc	
gets	putchr	
scanf	puts	
sscanf	sprintf	

printf( ) Functions

There are six different **printf( )** functions. The purpose of the **printf( )** functions is to format output. All of the **printf( )** functions will return the number of characters created by that call. All of the **printf( )** functions will accept format arguments. They are command codes that perform various operations, creating a string sent to a stream or stored in memory. Some of these operations require an argument list that will be converted to a sequence of characters.

Each of the **printf( )** functions performs a different task and has its own argument list. When a list is followed by three periods, this function can have a variable amount of arguments. These arguments are mostly to convert data values. Here is a list of the **printf( )** functions' prototypes:

```
1. int fprintf(FILE *stream, const char * string format, ...);
2. int printf(const char * string format, ...);
3. int sprintf(char *destination, const char * string format, ...);
4. int vfprintf(FILE *stream, const char * string format, va_list
         ap);
5. int vprintf(const char * string format, va_list ap);
6. int vsprintf(char *destination, const char * string format, va_
         list ap);
```

The purpose of the **printf( )** function is to write and format data values and character strings of variables. The distinctions are where the formatted output is sent, and in the acceptance of additional arguments. The ***const char *string*** format in the argument list is the format commands. The **fprintf( )** function will send the formatted output to a buffer. This buffer is specified by ***FILE *stream***. This buffer can be of any file type. The **printf( )** function differs from the **fprintf( )** function in that it can send only its formatted output to the **stdout**, which is usually the screen. The

sprintf( ) function writes to a string whose address is specified in ***char *destination***. The **vprintf( )**, **vfprintf( )**, and **vsprintf( )** functions perform identically to the **printf( )** function. The distinction in their argument list is a pointer to a list of arguments. The format commands will be applied to each in the argument.

Format Commands

As mentioned, each **printf( )** function uses format commands to format the output. They are specified in the ***const char *string format*** argument of the argument list. There are four possible components to the format command and all but the conversion specifier is optional. They are command codes that perform various operations, including creating a string sent to a stream or stored in memory. The format commands are with double quotation marks and preceded by a percent (%) sign. They are written in this order, following the percent (%) sign:

- *Flags*
- *Field width specifiers*
- *Precision*
- *Conversion specifiers*

Flags

Flags dictate variations on the standard conversions. There are five different variations:

(−)	A minus sign will justify output to the left, adding spaces to the right of the characters if needed.
(0)	Pads the output with leading zeros after any sign or prefix.
(+)	Places a + sign affixed to a positive signed value.
( )	Places a space where a sign would be affixed to a positive signed value.
(#)	Changes the behavior of certain conversions.

Field Width

A field width specifier pads the output to ensure that it is of a minimum length. The padding character can be placed before the decimal. The default character is a space. If the output is less than the minimum length, it will pad the output with the specified character or a space. If the output is greater than the minimum length, the entire string will be printed.

Precision

Precision commands will control:

1. The number of characters to be displayed
2. The number of digits behind a decimal

3. The number of significant digits

4. The number of digits to be displayed when converting an integer

The way the precision command is applied depends on the combination of precision and conversion specifiers. Table 1.5 shows how the precision will be interpreted with conversion specifiers. A precision command is a period (.) followed by a decimal.

Conversion Specifiers

Flags, field width specifiers, and precision are optional, but the conversion specifier is not optional and is needed to format output. The conversion specifier represents the data to be formatted. It is a one- or two-character sequence. Table 1.6 is a list of

Table 1.5   Interpretation of Combining Precision and Conversion Specifiers and Their Default Settings

Type	Meaning	Default
c	The precision is ignored.	A single character is output.
d u i o x X	The precision specifies the minimum number of digits to be output. If the value is less than precision, the output will be padded with zeros to the left of the value. If the value is more than precision, the value will be fully expressed.	A period alone sets precision to 0. A period followed by an asterick (*) sets the precision to the next *int* argument. If it is a negative value, precision is set to 0. If no precision is specified, precision is 1.
e E	The precision specifies the number of digits after the decimal point.	The precision is 6. If precision is 0, or no digits follow the decimal point, then the decimal is not output.
f	The precision specifies the number of digits after the decimal point. If the decimal is output, at least one digit is before the decimal point.	The precision is 6. If precision is 0, no decimal point is output.
g G	The precision specifies the maximum number of significant digits output.	All significant digits are output. If the precision is 0, the precision is set to 1. If no digits follow the decimal, no decimal point is output.
s	The precision specifies the maximum number of characters output, terminating at the null character. If the string is more than precision, only up to precision number of characters is output, and the array will contain a null character.	The string is output, terminating at a null character. The array will contain a null character.

Table 1.6   Conversion Specifiers and the Resulting Format

Type	Data Type	Resulting Format
c	*char*	Single character
d i	*int*	Signed decimal integer
hd hi	*int*	Short integer
ld li	*long int*	Long integer
e	*double*	Signed value in scientific notation
le	*long double*	Long integer
E	*double*	Signed value in scientific notation with uppercase *E*
LE	*long double*	Signed value in scientific notation with uppercase *E*
f	*double*	Signed value with a magnitude, decimal point, and digits behind the decimal determined by precision
Lf	*long double*	Signed value with a magnitude, decimal point, and digits behind the decimal determined by precision
g	*double*	Either *f* or *e* format
Lg	*long double*	Either *f* or *e* format
G	*double*	Either *f* or *e* format, with *E* in uppercase
LG	*long double*	Either *f* or *e* format, with *E* in uppercase
n	Pointer to *int*	Stores the number of characters output
hn	Pointer to *short int*	Stores the number of characters output
ln	Pointer to *long int*	Stores the number of characters output
o	Unsigned *int*	Octal digits
ho	Unsigned *short int*	Octal digits
lo	*long int*	Octal digits
p	Pointer to *void*	Implementation-defined sequence of characters
s	Pointer to *char*	Character string
u	Unsigned *int*	Unsigned decimal digits
hu	Unsigned *short int*	Unsigned decimal digits
lu	Unsigned *long int*	Unsigned decimal digits
x	Unsigned *int*	Unsigned hexadecimal digits
hx	Unsigned *short int*	Unsigned hexadecimal digits
lx	Unsigned *long int*	Unsigned hexadecimal digits
X	Unsigned *int*	Unsigned hexadecimal digits, with *A-F* in uppercase
hX	Unsigned *short int*	Unsigned hexadecimal digits, with *A-F* in uppercase
lX	Unsigned *long int*	Unsigned hexadecimal digits, with *A-F* in uppercase

field type conversion specifiers. Listing 1.1 is a program example demonstrating the use of flags, width specifiers, precision, and conversion specifiers.

Listing 1.1

```
// This program demonstrates some simple usages of flags, field
// width specifiers, precision specifiers, and conversion specifiers.

#include <stdio.h>
#include <math.h>

void main(void)
{
    int pI = 3.1416 * 10000;
    double Pi = M_PI;
    char Pie[3] = "pi";

    printf("%5d is an integer\n", pI);
    printf("%4.2f is a double\n", Pi);
    printf("%s is a string\n", Pie);
}
```

Output for Listing 1.1

31415 is an integer

3.14 is a double

pi is a string

These **printf( )** functions can be written into one **printf( )** function:

```
printf("%5d is a integer\n %4.2f is a double\n %s is a string\n", pI,
        Pi, Pie);
```

There is a format command string for each variable. The **%5d** format command string is for the integer variable **pI**. The number is the width specifier, and the **d** represents the integer to be output. The width specifier is the number **5**. The **d** means that it will output a decimal. The **%4.2f** format command string is for the floating point variable **Pi**. The **4.2** sets the precision to, at the most, four digits before the decimal and two digits behind the decimal. The **f** means that it will output a float. The format command string **%s** is for the string variable **Pie**. The **s** means that it will output a string.

scanf( ) Functions

There are three different **scanf( )** functions. The purpose of the **scanf( )** function is to read input from a specified input, then store it in a variable. The **scanf( )** functions return the number of items that were read successfully and saved to a variable. They can receive a variable number of arguments. These are the three **scanf( )** function prototypes:

1. `int scanf(const char *format,...);`
2. `int fscanf(FILE *stream, const char *format,...);`
3. `int sscanf(char *src, const char *format,...);`

The **scanf( )** function receives its input from the stream **stdin**, **fscanf( )** function receives its input from the ***FILE *stream***, and **sscanf( )** function receives its input from a null terminated string whose address is stored in ***src***. These functions will stop reading when an end-of-file or null terminator has been encountered. Similarly to the **printf( )** functions, the **scanf( )** functions also have formatting commands. These scan formats tell the function what arguments to expect and what if any conversion to perform.

Scan Format

Following the percent (%) sign, there are three components to the scan format commands in the following order (all but the conversion specifiers are optional):

1. Assignment suppression
2. Field width specifier
3. Conversion specifiers

Assignment Suppression

An assignment suppression prevents the storing of characters into a variable. An asterisk (*) following the percent (%) sign will cause the assignment suppression.

Field Width

The field width specifiers are decimals that determine the maximum number of characters for the conversion specifier.

Scan Conversion Specifier

The scan conversion specifier represents the data to be read to a variable, and determines the type of conversion to perform on that data. The specifier is a one- or two-character sequence. Table 1.7 is a list of the scan conversion specifiers, the input that the function expects, and the variable type the input will be stored. Listing 1.2 is a program demonstrating some **scan** format codes.

Listing 1.2

```
// This program demonstrates how the conversion specifiers can be used.
#include <stdio.h>
#include <string.h>

void main(void)
{
    char ch = ' ';
    float x = 0;
    double y = 0;
    int z = 0;
    char a[5] = " ";
```

```
            scanf("%c",&ch);
            scanf("%f",&x);
            scanf("%lf",&y);
            scanf("%d",&z);
            scanf("%s",a);
            printf("%c%f%lf%d%s",ch,x,y,z,a);
      }
```

Standard IOSTREAM Facility

The standard IOSTREAM facility consists of classes. A class is a level of abstraction that consists of the common characteristics of a group of things or objects. These classes are constructed to handle the input and output of a program, and can be

Table 1.7   scanf Conversion Specifiers, the Input Expected, and the Data Type Stored

Type	Variable Data Type	Input Expected
c	Pointer to *char*	Single characters, including white spaces
d	Pointer to *int*	Decimal integer
hd	Pointer to *short int*	Decimal integer
ld	Pointer to *long int*	Decimal integer
e E f g G	Pointer to *float*	Floating point
le lE lf lg lG	Pointer to *double*	Floating point
Le LE Lf Lg LG	Pointer to *long double*	Floating point
i	Pointer to *int*	Decimal, hexadecimal, octal
hi	Pointer to *short int*	Decimal, hexadecimal, octal
li	Pointer to *long int*	Decimal, hexadecimal, octal
n	Pointer to *int* (no conversion)	Stores the number of characters input
hn	Pointer to *short int* (no conversion)	Stores the number of characters input
ln	Pointer to *long int* (no conversion)	Stores the number of characters input
o	Pointer to unsigned *int*	Octal digits
ho	Pointer to unsigned *short int*	Octal digits
lo	Pointer to unsigned *long int*	Octal digits
p	Pointer to *void*	Pointer
s	Pointer to *char*	Character string
u	Pointer to unsigned *int*	Decimal integer
hu	Pointer to unsigned *short int*	Decimal integer
lu	Pointer to unsigned *long int*	Decimal integer
x X	Pointer to unsigned *int*	Hexadecimal digits
hx hX	Pointer to unsigned *short int*	Hexadecimal digits
lx lX	Pointer to unsigned *long int*	Hexadecimal digits

Table 1.8   Categorization of the IOSTREAM Classes

Type	Input	Output	I/O	Buffer	Format
Base	istream	ostream	iostream	streambuf	ios
File	ifstream	ofstream	fstream	filebuf	
Memory	istrstream	ostrstream	strstream	strstreambuf	

grouped as shown in Table 1.8. The **istream** class handles input data, and the **ostream** class handles output data, and **iostream** is derived from both **istream** and **ostream** classes. The other classes manage input from a file or memory, and output to a file or memory. The **ifstream** class handles input data from a file, and **strstream** class handles input data from memory. The **fstream** and **strstream** classes manage input and output from a file or memory, respectively. The **ofstream** class manages data to be output to a file, and **ostrstream** class manages data to be output to memory. Table 1.9 is the list of input functions and Table 1.10 is the list of the output member functions of the aforementioned input/output classes.

cout, cin, cerr, clog

The objects **cin**, **cout**, **cerr**, and **clog** are instances of the class **istream** and **ostream**. **cin** is an instance of **istream** class, and **cout**, **cerr**, and **clog** are instances of the **ostream** class. An instance is an object declaration of a class. Therefore, **cin** has the behavior or abilities of **istream** class; and **cout**, **cerr**, and **clog** have the behaviors or abilities of the **ostream** class. In most C++ environments, these objects have been declared in the IOSTREAM header file. The programmer does not need to declare them.

cout   The **cout** object has member functions that format data. It also has member functions that can send the data to the output device to which it is connected. The **cout** object is normally linked to the console, and is used with the overloaded left shift operators (<<). It can output any built-in data type and can be used to output user-defined data types by operator overloading. There will be nothing special to consider when outputting the different built-in data types. Listing 1.3 is a program using the **cout** object and the left shift operators to output to the screen built-in data types and a user-defined type, **rational_approximation**.

Table 1.9   Input Member Functions and Their Classes

Class	Input Member Functions
istream	get( ), getline( ), read( ), >>
streambuf	sgetn( ), sgetc( )

Table 1.10   Output Member Functions and Their Classes

Class	Output Member Functions
ostream	puts( ), write( ), <<
streambuf	sputn( ), sputc( )

Listing 1.3

```
// This program shows how to insert data into cout's stream.
// Some of the data are based on built-in data types, and
// some of the data are based on user-defined data types.

#include <iostream.h>
#include <math.h>
#include "r_approx.h"

void main(void)
{
    char PI = 227;
    float pi = 3.1416;
    double Pi = M_PI;
    int pI = 3.1416 * 10000;
    char Pie[3] = "pi";
    rational_approximation user_pi(3.1416);

    cout << PI << endl;
    cout << pi << endl;
    cout << Pi << endl;
    cout << pI << endl;
    cout << Pie << endl;
    cout << user_pi << endl;
}
```

Output from Listing 1.3

π

3.1416

3.141593

31415

pi

3927/1250

cin   The **cin** object has member functions that can read, format, then save data to variables. The **cin** object is normally linked to a console. The **cin** object is used with the overloaded right shift operators (**<<**). It can read any built-in data type, and can input data to a user-defined data type by operator overloading. Just like **cout**, there are no special considerations when reading in these different data types. Listing 1.4

is a program using the **cin** object and the right shift operators to input from the console built-in data types and a user-defined type, **rational_approximation**, into the appropriate variables.

Listing 1.4

```
// This program demonstrates how to extract data from the cin
// object. Some of the data that is extracted from the cin
// data type is based on built-in data types. Some of the
// data that is extracted from cin is based on user-defined
// data types.
#include <iostream.h>
#include <math.h>
#include "r_approx.h"

void main(void)
{
    char PI = ' ';
    float pi = 0;
    double Pi = 0;
    int pI = 0;
    char Pie[3] = " ";
    rational_approximation user_pi;
    cin >> PI >> pi >> Pi >> pI >> Pie >> user_pi;
}
```

Formatting Input and Output

The IOSTREAMS allow the programmer to format input and output by defining a number of member functions.

Flags

```
Prototype: long setf(long flags);
```

DESCRIPTION The **setf( )** member function sets a flag to format input or output. Table 1.11 lists the formatting flags and their descriptions.

```
Prototype: long unsetf(long flags);
```

DESCRIPTION The **unsetf( )** member function turns off a flag. The **unsetf( )** member function will return the current flags setting, then turns off the flags specified by *flags*. The flags will be applied to any data preceding the statements. The program in Listing 1.5 illustrates the use of the **setf( )** and **unsetf( )** member functions.

Listing 1.5

```
// This program demonstrates the setf( ), and unsetf( ) member
// functions.
```

Table 1.11   List of Formatting Flags, Their Values, Types, and Meanings (Values of the Format Flag May Vary Between Implementations)

Flags	Value	Type	Meaning
skipws	0x0001	input	set to skip leading white spaces from a stream, when cleared white spaces are not discarded
left	0x0002	output	set to add padding of the fill character to the left of data when output is less than precision
right	0x0004	output	set to add padding of the fill character to the right of data when output is less than precision
internal	0x0008	output	set to add space between the value and the base character or any sign preceding the value to fill a specified field
dec	0x0010	i/o	set to convert integer input or to generate integer output in the decimal number base
oct	0x0020	i/o	set to convert integer input or to generate integer output in the octal number base
hex	0x0040	i/o	set to convert integer input or to generate integer output in the hexadecimal number base
showbase	0x0080	output	set to display the base of a numeric value
showpoint	0x0100	output	set to display a decimal point of a floating point value
uppercase	0x0200	output	set to display lowercase characters in uppercase
showpos	0x0400	output	set to display a plus (+) sign for nonnegative values
scientific	0x0800	output	set to display floating point values in scientific notation
fixed	0x1000	output	set to display floating point values in normal notation
unitbuf	0x2000	output	set to flush output following each output operation
stdio	0x4000	output	set to flush stout and sterr following an output operations when using IOSTREAMS and stdio

```cpp
#include <iostream.h>
#include <math.h>

void main(void)
{
    float pi = 3.1416;
    double Pi = M_PI;
    int pI = 3.1416 * 10000;

    cout.setf(ios::scientific);
    cout.setf(ios::uppercase);
    cout << pi << endl;
    cout.unsetf(ios::uppercase);
    cout << Pi << endl;
    cout.unsetf(ios::uppercase);
    cout.unsetf(ios::scientific);
    cout.setf(ios::hex);
```

```
        cout.setf(ios::showbase);
        cout << pI << endl;
}
```

Output from Listing 1.5

> 3.1416E+00
>
> 3.141593e+00
>
> 0x7ab7

Field Width, Precision, and Fill

Besides formatting output by turning on flags, field width, precision, and fill character functions can be specified.

```
Prototype:int width(int length);
```

DESCRIPTION The **width( )** member function will return the current field width, and set the field width to its argument. The default width depends on the number of characters needed to represent data.

```
Prototype: int precision(int number);
```

DESCRIPTION The **precision( )** member function will return the number of digits displayed after the decimal, and set the precision value to its argument.

```
Prototype: int fill(char character);
```

DESCRIPTION The **fill( )** member function will return the current fill character used to pad output needed if the data takes up less space than the field width, and will set the character to what is specified by its argument. The default fill character is a space. The program in Listing 1.6 demonstrates the use of the **width( )**, **precision( )**, and **fill( )** member functions.

Listing 1.6

```
// This program demonstrates the width( ), fill( ), and precision( )
// member functions.
#include <iostream.h>
#include <math.h>
void main(void)
{
    char PI = 227;
    float pi = 3.1416;
    double Pi = M_PI;
    int pI = 3.1416 * 10000;
    char Pie[3] = "pie";

    cout.width(10);
    cout.setf(ios::right);
```

```
        cout.fill('^');
        cout << Pie << endl;
        cout.fill('-');
        cout.unsetf(ios::right);
        cout.width(10);
        cout << pi << endl;
        cout.unsetf(ios::right);
        cout.setf(ios::left);
        cout.width(10);
        cout << pI << endl;
        cout.precision(3);
        cout.fill('*');
        cout.width(10);
        cout << Pi << ' ' << PI << endl;
}
```

Output from Listing 1.6

^^^^^^^pie

----3.1416

31415-----

3.142*****π

Advantages of IOSTREAMS

There are four essential reasons that the IOSTREAM facility is an advantage over the standard I/O library; they are:

1. Reusability and extensibility
2. Type safeness
3. Single interface, multiple implementations
4. Ease of creation of input/output facility for user-defined data types

Reusability and Extensibility

When using the standard I/O library, the format conversion specifiers with the **printf( )** functions and the **scanf( )** functions are necessary. They represent the data that will be input to a variable or output to a device. In this example:

```
scanf("%d", &number);
printf("%d", number);
```

the **d** specifier represents the data as a decimal. For each piece of data, a conversion specifier has to be in place. If it becomes necessary to reuse this piece of code in another program, an issue may arise. In the original program, it asked for a decimal input, and output the decimal. The new program asks for a float as input and will also output a float. It will be necessary to change the format conversion specifiers to accommodate this change. It will be transformed to this:

```
scanf("%f", &number);
printf("%f", number);
```

This may seem a trivial matter in this situation; there are only two changes to be made. But in the case where there are hundreds or thousands of lines of code, it is no longer trivial.

The measure of reusability is based on the software or program's ability to be reused. Programs or software should be designed and written so that aspects of commonality among them are exploited to avoid reproducing the same code over and over again. Reusability leads to extendisility, the ability of software or a program to be adapted without major changes. If a program or software is reusable, then it is likely that it can be adapted to new systems without a major overhaul. Using the standard I/O library makes both extendisility and reusability difficult. Consider a function that accepts three numbers that will be displayed in a column:

```
int display(int num1, int num2, int num3)
    {
        printf("%-10d/n, %-10d/n,%-10d/n",&num1,&num2,&num3);
    }
```

In order for this function to be reused in a new system, it would have to display three characters instead of three names. The function's parameter list would have to be changed, as well as all of the conversion specifiers:

```
int display(char char1[10], char char2[10], char char3[10])
{
    printf("%-10c/n, %-10c/n, %-10c/n",char1,char2,char3);
{
```

To display different data types, all the conversion specifiers will have to be changed to accurately represent the data. Because the IOSTREAM facility does not use conversion specifiers, and there are no special considerations to make when displaying the built-in data type, only the parameter list would have to be changed to accommodate the new data type:

```
int display(char prompt1[10], char prompt2[10], char prompt3[10])
{
    cout << prompt1 << endl << prompt2 << endl << prompt3;
    cout <<endl;
{
```

This is the same function for displaying numbers:

```
int display(int prompt1, int prompt2, int prompt3)
{
    cout << prompt1 << endl << prompt2 << endl << prompt3;
    cout << endl;
}
```

This makes this procedure highly reusable, because it can be reused for any data type; and highly extensible, because only a small change was made (the parameter list) to accommodate the reuse.

Type Safeness

The format conversion specifiers have to match the data types in the parameter list. If they do not match, the compiler will not catch the error during compile time. When the program is run, unpredictable results may occur. Depending on whether the error is in a **scanf( )** or **printf( )** function, code or parts of the operating system can be output or an attempt made to input to a variable. Consider the aforementioned function:

```
int display(int num1, int num2, int num3)
{
    printf("%-10s\n,%-10s\n, %-10s\n",num1, num2, num3);
}
```

In this function, the format conversion specifier is not of the same type as the variables in the argument list. This version of the function will compile with no errors. During runtime, the specifier will look to display a null-terminated string. Since the data is a decimal, there is no null terminator. It will continue to look for it no matter where it is stored in memory. Subsequently, code or part of the operating system may be displayed. This would also occur if the **scanf( )** function was being used. An attempt would be made to store possibly part of the operating system or some part of the program code to a variable. This is called *weak type checking*. No attempt is made at compile time to check the specifiers with the data types to ensure that they match.

The IOSTREAMS have strong type checking or are type safe. Because the IOSTREAM does not use format conversion specifiers to represent the data, this type of runtime error will not occur. The correct implementation to display or scan in that data type will automatically be executed. This occurs because of the next advantage that the IOSTREAM has over the standard input/output library: one interface, multiple implementation.

One Interface, Multiple Implementation

One interface, multiple implementation means *there is one way to ask and many ways to perform*. In the IOSTREAM facility, when a message is sent to an object to perform a behavior, the data is sent to the object; then, the object determines which implementation (which of its member functions) will actually be activated. The correct implementation is not determined by the programmer, but rather the object that carries out the behavior.

In the standard input/output library, it is up to the programmer to decide what will be implemented. Therefore, it is the responsibility of the programmer to know what should be executed and when. When using the standard I/O library, there are several interfaces and many implementations, and the programmer has to be well versed in them all.

User-Defined Data Types and Input/Output

The standard input/output library makes it very difficult to create input or output capabilities for user-defined data types. With the IOSTREAMS, the right (>>) and left (<<) shift operators can be overloaded so that the programmer can continue to use **cout** and **cin** to output and input a user-defined data type. To create an operator overload member function for a user-defined class, the class must define what that operation will mean if applied to that class.

Because the advantages of the object-oriented IOSTREAM classes are obvious, the programmer may wonder why continue to use the nonobject-oriented I/O facilities. The answer is a simple and practical one. In many environments, C++ code must coexist with C code, and C++ I/O must coexist with C I/O. There are millions of lines of C code in place at installations that are moving to C++. There is no shortage of tested, debugged, true-and-tried libraries of C code that can be effectively used in a C++ environment. To maximize code reuse, it becomes imperative for the C++ programmer to be conversant with the C standard I/O functions, as well as with the C++ IOSTREAM input/output facilities.

From Device-Dependent I/O to Independent I/O

When the logic of a routine or a computer program relies on the specific structure or implementation of an I/O device that it accesses, this routine or program is said to be device-dependent. If the device for this routine is changed, then the logic of the routine must be changed also. There are various situations in which writing device-dependent code is desirable. Normally, these situations come down on the side of efficiency, mission-critical, real-time, or embedded systems. For instance, if a programmer needs to decode and display a PCX bitmap in real time, the program could contain code that looks something like Listing 1.7.

Listing 1.7

```
void pcx_image::displayPcxImage(void)
{
    unsigned int segment;
    unsigned int offset;
    segment = FP_SEG(BlueBitPlane);
    offset = FP_OFF(BlueBitPlane);
    outp(0x3c4,2);
    outp(0x3c5,1);
    movedata(segment,offset,0xa000,0x000,38400);
    segment = FP_SEG(GreenBitPlane);
    offset = FP_OFF(GreenBitPlane);
    outp(0x3c4,2);
    outp(0x3c5,2);
    movedata(segment,offset,0xa000,0x000,38400);
```

```
      segment = FP_SEG(RedBitPlane);
      offset = FP_OFF(RedBitPlane);
      outp(0x3c4,2);
      outp(0x3c5,4);
      movedata(segment,offset,0xa000,0x000,38400);
      segment = FP_SEG(IntensityBitPlane);
      offset = FP_OFF(IntensityBitPlane);
      outp(0x3c4,2);
      outp(0x3c5,8);
      movedata(segment,offset,0xa000,0x000,38400);
      outp(0x3c4,2);
      outp(0x3c5,0xF);
    }
```

In Listing 1.7, the **movedata( )** function contains specific references to addresses in video memory; for example, *0xa000,0x000*. The **outp( )** function also contains device-specific information. This routine is device-dependent. It was designed to access the color bit planes of a specific VGA adapter quickly. This block of code might have to be changed if another brand-name video adapter was used. If another type of video adapter was used, this routine would definitely have to be changed. Nevertheless, for necessary reasons, the particular hardware structure and memory configuration and location was relied upon.

It was necessary for the programmer to be aware of the specific structure of this video adapter; for example: How many registers does it have? What were their locations? How were they started? Where were the hardware errors posted? What is the read/write syntax for the registers and so on. Timing information was also needed. For instance, what is the exact data transfer rate between core memory and display adapter memory, and how is this accomplished. When an application program uses this amount of device-specific information, it is certainly device-dependent.

Needless to say, the program in Listing 1.7 and the routines it contained had a very low degree of reusability, and no degree of portability. Reusability and portability are usually major considerations in software design and development. However, they are not the only considerations and, within some classes of computer programs, they are not considerations at all. However, that device-dependence cannot be approached with reuse in mind. As we will see, the techniques that object-oriented programming can bring to I/O may redeem device-dependent programming after all. We will get back to this later.

First- and second-generation programmers were forced to use specific device architecture and addresses to do regular I/O. Once upon a time, this was the normal state of affairs. However, with the arrival of fourth-generation operating systems, the entire mind-set of how I/O should be accessed has changed. Now, conventional wisdom steers the programmer away from device-dependent programming.

To attain the goals of software reuse and portability, the notion of referencing the specific structure of I/O devices was deemed taboo. If we are to write programs that can be moved easily among a family of machines with possibly different video adapters, different pointing devices, and different memory configurations, then we can't include device-specific code in the programs. In fact, we want to consider all data as a generic stream of data coming from a generic I/O device, and going to a generic I/O device. To achieve this programming paradigm, some software component has to translate the generic stream of data into hardware-specific bytes, and the generic I/O devices into real-life hardware addresses, registers, interrupts, and memory configurations.

The component that presents the programmer with the generic device and generic data stream is made up of the operating system and a high-level computer language. The UNIX, OS/2, and NT operating systems all provide the necessary device-independence that allows the programmer to approach the *stream* concept of I/O. There are C++ compilers for each of these environments. The C++ environment includes two I/O facilities:

1. The nonobject-oriented I/O facilities
2. The object-oriented I/O facilities

The nonobject-oriented I/O facilities consist of low-level, unformatted I/O and stream (buffered) I/O. The object-oriented I/O facilities comprise the IOSTREAMS and the manipulators. The current trends in operating systems for the desktop provide device-independence through the concepts of *device contexts* and *presentation spaces*. Through a combination of IOSTREAM facilities provided by the C++ environment, and the *device contexts* and *presentation spaces* that are prevalent in the current trend of operating systems, the programmer can achieve a higher degree of device-independence, software component reusability, and software portability than is currently available through the use of the stream concept alone.

In this book, we will talk about the object-oriented input/output facilities that are part of the C++ environment. The input/output facilities are packaged in a set of classes called the IOSTREAMS. We will describe the function and purpose of the data members and the member functions that are within the set of IOSTREAM classes.

We will describe the relationships and interdependence between the classes in the IOSTREAM facilities. In this book, we will define what object-oriented input is as it relates to the IOSTREAM facilities. We will explore the new device-independence that is achieved, using the device context concepts used in the current trends in GUI programming. We will explore the new type of device-dependence achieved through hardware modeling, using object-oriented concepts and the IOSTREAMS. Finally, we will examine the application of the object-oriented IOSTREAMS to sound-card technology, communication technology, GUI programming, and graphics programming. We will begin our discussion with an introduction to the IOSTREAMS.

Object-Oriented Streams

By an aggregate, *we are to understand any collection into a whole* **M** *of definite and separate objects* **m** *of our intuition or our thought . . .*

GEORGE CANTOR—*CONTRIBUTIONS TO THE FOUNDING OF THE THEORY OF TRANSFINITE NUMBERS*

Introduction to C++ IOSTREAMS

A complete I/O library in a computer environment will cover the entire spectrum between physical devices and logical objects, with physical devices at one end of the spectrum and logical objects at the other end of the spectrum. A complete I/O library will serve the needs of the system programmers (those who write device drivers, operating systems, interrupt handlers, and such), as well as the needs of the application programmers (those who normally deal with higher-level constructs). In Figure 2.1, the hardware devices at the left end of the spectrum represent traditional system-level programming requirements and concerns. As we move toward the right end of the spectrum, we approach the multimedia concerns that normally fall in the domain of applications programming. If we are faced with programming I/O at the left end of the spectrum, we have to deal with myriad characteristics and attributes from a wide range of devices, such as keyboards, modems, monitors, printers, bar code readers, tape drives, fax cards, disk drives, serial ports, parallel ports, sound cards, disk controllers, data acquisition adapters, joysticks, video capture boards, pointing devices, pen input devices, scanners, NTSC adapters, memory chips—to name several.

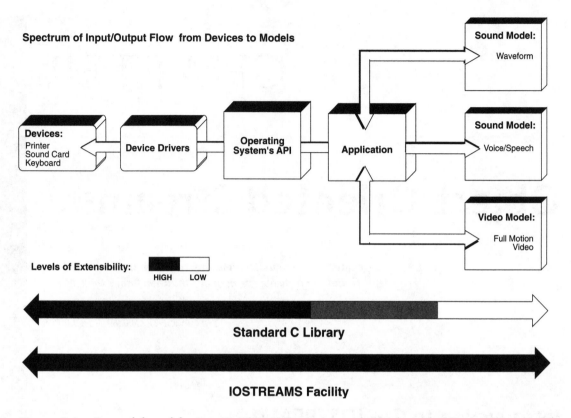

Figure 2.1   *Extensibility of the C++ IOSTREAMS in comparison to the **stdio** library of the I/O flow from models to devices.*

These devices have both physical characteristics and logical characteristics. Table 2.1 shows a list of some of the logical characteristics of hard disks, CD-ROMs, modems, graphic cards, and sound cards, along with some of the physical characteristics. A complete I/O facility will give the programmer an interface to the physical and the logical aspect of these devices. These devices have traditionally come in two flavors. They are usually classified as *block devices*, or *character devices*.

A *block device* accesses multiple bytes at a time usually in a direct manner. A block device does not need to access data sequentially; it can retrieve or place multiple bytes at a specific address or location. A disk drive is a good example of a block device. A disk drive can access data in chunks of 128, 256, 512, 1,024, 32,768 . . . bytes at a time. A *character* device accesses one character at a time in a sequential fashion. Character devices are normally associated with queues, stacks, or some derivative. A keyboard is a good example of a character device. It processes its input

Table 2.1   **Physical and Logical Characteristics of the CD-ROM, Hard Disk, Modem, and Graphics Adapter Devices**

Device	Physical Characteristics	Logical Characteristics
CD-ROM	Optical disk storage unit. Pits on the surface. Laser shines on a track that contains a pit. Light reflect indicates ON; absence of light indicates OFF. Read-only or write-once technology.	Divided into sectors.
Hard Disk	Data stored in magnetic patterns written in circles called tracks. Read/write heads read or write data. Read and write technology.	Divided into sectors. Divided into partitions. Has a directory file. Has directories, subdirectories.
Modem	RS-232C connector, speakers, batteries, dip switches, dialer	Baud rate is the number of times per second a signal changes state or varies channels. Parity, data bits, and stop bits.
Graphics Adapter Card	Color and control registers Memory Output connectors.	Palettes Coordinate system, coordinate pairs Pixels Resolution

in a serial mode, one keypress at a time. Table 2.2 lists the primary features of block devices and character devices.

A complete I/O facility will give the programmer the means to program block devices, character devices, or any combination there of effectively. At the other end of the input-output spectrum (Figure 2.1) dwell the logical entities: the objects that are input into the computer and/or its peripheral devices, and the objects that are output from the computer and/or its peripheral devices. These objects take the form of numbers, characters, text, sounds, speech, printed text, graphics, full motion video, voice activation, and so on.

Along with the access to physical devices, efficient access to the higher-level logical entities, structures, and data types represents the entire gamut that a programmer may face when implementing any given component of software. The IOSTREAM facilities in C++ take the concept of streams to a higher level by adding object-oriented capabilities to the input and output.

The IOSTREAMS are a set of C++ classes used to implement an object-oriented model of input and output. The IOSTREAM facilities packaged as a standard component with all C++ compilers is an object-oriented input/output facility, providing access to unbuffered (low-level) as well as buffered I/O operations. If for some reason, the IOSTREAM facilities that are available with any given C++ compiler are not sufficient for the job at hand, the programmer can improve them through inher-

Table 2.2   Characteristics of Block and Character Devices

Block Devices	Character Devices
Stores information in a fixed size called blocks.	Delivers or accepts a stream of characters without regard to block structure.
Does not need to access data sequentially.	Accesses data sequentially.
Can access a block independently from another, performs seek operations.	No seek operations.
Data files can be accessed by common system calls (read, write, etc.).	Data files can be accessed by common system calls (read, write, etc.).
Can retrieve or place multiple bytes at a specific address or location.	Accesses a character at a time in a stream; not addressable.
Files are mapped by a directory file.	Operates using a queuing process.
Example of block device is a disk.	Examples of character devices are: printers, screens, mice.

itance, polymorphism, encapsulation, and specialization. The I/O facilities in C++ are not restricted to a specific set of keywords. The class implementation of I/O adds extensibility and complete flexibility to the output capabilities of the C++ environment. Although the *stream* is a powerful programming construct, enabling the programmer to meet extremely challenging I/O demands, the object-oriented IOSTREAM has proved to be the proverbial silver bullet.

The Object-Oriented Paradigm

Object-oriented programming is an approach to programming in which the object is the fundamental unit of modularity. The *object* is a model or simulation of some person, place, thing, or idea.

Object-Oriented Programming

Any object-oriented programming environment must support at least the following basic concepts:

- Encapsulation
- Inheritance
- Polymorphism

Encapsulation

Encapsulation is an abstraction that combines operations and data into one unit or point of reference. This point of reference, or unit, is ultimately called an object.

Objects can be grouped into levels of commonness. *Classes* represent a set of attributes and characteristics that will be common among an entire family of objects. The class provides a blueprint or definition for an object or group of objects. It defines the characteristics, behaviors, or operations for those objects. Class relationship diagrams can be used to describe classes and their relationships with data, operations, or other classes. We will use *class relationship diagrams* in this book to talk about the relationships between the IOSTREAM family of classes, and the classes that we will model for input and output devices.

Figure 2.2 shows the encapsulation of a **graphics adapter card** class. The XGA graphics adapter card would be a specific type of graphics adapter card from the group of all graphics adapter cards. The class of graphics adapter card has behaviors that determine the color and resolution capabilities of a computer. Two examples of instances of graphics adapter cards are XGA and VGA. The **xga** object has the

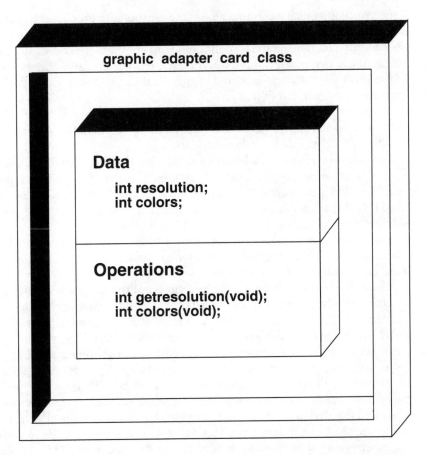

Figure 2.2 *Encapsulation of data and operations of the **graphics adapter card** class.*

capacity to display 320 × 200 to 1024 × 768 resolution, and as many as 65,536 colors simultaneously. The **vga** object has the capacity to display 320 × 200 resolution with 256 colors, to 640 × 480 resolution with 16 colors. The **graphics adapter card** class defines the group of adapter cards that give the computer graphics capabilities.

In a class, there is data and operations that access the data. Some of the data or some operations may be of interest only to the class, and of no interest to the outside world. In that case, the data and operations are internal and are used to carry out only some other behavior that is stereotypical of the class. This information hiding protects the integrity of the class, preventing accidental modification of the internal operations that may cause some type of behavioral failure. This welding together of operations and data with information hiding is one common form of *encapsulation*. Encapsulation gives the class its distinctive identity.

Inheritance

Inheritance is a mechanism that allows the creation of new classes by means of using already existing classes. The new class is the already existing class with added behaviors and/or data. The new class defines the qualities that make it distinctive. It reuses the qualities that make it similar to the existing class or classes. Instead of recreating those qualities, they are inherited. Those qualities will include both data and the operations. A class that inherits from another class is not an instance of the class, but rather an extension of the class. The existing class is traditionally called the **ancestor**, or **base**, class and the new class that inherits the qualities of the ancestor or base class is called the **descendant**, or **derived**, class.

For example, a **graphics adapter card** class has the ability to reveal the state of the currently installed graphics card on a system. The class can set the card to a text or graphics mode, and reveal the current mode of the card. Another class can be created called **vga** class. It would have the ability to reveal its current mode and set its adapter card to text or graphics mode. It could load an image into its video display memory, and it can display the image on a screen. The new **vga** class has common characteristics with the **graphics adapter card** class. In fact, it is a **graphics adapter card** class with added functionality.

The core similarity between the **vga** class and the **graphics adapter card** class is contained in the **graphics adapter card** class. The differences between the classes are contained in the new **vga** class. The *class relationship diagram* in Figure 2.3 shows the relationship between the **graphics adapter card** class and the **vga** class. The difference between the **base** class and the **derived** class occupies a peculiar place in the object-oriented paradigm. Because the **derived** class depends upon the **base** class for its definition, the **derived** class is not defined without its **base** class and cannot be referenced apart from the **base** class. Although the differences between the **base** class and the **derived** class are not enough to be a **stand-alone** class, the differences are more than just a data type. The differences can be member functions or data members, or a set of member functions and data members. This set of differences that is less than a complete class and more than a data type we call the **protoclass**.

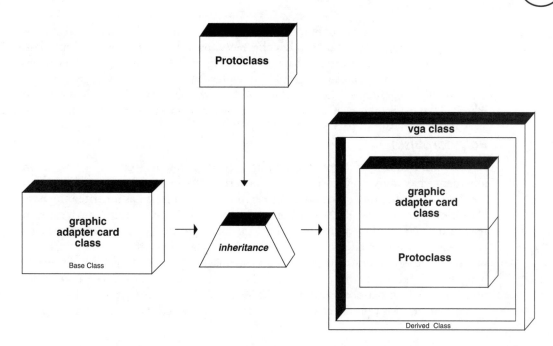

Figure 2.3 *Single inheritance of the **graphics adapter card** class and the protoclass by the **vga** class.*

The **protoclass** is the set of differences between a **base** class and the **derived** class. In the **derived** class, the **protoclass** cannot stand alone as a complete class. It may stand alone as a complete class in some context other than the **derived** class's context, but in the context of the **derived** class, the **protoclass** is incomplete. The **protoclass** requires the **base** class to become the **derived** class. In our graphics card example, instead of recreating the same abilities again in the new class, the **vga** class would inherit them from the **graphics adapter card** class. Figure 2.3 shows that the inheritance relationship exists between the **protoclass** and the **graphics adapter card** class to form a new class. The new **vga** class inherits the **graphic adapter card** class, then defines its ability to read and display images within itself. The new class has access to the data and the operations of the **graphics adapter card** class. Here, the **graphics adapter card** class is the **ancestor** and the new **vga** class is the **descendant**. The **base class** is also called **parent class**, and the **derived class** is also called **child class**.

This mechanism enhances the idea of program reusability and easily made modifications. Other classes can inherit these **base** classes. The new classes will contain only the differences between classes. Code will not be duplicated, and the model would be much smaller. Any class can be a **base** class creating a lineage of inheriting classes. Modifications made in the **ancestor** or **base** class will also be inherited by the descending or **derived** classes. Any modifications in the **descendant** will not affect the **ancestor**.

There are two basic types of inheritance: single and multiple. The example given was an example of single inheritance in which a new class inherits the ability of one class. It is also possible to inherit more than one class. Figure 2.4 shows an inheritance relationship between an **xga** class, a **graphics adapter card** class and a **vga** class. This is called *multiple inheritance*. The new class will have the ability of all the classes it is to inherit. All the advantages of single inheritance will also apply to multiple inheritance.

Polymorphism

Polymorphism allows the same name to be used for different forms of a task. In an inheritance hierarchy, polymorphism allows **derived** classes to redefine a task found in the **base** class using the same name. For example, the **vga** class has inherited the **base class graphiccard**. It has all the same operations as the **base** class except that it can also read into video memory an image and then display that image on the screen. A new class called **xga** is created and it will inherit the **vga** class. Therefore, the new **xga** class will reveal its state and read and display an image. However, there is a difference between the display memory in these card types. The **vga** class card display memory uses a multiplane-per-pixel approach. There are four bit planes stored in memory. Each bit plane has a primary color (red, green, blue, and intensity), and stores complete

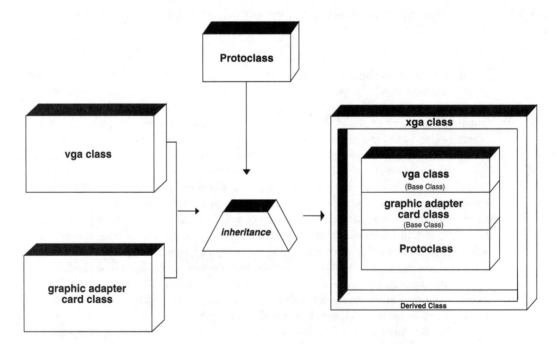

Figure 2.4 *Multiple inheritance of the **vga** class, **graphics adapter card** class, and the protoclass by the **xga** class.*

representation of the image. To display a pixel on the screen, the display controller reads a bit from each plane, and uses the collection of these bits to determine the color of the pixel. It has four bits per pixel. On the other hand, an **xga** class card has 16 bits per pixel in order to display 65,536 colors (1111111111111111) in 640 × 480 resolution. It uses 5 bits for red, 6 bits for green, and 5 bits for blue. To display an image for either of these card types will require different algorithms. Therefore, the implementations to load and display the **xga** class image must be redefined or overridden by the **xga** class to work properly. Both classes will use the same name to read and display an image (**load image**, **display image**), but depending on the class of the object during compile time, the appropriate form of **load and display image( )** will be executed.

Object-Oriented Concepts in C++

To implement object-oriented programming, the computer language should be able to support the object-oriented paradigm. The C++ language has keywords, operators, and constructs that allow the programmer to create types that support classes and encapsulation, inheritance, and polymorphism.

C++ and Encapsulation

In C++, the user-defined class type is declared by using the keyword **class**, **struct**, or **union**. In this book, when we refer to the C++ keyword **class**, we are also referring to **struct** and **union** when they are used to support object-oriented programming. The class is declared in a header file with a **.h** extension. A class has data members and member functions. These elements can be **private**, **public**, or **protected**. The elements declared as **private** are accessed only by member functions. They are used only by the internal of the class. They cannot be accessed outside the class, or by **derived** classes. These elements are encapsulated within the class. The elements declared as **public** can be accessed outside the **class** and by the **derived** classes. The **protected** elements can be accessed only by the **derived** classes.

By default, all elements are **private** when using the **class** keyword, and **public** when using the **struct** keyword. **Public, protected**, and **private** elements are preceded by the keywords **public, protected**, and **private**, followed by a colon. What follows is the list of data members and the prototypes for the member functions. The prototype tells the name of the member function, what the member function will return, and the argument list. There must be a prototype for all member functions. Listing 2.1 shows an example of a declaration of a *class graphiccard*.

Listing 2.1

```
class graphiccard {
private:
```

```
        boolean textmode;
        boolean graphicsmode;
        int mode;
        int currentmode;
        int driver;
        int initialize(int graphdriver);
    protected:
        boolean detectcard(void);
        int detectmode(void);
    public:
        boolean textmode(void);
        boolean graphicsmode(void);
        int mode(void);
        int driver(void);
        int getcurrentmode(void);
        boolean settextmode(void);
        boolean setgraphicmode(int graphdriver, int graphmode);
    }
```

The members' ***textmode, graphicsmode, mode, currentmode,*** and ***driver*** are all private elements of the class. They are preceded by the keyword **private**. They can be directly accessed only by the member functions. The only way these variables can be revealed is by the **public** member functions that bear the same names as the data members. These member functions will return the contents of the data members. They should not be able to alter the contents of the data members, because this will conflict with encapsulation. The member functions **initialize( )**, **detect-card( )** and **detectmode( )** are **protected**. They cannot be directly accessed outside the class. They can be accessed only by other member functions and **derived** classes. They are used by the **public** member function **setgraphicmode( )**. Figure 2.5 shows the access permission that is available to member functions, derived classes and the outside world.

The class declaration is placed in a file with an **.H** extension. The coding for these member functions is placed in a separate file with a **.CPP** extension. Each definition of each member function will have the member function name and argument list preceded by the return type and the class name to which the member function belongs. This will be followed by the scope resolution operator (::). The scope resolution operator informs the compiler that this version of the member function belongs to this class. Listing 2.2 is an example of how some member functions for the class **graphiccard** would appear in the **.CPP** file.

Listing 2.2

```
boolean graphiccard::detectcard(int graphdriver)
{
    program code
}
```

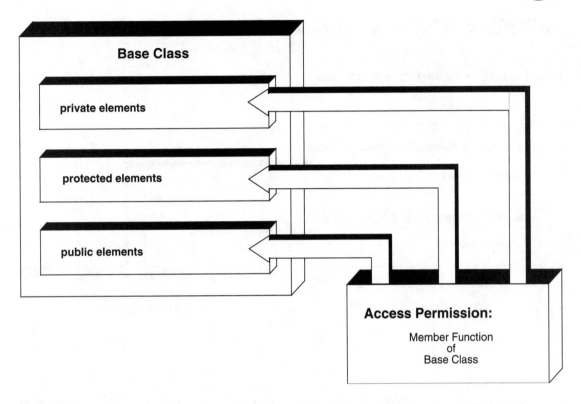

Figure 2.5   *(a) The access permission that is available to the member functions of the base class.*

```
int graphiccard::settextmode(void)
{
    program code
}
```

To declare an instance of the class **graphiccard**, declare a variable of that class type; for example:

```
graphiccard vga, xga;
```

In this case, **xga** and **vga** are instances of the class **graphiccard**. An example of a request to that object would appear like this:

```
vga.settextmode( );
```

C++ and Inheritance

As stated, inheritance allows the creation of new classes by means of using already existing classes. The new classes are a combination of the already existing classes

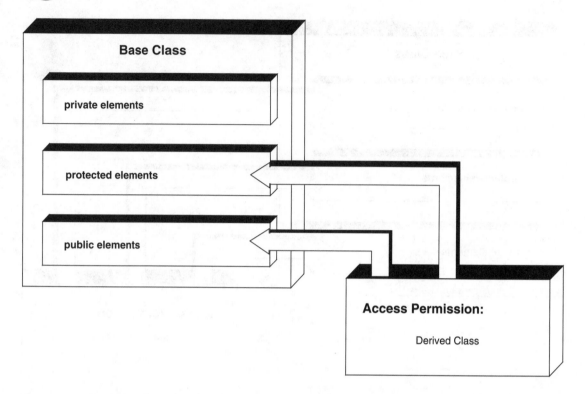

Figure 2.5 (*Continued*)   (*b*) *The access permission that is available to the derived class of the base class.*

with added abilities and/or data. The added abilities are defined in the new class. This makes the new class distinctive, and reuses the qualities that make it similar to the existing class. In C++, an existing class can be incorporated into another class's declaration. The new class is said to have **derived** from the existing class. The existing class is the **base** class.

To show inheritance, in the **derived** class declaration, the **base** class name is placed after the **derived** class name preceded by a semicolon and the type of access the relationship will have. The relationship the **derived** class has with the **base** class can be **public** or **private**. If the relationship is **public**, the public elements of the **base** class will also be considered public members of the **derived** class. If the relationship is **private**, then public and protected elements of the **base** class are considered private in the **derived** class. Figure 2.6 shows the transfer of data members and member functions during the inheritance process. The elements of the **base** class are incorporated into the private and public parts of the **derived** class. Listing 2.3 shows how the declaration of a derived class vga inherits the base class graphiccard as public.

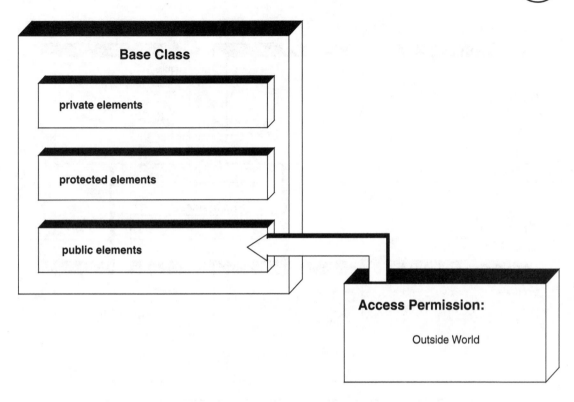

Figure 2.5 (*Continued*)   (*c*) *The access permission that is available to the outside world.*

Listing 2.3

```
class vga: public graphiccard{
private:
    int videopage;
    int size;
    char imageloc[4];
    char screenloc[4];

protected:
    int getvideopage(int graphdriver, int graphmode);

public:
    int loadimage(int imagesize, char *location);
    int displayimage(int imagesize, char *screen);
}
```

This example shows *single inheritance*. When the **graphiccard** class has a public relationship with the **derived** class **vga**, all the public elements of the **base** class

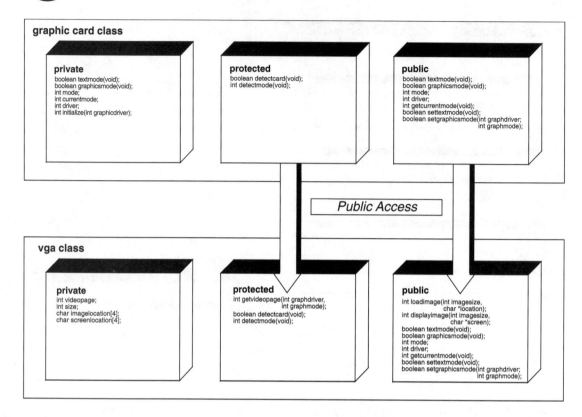

Figure 2.6   *(a) This diagram illustrates the transfer of code by public access through inheritance.*

graphiccard are incorporated into the public members of the **vga** class and the protected elements of the **base** class **graphiccard** are incorporated into the protected elements of the **vga** class. When the **graphiccard** class has a private relationship with the **derived** class **vga**, all the public elements of the **base** class **graphiccard** are incorporated into the private elements of the **vga** class, and the protected elements of the **base** class **graphiccard** are also incorporated into the private elements of the **vga** class (Figure 2.6).

A class can inherit more than one class. This is called *multiple inheritance*. The **base** classes appear in the same way as for single inheritance, but separated by a comma. Again, each of the **base** classes can have a private or public relationship with the **derived** class. Listing 2.4 shows an example of multiple inheritance.

Listing 2.4

```
class xga: public graphiccard, private vga{
private:
    int maxX;
```

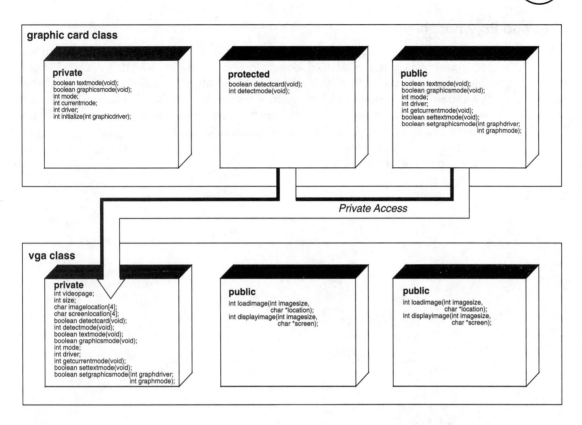

Figure 2.6 (*Continued*)   (*b*) *This diagram illustrates the transfer of code by private access through inheritance.*

```
        int maxY;
        int driver;
        int mode;
    protected:
        int determinemaxX(void);
        int determinemaxY(void);
    public:
        int resolution(int graphdriver, int graphmode);
        int maxX(void);
        int maxY(void);
```

This example shows a **derived** class **xga** that inherits **graphiccard** and **vga** class. The class **graphiccard** has a public relationship with the **derived** class **xga**, and **vga** class has a private relationship with the **derived** class. Figure 2.6 shows how the **base** classes are incorporated into the public and private elements of the **derived** class **xga**.

C++ and Polymorphism

One way polymorphism can be implemented in C++ is through *virtual* functions. Polymorphism allows a **derived** class to redefine a function that is declared in the **base** class. The **base** class can declare the functions as virtual. The keyword **virtual** precedes the declaration of the function in the header file. The **derived** class can then declare a function of the same name, and redefine the implementation of the function. The prototypes of the **virtual** function in the **base** class and the redefined function in the **derived** class must have the same prototypes. Listing 2.5 shows an example of how a virtual function is declared.

Listing 2.5

```
class vga: public graphiccard{
private:
    int videopage;
    int size;
    char imageloc[4];
    char screenloc[4];

protected:
    int getvideopage(int graphdriver, int graphmode);

public:
    virtual int loadimage(int imagesize, char *location);
    virtual int displayimage(int imagesize, char *screen);
}
class xga: public graphiccard, private vga{
private:
    int maxX;
    int maxY;
    int driver;
    int mode;
    int size;
    char imageloc[4];
    char screenloc[4];
protected:
    int determinemaxX(void);
    int determinemaxY(void);
public:
    int resolution(int graphdriver, int graphmode);
    int maxX(void);
    int maxY(void);
    int loadimage(int imagesize, char *location)
    int displayimage(int imagesize, char *screen);
}
```

An object declared of the **derived** class receiving a request to implement that function will execute the **derived** class version of the function. If the **derived** class does not redefine the virtual function, then the **base** class's version will be executed.

Classes and the IOSTREAMS

The IOSTREAMS are made of three fundamental types of classes:

- *stream state classes*
- *buffer classes*
- *conversion or translation classes*

The class relationship diagram in Figure 2.7 shows the fundamental relationships among the three types of classes. Notice that the buffer classes have contained relationships, as opposed to inheritance relationships, with the IOSTREAM classes.

The **stream state** classes contain the condition of a stream at any given point or time. The IOSTREAM has several predefined states. The IOSTREAM classes also support user-defined states. The stream may be in a *good* state, signaling that the previous operation on the stream was successful and the next operation on the stream can be attempted. The stream may be in a fail or bad state, signaling that the previous operations failed and, unless action is taken, any following operations will fail. The **stream state** class also contains specifications that represent the format of how data should be interpreted coming into or going out of the stream. For instance, the data may need to be read into a hexadecimal, binary, or double precision format. The data may need to be sent to the output in scientific notation.

The **buffer** classes specify a generic holding area for the data while it is in transit from an input device or to an output device. The buffer classes also contain the specifications for the operations that can be performed on the data in the generic holding area. The buffer classes specify position designators that determine where the next character in the holding area will be read from, or where in the holding area the next character will be written.

The **conversion** classes either convert the data types to an anonymous sequence of bytes on the output stream, or translate an anonymous sequence of bytes from the input stream into either user-defined data types, or built-in data types. The **conversion** classes are largely responsible for giving the programmer the device-independent look and feel that the IOSTREAMS have.

These classes are interconnected through inheritance and possession. The **conversion** classes are usually descendants of a **stream state** class. The **stream state** class may possess a **buffer** class. The **buffer** class may have buffer ancestors, and so on. Because the IOSTREAMS are a set of classes (not functions!), all the concepts and advantages of object orientation can be applied.

Inheritance allows the programmer to combine the data members and member functions of a class designed to model input, with a class designed to model output. This combination will give the programmer a class that is suitable for both input and output. Through inheritance, a **buffer** class can be combined with a **printer** class, producing a **buffered printer** class. Using inheritance, the programmer can specialize or modify the functionality of any of the IOSTREAM classes, through function

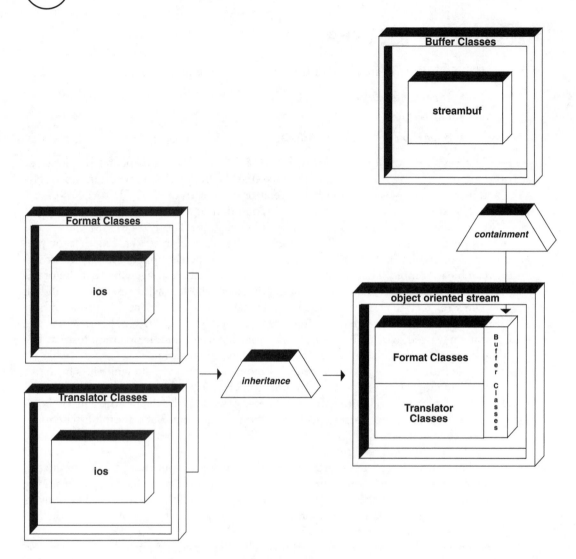

Figure 2.7   *Class relationship of the **format**, **translator**, and **buffer** classes of the IOSTREAMS.*

overloading or function overriding. Through polymorphism, the programmer can maintain a single input/output interface to multiple device types. This moves the program in the direction of device-independence. When the technique of polymorphism is properly applied, code reuse and modularity follow. Encapsulation gives the programmer the capability to combine I/O channels with the proper operations, ensuring that the channel is accessed only through or by intelligent type-safe member functions, preventing unauthorized access by rogue device drivers and the like.

The **stream state** class that forms an important **base** class for the **conversion** classes is called **ios**. The **ios** class contains information about how the stream has been opened. For instance, has the stream been opened in the *append mode*, or can the stream be *read* from and *written* to. Some streams are read-only, and some streams are write-only. Some streams can be opened for both read and write operations. The **ios** class holds the information that designates the attached stream as a binary stream or a text stream. The **ios** class controls the information that determines the base to which numbers will be formatted when being inserted into a stream or when extracted from a stream. That is, whether the numbers will be formatted as decimal, hexadecimal, or octal, or as scientific notation or in a fixed decimal format. The **ios** class also controls precision information for numbers entering or exiting a stream. We will explore the **ios** class in more detail in Chapter 3.

The buffer class that provides the base functionality of data sequence processing for the IOSTREAM classes is called **streambuf**. The **streambuf** class can process generic sequences of bytes. The **streambuf** class has methods that get bytes, put bytes, skip bytes, put back bytes, and so on. The **streambuf** class has the functionality that controls what happens with stream overflow or stream underflow conditions. From the **streambuf** class, other classes are derived to deal with file buffers, generic memory processing, and **stdio** synchronization. The **streambuf** class is usually contained as a data member of one of the other IOSTREAM classes. For instance, the **ios** class usually contains a **streambuf** data member. Positioning is another responsibility of the **streambuf** class. The **streambuf** family of classes control the movement of a **get** pointer and **put** pointer. The **get** pointer points to the next byte to be read, assigned, or viewed. The **put** pointer points to the next byte to be written, assigned, or viewed. We will have much to say about the **streambuf** family of classes throughout the remainder of this book. This family of classes provides a fundamental link to the operating system's I/O API.

There are two **conversion** classes that form the foundation of data translation within the IOSTREAM class hierarchy. These classes are called **istream** and **ostream**. The **istream** class models an input stream. The **ostream** class models an output stream. Both **istream** and **ostream** have **ios** as a **base** class. Both **istream** and **ostream** have access to a **streambuf** class. The **istream** and **ostream** classes encapsulate the primary object-oriented representation of a sink and a source. The **istream** and **ostream** classes provide the C++ programming environment with the notion of the *object-oriented stream*. The **istream** has member functions that accept into the stream generic sequences of data, and convert them to built-in types, user-defined types, or user-defined structures. The **ostream** accepts built-in types, user-defined types, or user-defined structures, and converts them to generic sequences of bytes that can be sent to the output (sink).

Together, the **istream** and **ostream** classes summarize the base functionality of the entire family of IOSTREAM classes. The **istream** and **ostream** classes are **base** classes for most of the other classes in the IOSTREAM hierarchy. Most IOSTREAM implementations have used multiple inheritance to derive a single class, called **iostream**, that is derived from **istream** and **ostream**. The reader should not confuse the iostream class with the IOSTREAM family of classes. The **iostream** class is a single entity that has been derived from an **istream** class and an **ostream** class. The IOSTREAM classes represent the entire object-oriented network of classes in the C++ environment that includes the **ios** class, **streambuf** family, **ostream** family, **istream** family, and the manipulators.

Packaging the I/O facilities in a set of classes allows the programmer to custom shape and mold the input and output to exactly fit the requirements of even the most demanding system. Classes provide the foundations for modeling I/O events, processes, devices, and operations. The notion of the *class* adds extensibility to I/O in C++. We cannot predict what types of devices will be connected to a computer at any given time in the future. We cannot modify the language every time a new peripheral is introduced. However, with the concept of classes and the IOSTREAMS, our ability to process I/O can evolve to adapt to whatever the prevailing environment is at that time.

Object-Oriented Input/Output

An object-oriented approach to the block and character devices give the programmer the ability to implement designs that match these devices in form and function. Although, in many applications, it is desirable to program independently of the structure of the devices that will be accessed. In some systems-level work, it is not only desirable, but also necessary to consider the structure to take full and efficient advantage of the specific capabilities of the device being accessed. Device drivers and interrupt handlers are examples of software components that usually require specific knowledge of the physical and logical structure of some I/O device.

An object-oriented I/O facility gives the programmer the power to model physical and logical characteristics of any device connected to or accessed by the computer. Modeling and simulations are natural activities in an object-oriented environment; the programmer has the option of programming at a high level, ignoring the underlying structure, or emulating the actual device he or she is programming to get maximum performance.

Using an object-oriented approach to input and output, the programmer can implement the input/output data structures directly from an I/O model. For example, the programmer might implement a voice object that accepts text input and sends speech output. If the programmer needs to access a character device for input and output (perhaps a VGA adapter), the programmer can simulate the attributes and functionality of the VGA adapter using object-oriented techniques. Any I/O facility that provides the low-level access, the stream paradigm, and object orientation also provides the programmer with a complete picture of input and output in a computer environment.

The **istream** class models an input stream in C++. When data is taken from a stream of type **ostream** and stored in a variable, it is called an *extraction*. The data is extracted from a stream in order to be input to a variable. The **>>** is called the *extraction operator*. The right shift operator is overloaded to perform input operations on built-in and user-defined data types.

The **cin** object is an instance of the **istream** class linked to the console. The **cin** object and the extraction operator **>>** can be used to input a built-in data type. Listing 2.6 is an example of a program that uses **cin** and the extraction operators to input to **char**, **float**, **double**, **integer**, and **string** built-in data types.

Listing 2.6

```
// This program demonstrates the uses of the cin object and polymor
// phism.

#include <iostream.h>
#include <math.h>
#include "r_approx.h"
void main(void)
{
    char PI;
    float pi;
    double Pi;
    int pI;
    char Pie[3];
    rational approximation user_pi;

    cin >> PI;
    cin >> pi;
    cin >> Pi;
    cin >> pI;
    cin >> Pie;
    cin >> user_pi;

}
```

The extraction operator can be overloaded to input user-defined data types. The extraction operator is declared as a friend function in the header file of the user-defined type. The friend function returns a reference to an object of type **istream**. It also accepts a reference of an object of type **istream** and the object of the user-defined class. Listing 2.6 also shows how **cin** and the extraction operator is used to input a user-defined data type.

istream's get( ), getline( ), and read( )

The **get( )** is a member function of the **istream** class. This is the prototype for **get( )**:

```
istream &get(signed char &character,int Delim);
istream &get(unsigned char &character, int Delim);
istream &get(char &character int Delim);
```

This member function will take a character from an input stream. The character can be a signed **char**, unsigned **char**, or **char**. A reference to the **istream** object will be returned. It will perform no translation or conversion on the character. The character will be taken from a stream of type **istream**, and stored into a variable.

The **getline( )** is a member function of the **istream** class. This member function will take a sequence of characters and store them in a variable. This is the prototype for **getline( )**:

```
istream &getline(signed char *buffer, int number, char = '');
istream &getline(unsigned char *buffer, int number, char = '');
```

It will accept a pointer to a signed or unsigned **char**, an integer, and a character. The pointer to the signed or unsigned **char** is the destination where the sequence of characters will be stored. The member function will accept characters up to the integer or the character pending, which is encountered first. If the pointer is to a signed **char**, the character delimiter will be stored in the string. If the pointer is to an unsigned **char**, then the character delimiter will not be stored.

read( ) is a member function of the **istream** class. It will read a block of binary data from an input stream. This is the prototype for **read( )**:

```
istream &read(signed char *buffer, int number);
istream &read(unsigned char *buffer, int number);
```

This member function will accept an array or a pointer to a buffer and the number of bytes to be read. The pointer to a buffer or an array will store the block of characters. It can point to a signed **char** or an unsigned **char**. Listing 2.7 shows an example of a program using the **read( )** member function on built-in data types.

Listing 2.7

```
// This program demonstrates the use of the read( ) member function and
// the cout object.

#include <fstream.h>
#include <stdlib.h>

struct ColorRegister{
    unsigned char Red;
    unsigned char Green;
    unsigned char Blue;
};

struct PcxFileHeader{
    unsigned char Header;
    unsigned char Version;
    unsigned char Encode;
    unsigned char BitPerPix;
    unsigned X1;
    unsigned X2;
    unsigned Y1;
    unsigned Y2;
    unsigned Hres;
```

```
        unsigned Vres;
};
struct PcxInfo{
    unsigned char Vmode;
    unsigned char NumberOfPlanes;
    unsigned BytesPerLine;
    unsigned char unused[60];
};
struct PcxFileInfo{
    PcxFileHeader PcxHeader;
    ColorRegister Palette[16];
    PcxInfo Info;
};
void main(void)
{
    char PcxCompressedFile[13] = "filename.pcx";
    ifstream In;
    PcxFileInfo *HeaderRecord;
    HeaderRecord = new PcxFileInfo;
    if(!HeaderRecord){
        cerr << "could not allocate header";
        exit(0);
    }
    In.open(PcxCompressedFile,ios::binary);
    if(!In){
        cerr << "could not open " << PcxCompressedFile;
        delete HeaderRecord;
        cin.get( );
        exit(0);
    }
    In.read((char *)HeaderRecord,sizeof(PcxFileInfo));
    cout << "Header Number: "
         << (unsigned) HeaderRecord->PcxHeader.Header
         << endl;
    cout << "Version: " << (unsigned) HeaderRecord->PcxHeader.Version
         << endl;
    cout << "Encoded: " << (unsigned) HeaderRecord->PcxHeader.Encode <<
endl;
    cout << "Bits Per Pixel: "
         << (unsigned) HeaderRecord->PcxHeader.BitPerPix << endl;
    In.close( );
    delete HeaderRecord;
```

Output from Listing 2.7

Header Number: 10

Version: 5

Encoded: 1

Bits Per Pixel: 1

The program in Listing 2.7 uses the **read( )** member function from the **ifstream** class to read in the header file for a **pcx** graphic image. The **read( )** member function has a counterpart in the **ofstream** class. These member functions perform unformatted reads and writes of blocks of data.

The **ostream** class models an output stream in C++. When data is sent to a stream of type **ostream**, it is called an *insertion*. The data is inserted to a stream in order to output it to an external device. The **<<** is called the *insertion operator*. The left shift operator is overloaded to perform output operations on built-in and user-defined data types.

The **cout** object found in standard IOSTREAM implementations is an instance of the **ostream** class linked to the console. The **cout** object and the insertion operator (**<<**) can be used to output built-in data types. Listing 2.8 is an example of a program that uses **cout** and the insertion operators to output **char**, **float**, **double**, **integer**, and **string** built-in data types.

Listing 2.8

```
// This program demonstrates how the insertion operator can be
// used with cout.

#include <iostream.h>
#include <math.h>

void main(void)
{
    char PI = 227;
    float pi = 3.1416;
    double Pi = M_PI;
    int pI = 3.1416 * 10000;
    char Pie[] = "Pie in the sky";

    cout << PI << endl;
    cout << pi << endl;
    cout << Pi << endl;
    cout << pI << endl;
    cout << Pie << endl;
}
```

Output from Listing 2.8

```
π
3.1416
3.141593
31415
Pie in the sky
```

The insertion operator can be overloaded to output user-defined data types. It is declared as a friend function in the header file of the user-defined type. The friend function returns a reference to an object of type **ostream**. It also accepts a reference to an object of type **ostream** and the object of the user-defined class. Listing 2.9

shows an example of **cout** and the insertion operator used to output a user-defined class rational number.

Listing 2.9

```
// This program shows how a user-defined object can be inserted into
cout.
#include <iostream.h>
#include "r_approx.h"

void main(void)
{
    rational_approximation user_pi(3.1416);

    cout << user_pi << endl;
}
```

Output from Listing 2.9

3927/1250

ostream Member Functions: put( ) and write( )

put( ) is a member function of the **ostream** class. This member function will place a character into an output stream. The character can be a signed **char**, unsigned **char**, or **char**. This is the prototype for **put( )**:

```
ostream &put(char character);
```

A reference to the **ostream** object will be returned. It will perform no translation or conversion on the character. The character will be sent to the external device to which the **ostream** object is linked.

write( ) is a member function of the **ostream** class. It will write a block of binary data to the output stream linked to an external device. This is the prototype for **write( )**:

```
ostream &write(const unsigned char *buffer, int number);

ostream &write(const signed char *buffer, int number);
```

This member function will accept an array or a pointer to a buffer and the number of bytes to be written. The pointer stores the block of characters. It can point to a constant of signed **char**, unsigned **char**, or **char**. Listing 2.10 shows an example of a program using the **write( )** function. This program reads a binary file into memory and writes it back out to disk using a different name.

Listing 2.10

```
// This program does a quick file copy, using the read( ) member
// function and the write( ) member function. This program also gets
// the file descriptor, using the fd( ) member function.
```

```
#include <fstream.h>
#include <io.h>
#include <stdlib.h>

void main(void)
{

    char PcxCompressedFile[13] = "pic1.pcx";
    char PcxCopy[13] = "newfile.pcx";
    ifstream In;
    ofstream Out;
    long FileSize = 0;
    unsigned char *GraphicImage;

    In.open(PcxCompressedFile,ios::binary);
    if(!In){
        cerr << "could not open " << PcxCompressedFile;
        cin.get( );
        exit(0);
    }

    Out.open(PcxCopy,ios::binary);
    if(!Out){
    cerr << "could not open " << PcxCompressedFile;
    cin.get( );
    exit(0);
    }
    cout << "File Size of "
    << PcxCompressedFile
    << " "
    << (FileSize = filelength(In.rdbuf( )->fd( )));
    GraphicImage = new unsigned char[FileSize];
    In.read(GraphicImage,FileSize);
    Out.write(GraphicImage,FileSize);
    In.close( );
    Out.close( );
    delete []GraphicImage;

}
```

The program in Listing 2.10 is file copy of a **pcx** compressed file. It shows several features of the **ostream** class.

Files

A file is a logical abstraction for any type of external device. A file is opened and associated with a stream in order for data to be exchanged to and/or from the program. There are two types of files: binary and text. The IOSTREAM classes can be used to write and read data for both types of files. To do file input and output, the **<fstream.h>** preprocessor must be included in the program header file.

Opening and Closing Files

To read or write to a binary or text file, the file has to be opened. Before the file is opened, an associated stream object is declared. Files and streams can be prepared as write-only, read-only, and read/write. There are two basic ways to declare a stream and open a file. The first way uses separate statements: one to declare a stream object, and the other to open the file. For an input stream, an object of class **ifstream** is declared. For an output stream, an object of class **ofstream** is declared. For a stream capable of both input and output, an object of class **fstream** is declared. The associated files for the declared stream are opened. A file can be opened by using the **open( )** member function of the **ifstream**, **ofstream**, and **fstream** classes. This is the prototype for the **open( )** member function:

```
void open(char *filename, int mode, int access)
```

Filename is the name of the file to be opened. It may include a path name. *Mode* specifies how the file will be opened, and *access* specifies how the file can be accessed. The mode values and their meanings are listed in Table 2.3. The mode can be one or more of the values combined by *or*ing two or more together. The access values are the same as DOS's file attribute codes shown in Table 2.3. They can also be combined by *or*ing two or more together.

The **ifstream** and **ofstream** classes have a default mode and access values. The **ifstream** class default value for mode is **ios::in**, and the default value for access is a normal file (0). The **ofstream** class default value for mode is **ios::out**, and it also has a normal file value (0) for access. If the default values for mode and access are to be used, it is not necessary to specify them in the parameters for **open( )**. In order to declare a stream capable of both input and output, both **ios::in** and **ios::out** must be specified in the parameter list. The constructor member functions of the **ofstream**, **ifstream**, and **fstream** classes can also be used to open a file and associate a stream for that file. The constructors will automatically open a file of that class type with

Table 2.3   Open Mode Values and Their Meanings

Open Mode Values	*Meanings*
ios::app	Output to a file is appended.
ios::ate	A seek to the end of a file occurs when a file is opened.
ios::in	A file is capable of input.
ios::out	A file is capable of output.
ios::nocreate	If the file does not already exist, the **open( )** function will fail.
ios::noreplace	If the file already exists, the **open( )** function will fail.
ios::trunc	Contents of a file that already exist by the same name are destroyed and truncated to a length of zero.

the default parameters. For example, declaring a stream capable of both input and output, and opening a normal file for that stream could be accomplished this way:

```
fstream <name of stream>("name of file");
```

To close a file, use the **close( )** member function of **ifstream**, **ofstream**, and **fstream** classes. The **close( )** has no return values or parameters.

Writing to a Text File

Inserters can be used to send built-in data types to a text file. In this case, the external device is a text file. A stream object of the class **ofstream** is declared and an output file is opened. The inserters are used in the same way as any other external device. Listing 2.11 shows an example of **char**, **integer**, **float**, **double**, and **string** data types being written to a text file.

Listing 2.11

```
// This program demonstrates how to write built-in data
// types and user-defined types to a text file.

#include <fstream.h>
#include <math.h>
#include "r_approx.h"

void main(void)
{
    char PI = 227;
    float pi = 3.1416;
    double Pi = M_PI;
    int pI = 3.1416 * 10000;
    char Pie[3] = "pi";
    rational_approximation user_pi(3.1416);
    ofstream Out(pi.dat);

    Out << PI << endl;
    Out << pi << endl;
    Out << Pi << endl;
    Out << pI << endl;
    Out << Pie << endl;
    Out << user_pi << endl;
    Out.close( );
}
```

To write a user-defined data type to a text file, a stream of type **ofstream** is declared and an output file is opened. The overloaded insertion operation for the user-defined class will send the data to the text file. Listing 2.11 also shows an example of a user-defined data type written to a text file. The rational class type shown earlier is used.

Reading from a Text File

Extraction operators can be used to read built-in data types from a text file. A stream object of the class **ifstream** is declared and an input file is opened. The data is read from the input file and stored into the appropriate variables. Listing 2.12 shows an example of **char**, **integer**, **float**, **double**, and **string** data types being read from the text file created by Listing 2.11, using the insertion operator.

Listing 2.12

```
// This program demonstrates how data can be extracted
// from a text file connected to the input stream.

#include <fstream.h>
#include <math.h>
#include "r_approx.h"

void main(void)
{
    char PI;
    float pi;
    double Pi;
    int pI;
    char Pie[3] = "";
    rational_approximation user_pi;
    ifstream In(pi.dat);

    In >> PI;
    In >> pi;
    In >> Pi;
    In >> pI;
    In >> Pie;
    In >> user_pi;
    In.close( );
}
```

To read a user-defined data type from a text file, a stream of type **ifstream** is declared and an input file is opened. The overloaded extraction operation for the user-defined class will allow the data to be read from a text file into appropriate variables. Listing 2.12 also shows an example of a user-defined data type being read from a text file.

Writing to a Binary File

The **put( )** member function is used to write a byte or character to a binary file. The **write( )** member function will write a block of binary data to the binary file and then return a stream of **ostream** type. Just like the text files, a stream has to be declared and a file associated with the stream has to be opened. The **put( )** and **write( )** member functions are used to write built-in data types to a binary file.

Reading from a Binary File

The **get( )** and **getline( )** member functions are used to read a character and a sequence of characters from a binary file. The **read( )** member function will read a block of binary data from the binary file and then return a stream of **istream** type. The **get( )**, **getline( )**, and **read( )** member functions are used to read built-in data types from a binary file.

Writing and Reading User-Defined Types from a Binary File

The **write( )** and **read( )** member functions can be used to write or read a user-defined data type to and from a binary file. The **write( )** and **read( )** member functions accept a pointer to a signed or unsigned **char** and the number of bytes to be written or read. The address of the user-defined type has to be converted to an address of a signed or unsigned **char**. The size of the user-defined type must be the second parameter in the list.

The IOSTREAMS in C++ provide the programmer with the complete I/O facility. From systems programming to multimedia level programming, the IOSTREAMS can be used to model I/O devices as well as I/O data structures. Now let's take a detailed look at the IOSTREAMS class hierarchy.

The IOSTREAM Class Hierarchy

> *. . . We shall thus see that a large amount of hereditary modification is at least possible; and what is equally or more important, we shall see how great is the power of man in accumulating by his selection successive slight variations.*
>
> CHARLES DARWIN—*THE ORIGIN OF SPECIES*

Relationship Overview

The IOSTREAM class hierarchy is a network of interrelated and interdependent classes. The IOSTREAM class hierarchy implements the object-oriented stream. Object-oriented input, output, and memory formatting can all be accomplished through the use and specialization of the IOSTREAMS. The basic structure of the IOSTREAM hierarchy can be seen in Figure 3.1, which is a class hierarchy relationship diagram of the **IOSTREAMS**. It shows the fundamental structure and relationships between the primary classes in the IOSTREAM family.

The input classes **istream**, **ifstream**, and **istrstream** are related through the inheritance mechanism. The ultimate base class for the istream family is **ios**. The output classes **ostream**, **ofstream**, and **ostrstream** are also related through the inheritance mechanism. The ultimate **base** class for the **ostream** family is also **ios**. Most IOSTREAM implementations will also contain an **iostream** class derived from **istream** and **ostream**; a **strstream** class derived from **istrstream** and **ostrstream**; and an **fstream** class derived from **ifstream** and **ofstream**. Some implementations also contain intermediate classes, such as **fstreambase** and **strstreambase**.

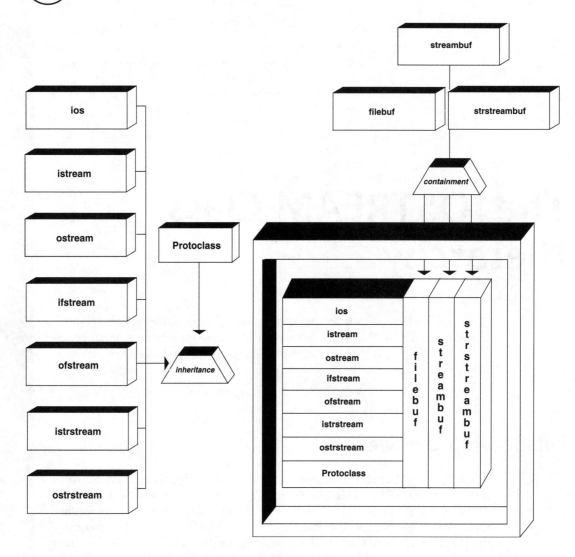

Figure 3.1   *Class relationship of the IOSTREAMS family of classes.*

The **istream** and **ostream** family of classes will also have a possession relationship with **streambuf** or one of its derivatives. The **istream** and **ostream** family of classes do not inherit the **streambuf** or its derivatives. Instead, they contain a **streambuf** or **streambuf** derivative as a data member. The fundamental **streambuf** derivatives are:

- filebuf
- strstreambuf
- stdiobuf

The **ios**, **istream** classes, **ostream** classes, and **streambuf** classes make up the foundation for the IOSTREAM input and output facilities in C++. Table 3.1 displays the entire set of classes for the IOSTREAMS. There will be other classes defined in the **ios.h**, **fstream.h**, **iostream.h**, or **strstream.h** that are part of the IOSTREAM classes, such as **fstreambase** or **strstreambase**. However, most of these other classes are implementation-specific or compiler-specific.

The C++ programmer is advised to open the header files that declare and define the **IOSTREAM** class libraries and examine the declarations and definitions that are in those header files. There are three basic interpretations for the exact structure of the **IOSTREAM** class library:

1. AT&T *de facto* standard
2. ANSI standard
3. Vendor's Standard(compiler-specific)

Although each of these interpretations may vary slightly in naming, immediate base class or immediate derived class, the primary functionality is the same. In this book, we are using the AT&T *de facto* standard and the latest ANSI discussion document to describe the primary classes of the IOSTREAMS in C++. The first class in the **IOSTREAM** class hierarchy that we will explore is **streambuf**.

The streambuf Class

The **streambuf** class can be divided into two levels: the buffer abstraction and the protected members that act on the buffer and the virtual methods used to permit specialization of any derived class. The **streambuf** class defines a buffer abstraction for IOSTREAMS. As a **base** class, it contains only the basic members to act on char-

Table 3.1   IOSTREAM Family of Classes Divided into Buffer, Format, and Translator Classes

Buffer Classes	Format Classes	Translator Class
streambuf	ios	istream
filebuf		ostream
strstreambuf		iostream
		ifstream
		ofstream
		fstream
		istrstream
		ostrstream
		strstream

acters in a buffer. The abstract buffer permits a persistent and theoretically unlimited storage or retrieval of sequential data. This abstraction requires one or two pointers that define the position in the buffer where characters are being inserted or extracted. Queuing buffers, such as **strstreambuf**, requires both a **put** and a **get** pointer. Input and output buffers, such as **filebuf**, may have one pointer or two pointers. The number of pointers a buffer has will depend on describing the buffer as performing **put**s and **get**s to the same pointer or having two pointers tied together. The implemented buffer is an extension of an I/O device. Because of the nature of block vs. character or block vs. block I/O devices, some buffering must occur in core memory.

What Is a Buffer?

A *buffer* is a contiguous set of bytes. These bytes are located in the computer's memory. The contents of the buffer are data items of the same type. The buffer is accessed by a pointer to the first byte. Arrays are similar to buffers except that an array sentinel is a null character (/0) and a buffer has a length. When a buffer is used by buffer manipulation routine, they require the number of bytes the buffer holds. The pointer to the buffer is an address. The address is composed of two parts: the segment and the offset. The segment address is shifted and the offset is added. The address is specified by an array name or a pointer to a variable.

The Structure of a streambuf

The class **streambuf** can be physically described as a set of memory areas with a number of protected methods that define the behavior of the memory areas. Three areas that make up the buffer are the *reserve, put,* and *get* areas. The reserve area is normally a fixed block of memory used as a memory resource by the other areas. The other two areas overlap (partially or fully) the reserve area but never meet each other. The get area could be divided into two areas: the get and *putback* areas. At least two flags indicate whether the reserve area exists and if it is owned by **streambuf**. All the areas are defined by a collection of character pointers.

The flags and collection of pointers are private to the **streambuf**. The minimum number of pointers is determined by the protected member functions that examine and set the state of the buffer. Usually, two pointers define the reserve area base and end. Three pointers define the put and get areas: their base or lower bound, start, and end. The start pointers indicate the next insertion or extraction point within a buffer. The value of these pointers (to adhere to the return values of the protected methods) must always fall between the base and end of their respective areas. The value of the base must be less or equal to the end pointer value. Methods to examine the **streambuf**'s pointers are nonvirtual and protected. They are used only for implementing derived buffer classes. Conceptually, pointers are between characters; however, in implementation they must point to characters. As a convention, all pointers should be viewed as pointing to just before the character at which they really point. This convention will be followed when describing **streambuf**'s methods.

Class Interface Specification:
```
streambuf
```

Declared in:
```
<iostream.h>
```

Derived from:
None

Base Class for:
```
filebuf
strstreambuf
stdiobuf (for mixing stdio with IOSTREAMS)
```

Constructors:
```
streambuf( )
streambuf (char * b, int n)
```

Destructors:
```
virtual ~streambuf( )
```

Public Data Members:
None

Protected Data Members:
None

Protected Member Functions:
```
int allocate(void)
char *base(void)
int blen(void)
virtual int doallocate(void)
char * eback(void)
char * ebuf(void)
char * egptr(void)
```

```
char * epptr(void)

void gbump(int n)

char * gptr (void)

char * pbase (void)

void pbump (int n)

char * pptr (void)

void setb (char * b, char * eb, int i = 0)

void setg (char * eb, char * g, char * eg)

void setp (char * p, char * ep)

int unbuffered(void)

void unbuffered(int)
```

Public Member Functions:

```
virtual streampos seekoff (streamoff ofs,
ios::seek_dir dir, int mode = (ios::in | ios::out))
virtual streampos seekpos (streampos pos,int mode = (ios::in |
                                ios::out))
virtual streambuf * setbuf (char * b, int n)
virtual int sync(void)
int in_avail(void)
int out_waiting(void)
virtual int pbackfail (int c)
virtual int overflow (int c = EOF)
virtual int underflow(void)
int sbumpc(void)
int sgetc(void)
int sgetn (char * s, int n)
int snextc(void)
int sputbackc (char c)
int sputc (int c)
int sputn (const char * s, int n)
void stossc(void)
```

DESCRIPTION streambuf is a class that models a buffer. It provides access to the buffer, along with position designators for the buffer.

The streambuf Constructors

The **streambuf( )** constructor with no arguments creates an empty buffer with all pointers and flags set to zero, which means that a buffer can be allocated when needed. If a **derived** class uses this constructor, then that class must make certain that **allocate( )** is called before the buffer is used. The **streambuf**(char * b,int n) constructor creates an empty buffer. The base will be set to the character pointer, and **ebuf( )** will be set according to the offset value of the second parameter. A call of **streambuf** (NULL, 0) is equivalent to the first constructor.

The allocate( ) Member Function

The **allocate( )** member function tries to set up the reserve area. If the area already exists or the unbuffered flag is not zero, then the **allocate( )** member function returns zero without doing anything. Otherwise, it should call the protected virtual function **doallocate( )** and return its value. The **allocate( )** member function will return one on success, or **EOF** on failure.

The doallocate( ) Member Function

The **doallocate( )** member function is called by the protected method **allocate( )** when a reserve area is required. It must call **setb( )** to supply the reserve area, or return **EOF** if it cannot. It will be called only if the **streambuf** can be buffered (**unbuffered( )** returns zero) and a reserve area does not exist (**base( )** returns NULL).

streambuf Reserved Area Access

The **base( )** member function returns the start of the reserve or buffer area. All other **streambuf** pointers must be greater than or equal to the returned value. The **eback( )** member function returns the lower bound of the get area. The differences between the get pointer, **gptr( )**, and the **eback( )** member function is the current size of the putback area. On putting data back into an input stream, the programmer must make certain that the current get pointer does not precede the **eback( )** member function. When refilling the get area from an input source, ensuring a minimum size for the putback area may be necessary. The **ebuf( )** member function returns a pointer to the byte after the last byte in the reserve or buffer area. All other **streambuf** pointers must be less than or equal to the returned value. The **egptr( )** member function returns a pointer to the byte after the last byte of the get area. The **epptr( )** member function returns a pointer to the byte after the last byte of the put area.

The **gptr( )** member function returns a pointer to the next byte of the get area. All consumable characters will be between **gptr( )** and **egptr( )** member functions. While **gptr( )** member function is less than **egptr( )**, the next character to be fetched will be *gptr( )**. Otherwise, the next character must come from an input source. The **pbase( )** member function returns a pointer to the first byte of the put base. Characters between **pbase( )** and **pptr( )** member functions are buffered for output consumption. Unlike the putback area, characters in this area should be viewed as inaccessible. The **pptr( )** member function returns a pointer to the next byte of the put area. The space between **pptr( )** and **epptr( )** member functions is available for buffering while the **pptr( )** member function is less than **epptr( )**. Otherwise, the output device must consume all data between **pbase( )** and **epptr( )** before any additional characters can be buffered.

streambuf Reserved Area Setup

The **setbuf( )** member function provides a means to specify the array *b* of length *n* to be used as the reserve area. If the supplied array is NULL or its length zero, then the usual interpretation is to make the **streambuf** unbuffered though the implementor of the derived class is not restricted to this behavior. However, to show that the request is accepted, the pointer must be returned; and if not accepted, a NULL pointer is returned. While this method is public in some implementations, it should be protected in derived classes. It was made public for backward compatibility.

The **setb( )** member function sets the reserve area and tells **streambuf** whether it can delete the buffer. The first two parameters are respectively assigned to **base( )** and **ebuf( )**. The third parameter indicates whether **streambuf** owns the buffer. When this parameter is nonzero, then the specified buffer will be deleted by any following call of **setb( )** member function or the buffer's destruction. The **setg( )** member function sets the putback and get areas within the reserve area. The putback pointer, **eback( )**, is set to the first parameter, the **gptr( )** is set to the second, and **egptr( )** to the last. There is no check for out-of-bounds values, so the programmer must ensure all fall within the reserve area. The **setp( )** member function sets the put area within the reserve area. The put pointer **pptr( )** is set by the first parameter, and **eptr( )** by the second. No method permits the programmer to change the put areas base pointer. There is no check for out-of-bounds values.

Getting Information about streambuf

The **blen( )** member function returns the length of the reserve area. It is equivalent to the statement: **(int) (ebuf( ) – base( ))**. There are two member functions that return information about buffering in the **streambuf** class: **int unbuffered(void)** and **void unbuffered(int)**. The first method returns the **streambuf**'s current buffering state and the second method sets it. Zero indicates that the **streambuf** can be buffered, and a nonzero value indicates that it is not buffered. This value does not indicate if a reserve area actually exists, only if it can or cannot exist.

The **in_avail( )** member function returns the number of characters that are available in the get area. It is equivalent to **egptr( ) – gptr( )**. However, it guarantees that a nonnegative value will be returned. The **out_waiting( )** member function returns the number of characters that are waiting in the put area to be written to the output device. It is equivalent to **pptr( ) – pbase( )**. However, it guarantees that a nonnegative value will be returned.

Positioning in the streambuf Class

The **gbump( )** member function adjusts **gptr** (get pointer) by the specified integer value that is either positive or negative. No check is made to ensure that the resulting value is within **eback( )** and **egptr( )**. The **pbump( )** member function adjusts **pptr** (put pointer) by the specified integer value that is either positive or negative. No check is made to ensure that the resulting value is within **pbase( )** and **epptr( )**.

The **seekoff( )** member function repositions the get and/or put pointers of the stream by the specified byte offset. The directions of the seek is from the beginning, current, or from the end of the stream. The offset may be negative. The pointers updated are specified by the third parameter. The put pointer is modified if **ios::out** is set, and the get pointer is modified if the **ios::in** bit is set. It must return the stream's current position (as a *magic cookie*) if successful, and **EOF** otherwise. If the derived class does not support file positioning, then **EOF** is returned. The **seekpos( )** member function returns **seekoff (streampos (pos), ios::beg, mode)** making it necessary to only overload the **seekoff** (void) method. The **pbackfail( )** member function normally returns **EOF**. If it is redefined in a **derived** class, then the supplied character *c* is returned on success or **EOF** on failure. The **sbumpc( )** member function returns the character get pointer is currently pointing, and then increments the get pointer. If the get pointer is at the end of the get area, then **EOF** is returned. The **stossc( )** member function increments the get pointer. If the get pointer is at the end of the get area, then this method has no effect.

Underflow and Overflow in the streambuf Class

If the programmer creates a derived class from **streambuf**, this method should be overloaded. Some implementations define this as a pure virtual. Others just return the default error value of **EOF**. The **overflow( )** member function is used to transfer data from a stream's put area to an output device. It is usually called when the put area is full but it can be called at other times; for instance, by a stream flush call. The supplied character should be saved within the method; then, the following default behavior occurs: First, all characters between **pbase( )** and **pptr( )** are sent to the output device. Next, **setp( )** is called to update the put area. Generally, the put pointer is set to **pbase( )** and the end of put area is left alone. Then, the supplied character, **c**, if not **EOF**, is placed in the restored put area and the put pointer updated. The **overflow( )** member function will return a zero on success, or **EOF** on failure (the AT&T document says return "something else" rather than **EOF**).

Just like the overflow method, this method should be overloaded in any class derived from **streambuf**. The **underflow( )** member function is called when data is requested from the stream but there is no information in the get area. If it is called when the get area is not empty, it returns the character at the get pointer. Otherwise, it resets the get area (set **gptr( )** to **eback( )**, plus an implementation-defined put-back size) and fills the get area with any available data from the input device. Reducing or enlarging the get area, within the reserve area, according to the size of data most efficient for the input device is not unusual.

streambuf Insertion and Extraction

The **sgetc( )** member function peeks at the first character after the get pointer. There are two conflicting requirements in the AT&T document: Calling this function does not change the value of the get pointer and returning **EOF** if no more characters are available. The conflict comes when this function is called. The get pointer is at the end of the get area, but more characters could be available from the source. In other implementations, the virtual method **underflow( )** is called when the get pointer is at the end of the get area and its value returned.

The **sgetn( )** member function retrieves n characters and places them in the supplied buffer, s. If there are fewer than n characters in the get area, then the **sgetn( )** member function will request additional input from the source. It will then reposition the get pointer and return the actual number of characters retrieved. Many implementations use an occasionally *undocumented virtual* method to refill the get area when it is empty. The **snextc( )** member function increments the get pointer and returns the character to which it is pointing. It will return **EOF** if already at the end of the get area, or if the end of the buffer is reached after the increment at which it is pointing.

The **sputback( )** member function decrements the get pointer by one position and assigns the supply character, c, to the get area. The AT&T document specifies that the supplied characters are the same as the value at the get pointer. The AT&T document later goes on to call this requirement a "botch." Regardless, when **gptr** (void) equals **eback( )**, this method calls the virtual method **pbackfail( )** and returns its value. **EOF** is returned on any failure. The **sputs( )** member function stores the character, c, at the current position referenced by the put pointer, then increments the put pointer. It returns **EOF** on any failure. If the put pointer is at the end of the put area, then the virtual method **overflow( )** is called to clear out as much of the put area as possible. If this occurs, then it returns the result from **overflow( )**. The **sputn( )** member function stores n characters from the buffer s into the put area. It will then reposition the put pointer and return the number of characters inserted.

The sync( ) Member Function

The **sync( )** member function tells the derived **streambuf** to check its internal pointers, compare them with any external devices, and update the internal pointers as necessary. The normal behavior of this method is to write out any waiting characters in the put and, if possible, get areas. When the **sync( )** member function returns the put area, it is empty. In other words, **pbase( )** and **pptr( )** are equal. **EOF** is returned on failure.

Implementation Considerations

Virtual methods, protected with noted exceptions, are used to customize any class derived from **streambuf**. While the programmer is free to overload these methods as seen fit, their interface and domain of return values must be followed explicitly. Also, if a derived class does not support the virtual method's default behavior, then its specified error value should be returned. Not doing so may cause the public methods of **streambuf** to behave unexpectedly.

Debugging streambufs

A method to examine a **streambuf**'s state has not yet been presented. The classes of **streambufs** are used as an attribute of **iostream**'s **ios** stream interface class that cannot access the protected **streambuf** methods of **gptr( )**, **base( )**, and so on. The **streambuf** class does define a public, nonvirtual method that will return its current state:

```
void dbp( );
```

This method is meant only for debugging. Its output is restricted to **stderr** (file descriptor 1). The form of its output is implementation-specific. The programmer will have to decide how useful is its output. A symbolic debugger may be as useful.

strstreambuf Class: An Object-Oriented Model for Buffering Data

As noted earlier, the **streambuf** class provides a defined interface for sending data to and from input/output devices, buffering this data as necessary. In the older stream library, this buffering behavior was implemented using byte arrays for storage of input and output data. While the definition of this behavior has been preserved, its implementation, which is now considered obsolete, has not. The actual implementation of this behavior is done by ancestors of the **streambuf** class. The basic buffering behavior is implemented in the **strstreambuf** class. Figure 3.2 is the class relationship diagram of the **strstreambuf** class.

The buffering that the **strstreambuf** class provides is simple and straightforward. It is a first-in, first-out (FIFO) list, or array, that is generally implemented as an array of bytes. Depending on the **strstreambuf** constructor used, this list may be a specific area of core memory or it may be allocated dynamically. The first constructor may be used to perform direct memory access.

The constructors that permit dynamic allocation permit the programmer control over the initial size and the secondary size of the buffer. After increasing once, or if the first growth delta is not specified, any additional increase in size is implementation-specific minimum. The overloaded virtual member function, **setbuf( )**, permits the programmer to modify these later buffer increases. After the next increase, any following increases will be by implementation's minimum.

Two member functions, in addition to the member functions inherited from **streambuf**, permit the programmer extended control over the array within **strstreambuf**. The freeze member function can be used to temporarily disable dynamic allocation of the array—an important ability if it is necessary to guarantee the memory address of the array for any length of time. The second member function, **str( )**, is used to get the memory address of the array. This member function calls the **freeze( )** member function for the programmer so that the general sequence of these member functions is a call to the **str( )** member function followed by one to freeze.

Besides the **setbuf( )** member function, **strstreambuf** generally overloads the **doallocate( )**, **overflow( )**, **underflow( )**, **sync( )**, and **seekoff( )** virtual member func-

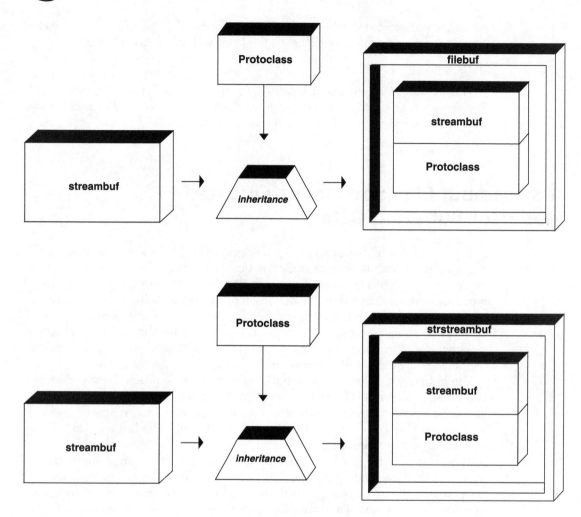

Figure 3.2   *Class relationship of the **strstreambuf** and **filebuf** classes.*

tions. The **doallocate( )** member function follows the behavior defined in **stream-buf**, increasing the reserve area when called. This increase, as noted earlier, will be either an implementation-specific minimum or the size last specified by **setbuf( )**. After the call, the next increase defaults back to the minimum. The **overflow( )** member function, undefined in **streambuf**, determines whether the buffer may grow, as specified by the constructor used. The **underflow( )** member function determines if there are any characters between the put area base and the put indi-cators, and turns them over to the get area. The **sync( )** member function simply returns zero, since there are no external devices to synchronize with. The **seekoff( )**

member function provides the ability to adjust the get and put indicators, as defined in **streambuf**.

The limited nature of **strstreambuf** is purposeful. It provides the basic functionality of buffers without the additional baggage of having to deal with external devices. Combining buffering and external device access in a single class restricts its reuse through inheritance. **strstreambuf** may be used to directly access video memory, or used by an IOSTREAM formatting object that converts standard text to bold text. **strstreambuf** can still be used as an ancestor class to a **streambuf** class that will communicate with external devices that do not provide their own data buffering.

Class Interface Specification:

```
strstreambuf
```

Declared in:

```
<strstream.h>
```

Derived from:

```
streambuf
```

Base Class for:

None

Contains:

None

Constructors:

```
strstreambuf::strstreambuf ( )
strstreambuf::strstreambuf (int)
strstreambuf::strstreambuf(void * (*a) (long), void (*f) (void *))
strstreambuf::strstreambuf(signed char *, int, signed char * = 0)
strstreambuf::strstreambuf(unsigned char *, int, unsigned char * = 0)
```

Destructors:

```
strstreambuf::~strstreambuf( )
```

Protected Data Member:

None

Protected Member Functions:

```
virtual int strstreambuf::doallocate( )
virtual int strstreambuf::overflow (int)
virtual int strstreambuf::underflow( )
virtual int strstreambuf::sync( )
virtual streambuf * strstreambuf::setbuf(char *, int)
virtual streampos * strstreambuf::seekoff (streamoff, ios::seek_dir,
    int)
```

Public Data Members:

None

Public Member Functions:

```
void strstreambuf::freeze (int = 1)
char * strstreambuf::str( )
```

DESCRIPTION strstreambuf is a class that models a buffer for memory location input and output. It provides access to the buffer, along with position designators.

strstreambuf's Constructors and Destructors

A **streambuf** can be implemented in two modes: *dynamic* and *static*, depending on the constructor used. Regardless of mode, the actual buffer used is treated as an array of characters. The abstract get and put indicators correspond to character pointers. Adjusting these indicators is equivalent to performing pointer arithmetic to increment or decrement the character pointers.

The constructor:

```
strstreambuf::strstreambuf ( );
```

creates an empty **strstreambuf** in dynamic mode. The reserve area is not allocated until needed. This allocation size is an implementation-specific minimum—generally, less than 10 bytes. So, if the number of characters to be stored is known to be large, it is not advisable to use this constructor. For example:

```
#include <strstreambuf.h>
#include <string.h>

char ac[256];
strstreambuf sb;

memset (ac, ' ', 256);
sb.sputn (ac, 216);
sb.sputn ("A short string with many leading spaces.", 40);
```

will cause 64 allocations and 63 copies (assuming the implementation uses 4 as its minimal growth factor) before storing the string completely. In cases similar to the preceding, either the following constructor should be used, or a call to the **setbuf( )** member function should be made before the put operation is performed.

The constructor:

```
strstreambuf::strstreambuf (int n);
```

is similar to the first constructor except, here, the programmer may specify the initial allocation of the reserve area. The reserve area still remains unallocated until needed.

The constructor:

```
strstreambuf::strstreambuf (void * (*a) (long), void (*f) (void *));
```

is the last of the dynamic mode constructors. Here, the programmer may supply the functions to allocate and dispose of the reserve area. If the first argument is NULL, then the new operator is used. If a function is supplied, then it must accept the number of bytes to allocate as its argument, and return a pointer to the allocated object. If the second argument is NULL, then the delete operator is used. Otherwise, it must be a function that will accept a pointer to an object created by the first function, and must be able to dispose of it. Declaring a **strstreambuf** instance with:

```
streambuf sb (NULL, NULL);
```

is equivalent to:

```
streambuf sb;
```

The constructors:

```
strstreambuf::strstreambuf (signed char * ptr, int n, signed char *
                            pstart = 0);
strstreambuf::strstreambuf(unsigned char * ptr, int n, unsigned char
                           * pstart = 0);
```

are the last two constructors that create a static **strstreambuf** using the supplied character arrays for the reserve area. They differ only in the typing of their first and third arguments. The first argument is used as the beginning of the reserve area. If the second argument, *n*, is positive then the reserve area will be *n* bytes in length from *ptr.* If *n* is zero, then *ptr* is assumed to point to a NULL-terminated, or ASCIZ, string. If *n* is negative, then the reserve area is assumed to continue indefinitely from *ptr.* The final argument specifies the start of the put area. If it is NULL (the default state), then the **strstreambuf** will be read-only; any stores will be treated as errors. Otherwise, *pstart* should be between *ptr* and *ptr + n*, inclusively.

The destructor:

```
virtual strstreambuf::~streambuf( );
```

deletes a **strstreambuf**. It will also delete the reserve area, provided it was constructed for dynamic allocation and is not frozen in a frozen state. A frozen state exists after either calling the frozen member function with a nonzero argument, or calling the **str( )** member function. **strstreambufs** may be unfrozen by calling the frozen member function with a zero argument.

The Public Member Functions

These member functions will generally be used by **strstreambufs** that were dynamically allocated. Both the **setbuf( )** and **freeze( )** member functions have no effect on **strstreambufs** that are dynamically allocated. The **str( )** member function will simply return the base pointer supplied to its constructor.

The setbuf( ) Member Function

The member function:

```
virtual streambuf * setbuf (char * p, int n);
```

returns a pointer to the **strstreambuf** if it is static. Otherwise, when the **strstreambuf** is dynamic, it will return NULL if the first argument is not NULL or zero; or, the request was honored and, on the next call to the **doallocate( )** member function, the **strstreambuf** will be increased by *n* bytes. After the next allocation, any further increases will be by an implementation-specified minimum increase.

```
#include <strstreambuf.h>
#include <string.h>

char ac[256];
strstreambuf sb;

memset (ac, ' ', 256);
ac[216] = (char) 0;
strcpy (ac, "A short string with many leading spaces.");
sb.setbuf (0, 256);
sb.sputn (ac, 256);
sb.sputn (" Just a few more characters.\n", 30);
```

In the preceding example, using the **setbuf( )** member function before the first **sputn( )** function will cause the **strstreambuf** to allocate sufficient memory and store the first sentence with a single memory copy call. Next, we will assume that the implementation minimum allocation size is 4 bytes. This means that the next **sputn( )** function will require eight more allocations and memory copy calls to store the second sentence. If *n* is less than the implementation-defined minimum, it is likely that this minimum will be used instead.

The freeze( ) Member Function

The member function:

```
void strstreambuf::freeze (int n = 1);
```

is ignored if the **strstreambuf** is static. Otherwise, it will freeze the **strstreambuf**'s reserve area if its argument is a nonzero value (the default call). It will unfreeze the reserve area if zero is passed. *Freezing* a **strstreambuf** is essentially making it static on a temporary basis. A dynamic **strstreambuf** will continue to behave as static until it is *unfrozen*. The effect of performing a put on a frozen **strstreambuf** is undefined. It is permitted to resume puts after the **strstreambuf** has been thawed.

The str( ) Member Function

The member function:

```
char * strstreambuf::str( );
```

may be used with static and dynamic **strstreambufs.** It will freeze the **strstreambuf** and return a pointer to the beginning of the reserve area. Whenever this member function is used, it is important that a corresponding call of **freeze(0)** be made to restore dynamic **strstreambufs** before any following puts are performed or their destructors are called. Failing to do so will cause undefined behavior, the most likely being memory leaks.

filebuf: Derived streambuf Class for Files

The **filebuf** class is derived from **streambuf.** Figure 3.2 is the class relationship diagram showing the relationship between **streambuf** and **filebuf. filebuf** serves as a buffer for output or input to or from a file. The file buffer is composed of the put and get areas. Characters are removed from the put area with write operations and placed in the get area by read operations. The file get/put pointer is considered a single pointer that indicates the current position where information is read or written. **filebuf** attempts to synchronize the get and put pointers when operations change from getting to putting or from putting to getting. The stream buffer is automatically allocated if a buffer is not specified with a constructor or the **setbuf( )** member function with the appropriate arguments.

Class Interface Specification:

```
filebuf
```

Declared in:

```
<iostream.h>
```

Derived from:

```
streambuf
```

Contains:

None

Constructors:

```
filebuf( )
filebuf (int)
filebuf(int _f, signed char _FAR *, int)
filebuf(int _f, unsigned char _FAR *, int)
```

Destructors:

```
~filebuf( )
```

Protected Data Members:

```
int xfd
int mode
short opened
char lahead[2]
```

Protected Member Functions:

None

Public Member Functions:

```
int _Cdecl is_open( )
int _Cdecl fd( )
filebuf _FAR * _Cdecl open(const signed char _FAR *, int, int =
                        filebuf::openprot)
filebuf _FAR * _Cdecl open(const unsigned char _FAR *, int, int =
                        filebuf::openprot)
filebuf _FAR * _Cdecl close( )
filebuf _FAR * _Cdecl attach(int)
virtual int _Cdecl overflow(int = EOF)
virtual int _Cdecl underflow( )
virtual int _Cdecl sync( )
virtual streampos _Cdecl seekoff(streamoff, ios::seek_dir, int)
virtual streambuf _FAR * _Cdecl setbuf (char _FAR *, int)
```

DESCRIPTION **filebuf** is a buffer for files. It provides access to the buffer, along with position designators for the buffer.

Constructors and Destructors of filebuf

The default constructor:

```
filebuf( );
```

has no arguments. It constructs a file buffer. The file buffer has a dynamic get and put area allocation. The file descriptor is set to **EOF** to signify that the object is unattached.

The constructor:

```
filebuf(int d);
```

constructs a **filebuf** object that is attached to the file descriptor specified in the argument. This constructor is also dynamically allocated. The default *io_mode* specifies an input/output file.

The constructor:

```
filebuf(int d, char *p, int len);
```

constructs a file buffer with memory specified for its get and put areas in the argument *p*. The object uses the stream buffer at the position pointed to by *p* with a length stored in the *len* argument. If the length is less than or equal to zero, then operation on the object is unbuffered. Each character transaction will be directly to or from the associated file. The destructor calls the **fb.close( )** function.

The destructor:

```
~filebuf( );
```

deallocates the file buffer by calling the **fb.close( )** member function.

The open( ) and close( ) Member Functions

The **open( )** function opens a file. The function:

```
open(char *fname, int omode, int prot=openprot);
```

opens a file specified by the *fname* argument and attaches a file buffer to it. The *fname* can be an unsigned or signed **char** string. The *omode* will be one of the open mode values. If the *omode* parameter is not equal to *ios::nocreate* and *fname* does not already exist, the **open( )** member function will try to create the file with the protection mode that is equal to *openprot* default file protection.

The default protection mode is *S_IREAD|S_IREAD*. The file is created with both the read and write permissions. If the protection mode is set to *S_IREAD* only, the file will be created with a read-only permission. It cannot be removed by using the **stdio.h remove( )** function.

The **close( )** member function flushes any output in the put area to a file. The file buffer is disconnected from the file, and the file descriptor is set to the **EOF**, meaning that it is unattached. If this is successful, the function will return a pointer to the file buffer. If an error occurs, the **close( )** function will return a zero. The file buffer will still be disconnected, and the file marked as unattached.

The attach( ) Member Function

The **attach( )** member function:

```
filebuf* attach(int descrip);
```

has an *int* argument. It attaches a file buffer to the file descriptor specified in the argument. It returns a pointer to the file buffer. If the file buffer is already open or if the *int* argument is not open, the **attach( )** function will return a zero.

The fd( ) Member Function

The **fd( )** member function returns the file descriptor that is attached to the file buffer. If the **filebuf** is not attached, the function will return an **EOF**.

The Virtual Functions

underflow( ); overflow( ), sync( ), setbuf( ), and seekoff( ) member functions are declared as virtual functions. They can be redefined by classes derived from filebuf.

Underflow and Overflow Member Functions

The **underflow( )** and **overflow( )** member functions are explained in the **streambuf** section of this chapter.

The sync( ) Member Function

The **sync( )** member function attempts to synchronize the get/put pointer and the file get/put pointer. If the **sync( )** member function synchronizes the pointers, it will return a zero. It flushes the buffer to the file or repositions the file get/put pointer if characters read in are waiting in the buffer. If the pointers cannot be synchronized, the function will return an **EOF**.

The setbuf( ) Member Function

The **setbuf( )** member function:

```
streambuf* setbuf(char* pbegin, int len);
```

sets up a stream buffer with a length specified in the *len* argument, beginning at the position specified by *pbegin* argument. The stream buffer is actually an array of *len* single-byte characters. If the beginning position is zero and the length is a nonpositive integer, the **filebuf** object will be unbuffered. If the **filebuf** object is open and the stream buffer has been allocated, there will be no changes made to the stream buffer. The **setbuf( )** member function will return a zero. If the file is a null pointer, the function will return a null pointer. Otherwise, it will return a pointer to the file buffer.

The seekoff( ) Member Function

The member function:

```
streampos seekoff (streamoff so, seek_dir sd, int omode);
```

moves the get/put file pointer to a position specified by the *sd* argument with an offset specified by the *so* argument. The *so* argument can specify the beginning of a file, the current position of the file get/put pointer, or the end of a file. The *so* argument can be either positive or negative.

If the file buffer is attached to a file that cannot perform a seek operation, or if the value of the sum of *so* and *sd* arguments are a position that is before the beginning of the file, the function will return an **EOF** and the position of the file pointer will be undefined. Otherwise, the **seekoff( )** function will return a value of **streampos**. Depending on the implementation, this value is the new position of the file pointer.

The Protected Data Members

The *xfd* data member is an integer; it is the file descriptor. If the **filebuf** is closed, the value of *xfd* is **EOF**. The mode is also an integer; it is the open mode of the file buffer. The *opened* member function is a short integer in which its value will be nonzero if the file is opened. The *lahead* is an array of two characters. It is the current input character if the filebuf is unbuffered.

ios Class—The Ultimate Base Class

The **ios** class is the ultimate base class of the entire IOSTREAM family of classes. Every major class in the IOSTREAM class hierarchy, except for **streambuf** family, has an **ios** component. This means that all the protected and public data members and member functions of **ios** are accessible to all the derived IOSTREAM classes. The immediate derived classes of **ios** are **istream** and **ostream**. The class relationship diagram in Figure 3.3 shows the relationship between **ios**, **istream**, **ostream**, and **streambuf**. The **istream** and **ostream** classes form the base classes for the remainder of the IOSTREAM hierarchy.

The **ios** class is the state component of the IOSTREAM class hierarchy. All classes that are derived from **ios** have several states associated with them:

- *Open state*
- *Buffer state*
- *Format state*

These states are encapsulated within the **ios** class. The open state designates how the stream has been opened. The stream can be opened for reading, writing, or appending. The open state can specify that a new file be created. The open state can describe a stream as either binary or text. The format state determines what type of conversion takes place when objects are inserted into the stream or when objects are extracted

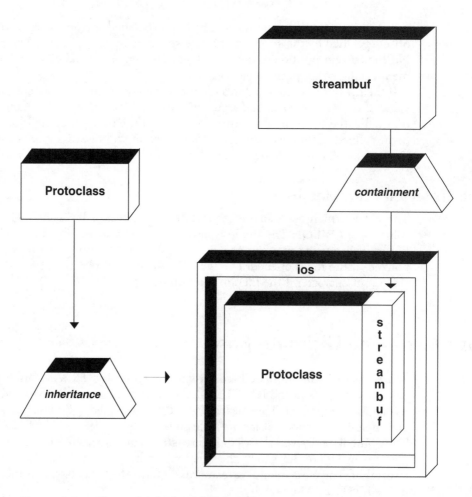

Figure 3.3 *Class relationship of the **ios** class.*

from the stream. For example, 4 bytes may be extracted from the stream and interpreted as hexadecimal during the input process. The format state describes whether objects are left justified or right justified as they are inserted into a stream. The format state describes how numbers are represented as they are inserted or extracted to or from a stream. The base of the numbers can be decimal, hexadecimal, or octal. The numbers can be formatted as fixed floating point or in scientific notation. The format state describes the fill character that will be used for padding during stream operations.

The **ios** class also contains the buffer component of the **istream** and **ostream** family of classes. This buffer is a **streambuf** class. The **streambuf, filebuf, strstreambuf,** and **stdiobuf** have an associated state. We call this state the buffer state. These buffer classes can either be in a *good state,* an **EOF** state, or an *error state.* If the buffer is in a good state, then the next insertion or extraction operation can be attempted. If the buffer is in an error state, then the next insertion or extraction operation will be ignored. Because the **ios** class is the ultimate base class for the IOSTREAM classes, every IOSTREAM object has an internal state that can be accessed through the member function of the **ios** class. The **ios** class relationship diagram shows the relationship between the **ios** protoclass and the **streambuf** class as a containment relationship. The **ios** class does not inherit the **streambuf**. Instead, the **ios** class contains a pointer to a **streambuf**. This means that the **ios** class and its derived classes can access only the reserved area of the **streambuf** through the **streambuf**'s public member functions.

The **ios** interface specification shows the protected and public interfaces to the **ios** class.

Class Interface Specification:

```
ios
```

Declared in:

```
<iostream.h>
```

Derived from:

None

Base Class for:

```
istream
ostream
```

Contains:

```
streambuf *
```

Constructors:

```
ios (streambuf*)
ios( )
```

Destructors:

```
virtual ~ios( )
```

Protected Data Members:

```
streambuf* bp
ostream* x_tie
int state
int ispecial
int ospecial
long x_flags
int x_precision
int x_width
int x_fill
int isfx_special
int osfx_special
int delbuf
int assign_private
enum { skipping = 0x100, tied = 0x200 }
```

Public Data Members:

```
enum io_state {
  goodbit = 0x00
  eofbit = 0x01
  failbit = 0x02
  badbit = 0x04
  hardfail = 0x80
}

enum open_mode {
  in = 0x01
  out = 0x02
  ate = 0x04
  app = 0x08
  trunc = 0x10
  nocreate = 0x20
  noreplace = 0x40
  binary = 0x80
}
```

```
enum {
  skipws = 0x0001
  left = 0x0002
  right = 0x0004
  internal = 0x0008
  dec = 0x0010
  oct = 0x0020
  hex = 0x0040
  showbase = 0x0080
  showpoint = 0x0100
  uppercase = 0x0200
  showpos = 0x0400
  scientific = 0x0800
  fixed = 0x1000
  unitbuf = 0x2000
  stdio = 0x4000
}
enum seek_dir { beg=0, cur=1, end=2}
  static const long basefield;      // dec | oct | hex
  static const long adjustfield;    // left | right | internal
  static const long floatfield;     // scientific | fixed
```

Member Functions:

```
long flags( )
long flags(long)
long setf(long _setbits, long _field)
long setf(long)
long unsetf (long)
int width( )
int width(int)
char fill( )
char fill(char)
int precision(int)
int precision( )
ostream* tie(ostream*)
ostream* tie( )
```

```
int rdstate( )
int eof( )
int fail( )
int bad( )
int good( )
void clear(int = 0)
operator void* ( )
int operator! ( )
streambuf* rdbuf( )
static long bitalloc( )
static int xalloc( )
long & iword(int)
void*& pword(int)
static void sync_with_stdio( )
void init(streambuf*)
void setstate(int)
```

DESCRIPTION The **ios** class encapsulates the stream state and the buffer state. It represents the format and condition of the stream, and any objects that have been inserted in or extracted from the stream. The **ios** class provides the **istream** class and the **ostream** class with a buffer.

The Open Mode of the ios Class

The **open_mode** enumeration is a data member of the **ios** class. Through this data member, the **ios** class supports several modes for opening streams. These modes are declared as enumerated data types:

```
enum open_mode {
in = 0x01,
out = 0x02,
ate = 0x04,
app = 0x08,
trunc = 0x10,
nocreate = 0x20,
noreplace= 0x40,
binary = 0x80
};
```

These modes are specified in either the declaration of the stream, for example:

```
fstream Out ("Myfile",ios::out);
```

or in a call to the **open( )** member function, for example:

```
fstream Out;
Out.open("Myfile",ios::in | ios::out);
```

These modes specify the manner in which the stream is treated upon opening, reading, and writing. The *in* mode specifies that the stream is opened for reading. If a stream has been opened only for reading, then the programmer cannot send output to this stream. The *out* mode specifies that the stream is opened for writing. If a stream has been opened only for writing, then the programmer cannot extract data from this stream. A stream can be opened for reading and writing by *or*ing these two modes together:

```
fstream Device;
Device.open("Myfile",ios::in | ios::out);
```

The *ate* mode specifies that the position pointer should be set to the end of the file upon initial opening. The *app* mode specifies that the file should always be appended. The *ate* mode, *app* mode, and *trunc* mode can also be used with **ostrstream** and **strstream** constructors. For example:

```
char Buffer[80];

strstream Memory(Buffer,79, ios::app);

ostrstream Memory(Buffer,79,ios::ate);

strstream Memory(Buffer,79,ios::trunc);
```

When *ate* and *app* modes are used, the position pointer is moved to the null value in the character array upon construction of these objects. The *trunc* mode is basically a start-from-scratch mode. If the stream's object previously exists and the stream is opened in *trunc* mode, then the contents of the stream's object is destroyed. The *nocreate* mode specifies that the file should be opened only if it already exists. If the file does not exist, the **open( )** member function fails. The *noreplace* mode specifies that the file can only be appended to, or, when opened, the position pointer must move to the end of the stream's object. This is accomplished by specifying either the *app* mode or *ate* mode.

The *binary* mode specifies that the stream be opened for raw binary processing as opposed to a *text* or ASCII processing. This mode affects how the \n is handled. When a stream is in *text* mode, the \n newline character is converted into two characters: a carriage-return character and a line-feed character upon output. The carriage-return, line-feed pair (crlf) are converted to a \n upon input. This is in contrast to processing on a binary stream. When a stream is opened in *binary* mode the \n is written as a \n character on output, and the \n is read as a \n on input. When a stream is opened in *binary* mode, numbers are written in binary form upon output, and are read in as binary upon input. When a stream is opened in *text* mode, numbers are written to the output using their ASCII representation—that is, numbers are written as characters, as opposed to absolute binary bytes. The same is true upon input in *text* mode. Numbers are translated from ASCII to the targets to which they are input. The *text open* mode is not applicable to UNIX environments.

The Buffer Component of the ios Class

The **bp** data member is a pointer to the buffer component of the **ios** class. This pointer provides the **ios** family of classes with a buffer area to store characters. The buffer component of the **ios** class is a pointer to a **streambuf** object. The **streambuf** object specifies a generic holding area for the data while it is in transit from an input source or to an output destination. The source or destination may be a block of memory, a file, or an I/O device. Through the pointer to the **streambuf** object, the **ios** class and any of its derived classes have access to all the functionality of the **streambuf** object.

This pointer can be accessed through the **rdbuf( )** member function, which takes no arguments and returns the **streambuf** pointer contained in the **ios** class. Some implementations may declare the pointer to the buffer component to be private.

The Buffer State Component of the ios Class

The **ios** class maintains a state variable that describes the associated buffer at any given time. The state variable is normally represented by an *int* data type. The *int* data type is then further divided into bits, with specific combinations of bits representing the state of the buffer. These bits are set (turned on) or unset (turned off). The bits are normally declared as enumerations with certain values (bitmasks):

```
enum io_state{
goodbit = 0x00,
eofbit = 0x01,
failbit = 0x02,
badbit = 0x04,
};
```

These bits represent four basic states in which the streambuf component can be:

Good

EOF

Fail

Bad

We refer to these states as buffer states. Sometimes, these states are referred to as error states. Since only two of these conditions are strictly error conditions, we will use buffer states when referring to the condition of the buffer component. If the buffer is in a good state, then no bits are set in the *state* variable. The **good( )** member function returns a nonzero value if the buffer component is in a *good* state. If the buffer is in an **EOF** state, then the **EOF** bit is set (turned on) within the *state* variable. The **eof( )** member function returns a nonzero value if the **EOF** bit is set. If the buffer is in a *bad* state, then the *badbit* is turned on. The **bad( )** member function will return a nonzero value if the *badbit* is set. The *badbit* is set when some operation on the **streambuf** object has failed. If *failbit* or *badbit* is set within the *state* variable, the buffer is said to be in a *fail* state. The **fail( )** member function returns a nonzero value if either the *badbit* is set or the *failbit* is set.

The *fail* state and the *bad* state are not exactly the same. If a buffer is in a *bad* state it is also in a *fail* state. However, a buffer can be in a *fail* state without being in a *bad* state. For example, if an operation tries to read past the end of file, the operation will fail. This puts the stream in a *fail* state. This does not necessarily mean that the stream is unusable. When a stream is in a *bad* state, this normally signals that the stream is unusable. The value of the state variable is returned by the **rdstate( )** member function. The state of the buffer is propagated through the operations on that buffer. This means that all the operations that access the buffer are aware of the buffer state. If the buffer is in a *good* state, then insertion and extraction operations can be attempted. However, if the buffer is in a *bad* state, all insertion and extraction operations will be ignored. The **clear( )** member function must be called in this circumstance. The buffer is unusable unless the **clear( )** member function is called.

The **clear( )** member function serves two primary functions: The first function is to clear the *error* state of a buffer associated with an **ios** class. The second primary function of the **clear( )** member function is to set bits within the *state* variable. The **clear( )** member function takes an *int* data type as an argument and returns void. If the **clear( )** member function is called with an argument of zero, the *state* variable for the buffer is reset to zero. If the **clear( )** member function is called with the value of one of the states that the buffer can be in, for instance:

```
ios Object;
Object.clear(ios::failbit | Object.rdstate( ));
```

then the *failbit* is set in the *state* variable. Notice that the technique for doing this involves a bitwise *or*ing of the *state* variable with the desired bit to be set. Table 3.2 shows the four fundamental states the stream can be in, and what conditions are sufficient to cause those states to be entered. Examples of accessing the buffer component of **ios** are at the end of this chapter (see also: **streambuf** class).

The Format State Component of the ios Class

The *format* state determines the type of conversion that will take place when objects are inserted or extracted to or from the stream. Some of the data members of the **ios** class that relate to the *format* state are:

```
x_flags
x_precision
x_width
x_fill
floatfield
```

Table 3.2   Four Fundamental States of the Streams and the Condition in which They Are Set

Function/Bit	*Condition When Set*
goodbit **int good( )**	A nonzero value if no ***error*** state is set.
eofbit **int eof( )**	A nonzero value when set; otherwise, zero.
	Normally set when an end of file has been encountered during an extraction.
	No further characters are available from **streambuf**, or an attempt to output characters failed because the **streambuf** could not accept more.
	Normal EOF condition when outputting to a full disk, printer with no paper, no hardware error.
	EOF condition while skipping white space.
	EOF condition detected while incomplete inputting of required type.
	EOF condition if characters input are incomplete (e.g., 2.3 e).
	Transfer stopped due to EOF encountered immediately on extraction characters.
	EOF condition encountered before *n* characters are transferred by a **read( )** function.
	EOF condition occurs while **ipx( )** function extracting white space, and the extraction argument character has changed.
failbit **int fail( )**	A nonzero value when ***badbit*** or ***failbit*** is set the ***error*** state; otherwise, zero.
	Normally, this indicates that some extraction or conversion has failed but the stream is still usable after the failbit has been cleared.
	Characters lost due to ***error*** state detected before characters are passed during input.
	Input of an integer requested but only white spaces are encountered.
	Input of integer requested but only characters are encountered.
	Input request from stream set up without a source or destination (source/sink).
	Failure if output stream does not support seeking when seek operations are performed.
	ipfx( ) function receives a nonzero status.
	EOF condition encountered during the extraction of ***ws.***
	Input causes overflow of specified type.
	Input integer requested but no integers are encountered.
	Input request for double, but scientifically notated value is encountered.
	Transfer stopped immediately on extraction characters.
	No characters extracted before EOF condition.
	EOF condition encountered before *n* characters are transferred by a **read( )** function.
	Error occurred while flushing a **filebuf**, or file closed failed.
	attach( ) function called when stream is already attached.
	EOF condition occurs while **ipx( )** function extracting white space, and the extraction argument character has changed.

Table 3.2 (*Continued*)   **Four Fundamental States of the Streams and the Condition in which They Are Set**

Function/Bit	Condition When Set
badbit **int bad( )**	A nonzero value when an error state occurs; otherwise, nonzero.
	Usually indicates that some operation on **s.rdbuf( )** has failed; a severe error from which recovery is probably impossible (cannot perform IO operation on the stream).
	streambuf object has not been connected to a source or destination.
	Input requested without source or destination.
	Characters lost due to an error state after some characters were processed.
	Input request for double but scientifically notated value is encountered.
	The **stream_with assign** constructors are used but are not functional.
	File for a **filebuf** is closed and **filebul** is unattached when using the **fstream_comm close( )** function.
	ifstream constructor creates an object that is not associated with a file.

```
base field
adjustfield
```

The **x_flags** data member contains the bit pattern for the format flags. This data member represents the *format* state. Each bit in the *format* state represents a *format* flag. The **flags( )** member functions can return or set the *format flag* state. The **flags( )** member function is used to access the *format state* variable. This **flags( )** member function takes no arguments and returns a *long int*, which is the decimal representation of the value stored in the *format* state. The overload of the **flags( )** member function will set the *format* state to that specified in its argument, and return the previous value. The argument is a *long int* as well as the return value. **flags(0)** will reset the *format* state to its original value. The value of **x_flags**, along with the initialized values of the *format* flags, designate how objects are formatted into and out of the stream.

Each *format* flag controls a specific way the information is formatted. These *format* flags have values that may differ between implementations:

```
skipws = 0x0001
left = 0x0002
right = 0x0004
internal = 0x0008
dec = 0x0010
oct = 0x0020
```

```
hex = 0x0040
showbase = 0x0080
showpoint = 0x0100
uppercase = 0x0200
showpos = 0x0400
scientific= 0x0800
fixed = 0x100
unitbuf = 0x2000
stdio = 0x4000
```

When the *skipws* flag is set, the *format* state of the stream specifies that white-space characters will be ignored for input. If the flag is not set, then white-space characters will not be ignored. White-space characters include spaces, tabs, and new-line characters. In an attempt to extract numeric data preceded by a white space with the *skipws* flag not set, the *failbit* flag would be set and extraction would discontinue until the *failbit* flag was cleared. When the *left* format flag is set, the *format* state of the stream specifies that padding used to meet a field width is placed after the actual data value. If the *right* format flag is set, the *format* state of the stream specifies that padding used to meet a field width is placed before the actual data value. A set *internal* format flag describes a *format* state of the stream that pads a field width between any sign type (base information or integer sign) and the actual data value. The data will appear to be right-justified. By default, the *right* format flag is set.

When the *showbase* format flag is set, the *format* state of the stream specifies that numeric data will display its base convention for output. The default is numeric data absent of the base conventions. The base convention for hexadecimal numbers is *0x* and the base convention for octal numbers is *0* placed before the number. There is no base convention for decimal numbers. Setting a *showpoint* format flag describes the *format* state of the stream in which floating point numbers will display a decimal point and trailing zeros for output. The decimal point and trailing zeros will be displayed only with a floating point number with precision greater than zero. There will be as many trailing zeros as needed to meet precision. If this flag is set and precision is zero, there will be no decimal point or trailing zeros. The *showpos* format flag when set specifies a *format* state of the stream that displays a plus sign for positive integers for output. Negative integers will automatically display a minus sign regardless of the setting of this flag. The other bases are unsigned. The *uppercase* format flag when set specifies a format state in which numeric data represented with hexadecimal digits will display the hex base indicator and hexadecimal digits *A-F* in uppercase. The floating point numbers represented in scientific notation will display an uppercase *E* for output. The default is lowercase.

Setting the *unitbuf* format flag causes the *format* state of the stream to specify that output is flushed after each output operation. When the **stdio** format flag is set, the *format* state of the stream specifies that the **stout** and **sterr** are flushed after an insertion operation when using both the **iostreams** and the **stdio** functions for output. This flag is used by **sync_with_stdio( )** and should not be set directly. Therefore, if the **iostreams** and the **stdio** library are to be combined for output, the **sync_with_stdio( )** should be used.

The *hex*, *oct*, or *dec* format flags can be set in order for integer data inserted or extracted from or to the stream to be represented in these various bases. If the *dec* format flag is set, integers will be represented in the decimal base. If the *hex* format flag is set, integers will be represented in the hexadecimal base. If the *oct* format flag is set, integers will be represented in the octal base. By default, numeric values retain their original base.

Floating point numbers can be represented in scientific or fixed notation by setting the *scientific* or *fixed* format flags. If the *scientific* format flag is set, the format state of the stream will represent floating point data in scientific notation. Scientific notation expresses floating point numbers with the decimal placed behind the first digit. The *e* represents exponentiation of 10 to a power. Floating point data will be represented in scientific notation if the exponent after the conversion is less than -4 or greater than or equal to the current precision. When the *fixed* format flag is set, the format state of the stream specifies that floating point numbers will be displayed in decimal notation with a set number of digits after the decimal. The number of digits after the decimal is determined by the precision currently set.

The **basefield**, **floatfield**, and **adjustfield** are collective data members. These data members contain the values of a group of format flags. The **basefield** data member contains the values of *dec*, *oct*, and *hex* format flags. The **floatfield** data member contains the values of scientific and fixed *format* flags. The **adjustfield** data member contains the values of *right*, *left*, and *internal* format flags. These data members are used to collectively clear the format flags for which they represent, and to set an individual flag within the group.

To set format flags, the **ios** class provides a number of member functions for this purpose. The **flags( )** member function can set all the format flags at one time to the *long int* supplied by its argument. The **setf( )** member function is used to set an individual flag. The **setf( )** member function will set a format flag to that specified in its argument, and return the previous format flag. For instance, here is an example of the setting of a format flag:

```
long prevflag;
prevflag = cout.setf(ios::scientific);
```

This will set the *scientific* format flag. The member function returns the previous format flags (the value stored in the *format flag* variable) as a *long int.* This value can be used or discarded. **flag(0)** will reset the format flags to their default values.

The overload of **setf( )** will clear a collection of flags and set an individual flag to that specified in one of its arguments. This member function has two arguments:

The first argument is the individual flag to be set, and the second is the group of flags to be cleared specified by **adjustfield**, **basefield**, or **floatfield**. Both of these arguments are *long int.* The **setf( )** member function will clear the flags specified by the second argument, then set the individual flag (one of the collection) specified by the first argument. Then the member function will return the previous value of the *format state* variable as a *long int.* Here is an example of the use of this member function:

```
long prevflag;
prevflag = cout.setf(ios::scientific, ios::floatfield);
```

This will clear the **floatfield** flags, scientific and fixed, then set the **scientific** format flag. Then it will return the previous value of the *format state* variable.

The **unsetf( )** member function is used to clear an individual format flag. This individual format flag is specified in the **unsetf( )** argument as a *long int.* This member function will return the previous value of the *format flag state* variable also as a *long int.* For example, this will clear the *scientific* format flag:

```
long prevflag;
prevflag=cout.unsetf(ios::scientific);
```

Format flags can be *or*ed together in a single message to combine numerous settings of different flags. This can be used to set or unset format flags. This is an example of setting and clearing format flags using this technique:

```
cout.unsetf(ios::scientific |ios::uppercase);
cout.setf(ios::fixed | ios::showpoint);
```

The **x_precision** data member contains the precision, the number of digits after the decimal, for a floating point number. The value of precision can be accessed through the **precision( )** member function. The **precision( )** member function takes no arguments and returns an integer. The integer is the value stored in the *precision* variable. The default precision is 6. The overload of the **precision( )** member function sets the value of precision. The **precision( )** member function has an integer argument that is the value stored in the *precision* variable. It returns the previous value of precision as an *int.* The **fill( )** member function returns the fill character and takes no arguments. The fill character is used to pad a field in which the data takes less space than the field width specifies. The field will be padded according to the setting of the **adjustfield** bits. The default fill character is a space. The overload **fill( )** member function will set the fill character to the character passed in its argument, and return the previous fill character.

The **x_width** data member contains the width specification for objects that will be inserted into or extracted from a stream. The width of the field specifies the amount of space that will be used for data, string, or numeric. A call to the **width( )** member function will return the value of width as an *int.* The **width( )** member function takes no arguments. The overload **width( )** member function will set the width value to its integer argument, and return the previous value of width as an *int.* If the data inserted is less than the field width, the data will be padded. If the data to be inserted is more than the field width, the data will be expressed completely and not truncated. The default width is *0*, which means the width will be the length necessary to express the data completely. The **width( )** member function is set for only the immediate input or output operation and will have to be reset for each subsequent operation. The **x_fill** data member contains the fill character used to pad a field width.

The program in Listing 3.1 demonstrates how flags are set and cleared, how they affect integer values and floating point values, and how flags set in combination with other flags affect output.

Listing 3.1

```
// This program demonstrates the uses of flags on integers and floating
// point values.
#include <iostream.h>
#include <math.h>
#include <conio.h>

double AvogadroNumber = 6.023e23;
float SpeedOfLight = 3.00e8;
double PlanckConstant= 6.63e-34;
int EarthDensity = 5570;
char PlanckUnits[13] = "(Joules*sec)";
char AvogadroUnits[20] = "(particles/g*atom)";
char LightUnits[12] = "(miles/sec)";
char DensityUnits[10] = "(kg/m^3)";

void main(void)
{
    cout.width(30);
    cout<< "Avogadro's";
    cout.width(27);
    cout << "Speed of" << endl;
    cout.width(20);
    cout.setf(ios::left);
    cout << "Flags";
    cout.width(7);
    cout << "Number";
    cout.width(22);
    cout << AvogadroUnits;
    cout << "Light " << LightUnits << endl;
    cout.width(20);
    cout << "—-";
    cout.width(29);
    cout << "——————-";
    cout << "———--" << endl;

    cout.width(6);
    cout << "number";
    cout.setf(ios::right);
    cout.width(39);
```

```
cout << AvogadroNumber;
cout.width(27);
cout << SpeedOfLight << endl;

cout << endl<< "right" << endl;
cout << "showpoint" << endl;
cout << "scientific";

cout.setf(ios::scientific|ios::showpoint);
cout.width(35);
cout << AvogadroNumber;
cout.width(27);
cout << SpeedOfLight << endl;

cout << endl<< "right" << endl;
cout << "uppercase" << endl;
cout << "scientific";

cout.unsetf(ios::showpoint);
cout.setf(ios::uppercase);
cout.width(35);
cout << AvogadroNumber;
cout.width(27);
cout << SpeedOfLight << endl;
cout << endl << "right" << endl;
cout << "precision 4" << endl;
cout << "fixed";

cout.unsetf(ios::scientific);
cout.setf(ios::fixed);
cout.width(40);
cout.precision(4);
cout << AvogadroNumber;
cout.width(27);
cout << SpeedOfLight << endl;

cout << endl << "right" << endl;
cout << "showpoint" << endl;
cout << "precision 4" << endl;
cout << "fixed";

cout.unsetf(ios::scientific);
cout.setf(ios::fixed|ios::showpoint);
cout.width(40);
cout.precision(4);
cout << AvogadroNumber;
cout.width(27);
cout << SpeedOfLight << endl;

cout << endl;
cout.width(28);
cout << "Planck's";
cout.width(27);
cout << "Earth" << endl;
cout.width(20);
```

```
cout.setf(ios::left);
cout << "Flags";
cout.width(9);
cout << "Constant ";
cout.width(21);
cout << PlanckUnits;
cout << "Density " << DensityUnits << endl;

cout.width(20);
cout << "—-";
cout.width(30);
cout << "——————————-";
cout << "————————" << endl;
cout.unsetf(ios::right);
cout.setf(ios::left);
cout.width(20);
cout << "number";
cout.width(30);
cout.unsetf(ios::fixed|ios::showpoint);
cout.unsetf(ios::scientific);
cout << PlanckConstant;
cout << EarthDensity << endl;

cout << endl<< "left" << endl;
cout << "showbase" << endl;
cout << "uppercase" << endl;
cout.width(20);
cout << "octal";

cout.unsetf(ios::right|ios::showpoint|ios::fixed);
cout.setf(ios::left|ios::showbase|ios::uppercase|ios::oct);
cout.width(30);
cout << PlanckConstant;
cout << EarthDensity << endl;

cout << endl<< "internal" << endl;
cout << "showpos" << endl;
cout.width(20);
cout << "decimal";
cout.unsetf(ios::left|ios::showbase|ios::uppercase|ios::oct);
cout.setf(ios::internal|ios::showpos|ios::dec);
cout.width(20);
cout << PlanckConstant;
cout << " ";
cout.width(20);
cout << EarthDensity << endl;

cout << endl << "left" << endl;
cout << "showpos" << endl;
cout << "fill"<< endl;
cout.unsetf(ios::internal);
cout.setf(ios::left);
cout.width(20);
cout << "decimal";
```

```
      cout.fill('\');
      cout.width(20);
      cout << PlanckConstant;
      cout << " ";
      cout.width(20);
      cout << EarthDensity << endl;
}
```

Output for Listing 3.1

Flags	Avogadro's Number (particles/g*atom)	Speed of Light (miles/sec)
number	6.023e+23	3e+08
right showpoint scientific	6.023000e+23	3.000000e+08
right uppercase scientific	6.023E+23	3E+08
right precision 4 fixed	60229999999999975891853.9649	300000000
right showpoint precision 4 fixed	60229999999999975891853.9649	300000000.0000

Flags	Planck's Constant(Joules*sec)	Earth Density (kg/m^3)
number	6.63e-34	5570
left showbase uppercase octal	6.63E-34	012702
internal showpos decimal	+ 6.63e-34	+ 5570

```
left
showpos
fill
decimal        +6.63e-34//////////        +5570///////////////
```

All of the flags and the **fill( )** and **precision( )** member functions will affect all proceeding values until the flag is cleared or reset to its default values. The **width( )** member function has to be set before the value that it is to affect. The *adjustfield*, *basefield*, and *floatfield* flags are mutually exclusive flags. Only one flag from each group should be set at one time. If more than one flag from a group is set, it will have no effect on the output. For example, if the *right* and *left* adjustfields are set, only one of them will affect the output. If the octal and hexadecimal *basefield* flags are set, only one flag will be recognized.

Flags for integer values will have no effect on floating point values, and flags for floating point values will have no effect on integer values. For example, in the output for Listing 3.1, the *basefield* flags convert integers to another number base. The *octal* flag is set for Planck's constant, which is a floating point value. No conversion takes place and the number is displayed as a decimal. No error will occur, neither the *failbits* nor the *badbits* will be set. The flag is simply ignored.

Some flags work in conjunction with other flags. For example, if the **width( )** member function is not set to a value that is larger than the field that the output occupies, the **fill( )** member function will have no effect on the output. Other flags have no effect on output. If the *showbase* flag is set for a decimal value, this will have no effect on the output. If the *uppercase* flag is set for a numeric value that is not in scientific notation or does not display a character for its base, this will have no effect on the output. Other flags have no effect on output if a certain flag was previously set. For example, the *fixed* flag was set for Avogadro's number and then the *showpoint* flag was set without clearing the *fixed* flag. As the output displays, this had no effect on the output.

Interactive I/O and the ios Classes

An **ostream** object can be tied to an **istream** object for purposes of *buffer flushing*. Buffer flushing sends output immediately to an output device. This can be useful when calling insertion operations immediately followed by extraction operations, or an extraction operation immediately followed by an insertion operation. For example:

```
#include <iostream.h>

void main(void)
{
    double PI;
    double Speed;
    double AvNum;
    cout << " What is the value of pi ? " << endl;
    cin >> PI;
```

```
        cout << "What is the speed of light ? " << endl
        cin >> Speed;
        cout << "What is Avogadro's number ?" << endl
        cin >> AvNum;
    }
```

When concurrent insertions and extractions are intermixed without explicitly flushing the buffer, the prompts may not be displayed on the console until after the input is extracted from the stream. Buffers are implicitly flushed when they are full or some other buffer flushing condition has occurred. If the buffer is not full and no other buffer flushing condition has occurred, then data may remain in the buffer and not be sent to the output until explicitly flushed. The predefined stream *cin* is tied to *cout* by default to prevent this subtle problem during intermixing insertions and extractions.

An **ostream** object is tied to an **istream** object using the **tie( )** member function. The **x_tie** data member holds a pointer to the **ostream** object that is tied to this **ios** object if an **ostream** is tied to it. In a user-extended **istream**, there may be no **ostream** tied to it. Tying is not mandatory. However, if the buffers are not flushed properly, output to a device may occur in an unnatural sequence. The **tie( )** member function has two forms: The first form, **ostream *tie( )**, returns a pointer to the stream that has been tied if a stream has been tied. The second form, **tie(*ostream)**, accepts a pointer to an **ostream**. The **istream** is then tied to an **ostream** through this pointer.

When two streams are tied while one stream is processed, the other is affected. For example, when a *cin* object is getting ready to extract some characters from the stream, if an **ostream** object is tied to it, the **ostream** will be flushed first, then the extraction will take place. Calling the **tie( )** member function with an argument of *0* separates the object from its tied stream if there was one.

Mixing stdio with IOSTREAMS

As stated in Chapter 1, the C++ object-oriented I/O facilities can be used and intermixed with the **stdio** nonobject-oriented facilities. These nonobject-oriented I/O facilities are found in C and C++ environments. Because of memory management and buffer handling differences between the IOSTREAM facilities and the standard I/O facilities, the **sync_with_stdio( )** member function must be called prior to intermingling the two I/O facilities. The call to the **sync_with_stdio( )** member function synchronizes the I/O facilities.

istream Class—An Object-Oriented Model of Input

The **istream** class is a twin class to the **ostream** class. What the **ostream** class is to output, the **istream** class is to input. The **istream** class is the foundation for the object-oriented input stream in the C++ environment. The **istream** class encapsulates the input model in the C++ environment. In fact, it is the object-oriented equivalent of the input stream concept. The **istream** class is derived from the **ios** class. This means that the characteristics and attributes that are contained in the **ios** class are also contained in the **istream** class and its derived classes. All the member functions that are callable from an **ios** class are callable from an **istream** class. All the protected and public data members that are contained in the **ios** class are contained in the **istream** class.

The **ios** class contains a pointer to a **streambuf** class. The **istream** class inherits this pointer to the **streambuf** class. This means that the **istream** class has full access to the functionality of the **streambuf** class and the services that it provides. The class relationship diagram in Figure 3.4 shows the relationship between the **istream** class, **ios** class, and the **streambuf** class. The relationship between **istream** and **ios** is an inheritance relationship. This inheritance relationship means that **ios** is a subset of the **istream** class. The class relationship diagram in Figure 3.4 shows that **istream** will contain a **streambuf** component. This means that the **istream** class can access the functionality of the **streambuf** class only through its public members.

Through encapsulation and inheritance, the **ios** class and **streambuf** class are combined with the **istream** *protoclass* to form the **istream** class. The **istream** protoclass contains member functions and data members that do not represent a complete class in the context of an input stream. Only when the **istream** protoclass is combined with the **ios** component does the resulting class represent a complete class.

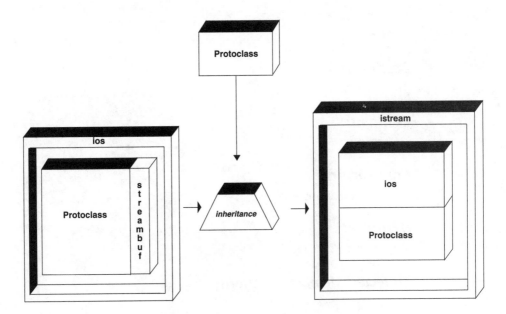

Figure 3.4 *Class relationship of the **istream** class.*

The **istream** class implements the notion of the *object-oriented input* stream. This object-oriented input stream can be a **binary stream** or a **text stream.** The object-oriented stream can be buffered or unbuffered. An **istream** object can be tied to such input devices as keyboards, disk drives, and CD-ROMs. The **istream** class has facilities to process single characters or blocks of characters. When characters or blocks of characters are taken from an **istream** object, the operation is referred to as *extraction.* Data is extracted from an input stream and stored in some data object or data structure. A C++ program can contain multiple **istream** objects. There can be a separate **istream** object for every input device and input file in the program. This gives the programmer maximum flexibility in I/O design.

The **istream** class is the fundamental base class for the **ifstream** and the **istrstream** classes. These two classes are a specialization of **istream** that deal with files and memory areas, respectively. Familiarity with the structure and operations of the **istream** and **ostream** classes are necessary for a good understanding of the IOSTREAM class hierarchy.

Class Interface Specification:

```
istream
```

Declared in:

```
<iostream.h>
```

Derived from:

```
ios
```

Base Class for:

```
ifstream,istrstream
```

Contains:

```
streambuf *
```

Constructors:

```
istream(streambuf*)
```

Destructor:

```
virtual ~istream( )
```

Protected Member Functions:

```
istream( )
void eatwhite( )
```

Public Member Functions:

```
int ipfx(int = 0)
void isfx( )
istream& seekg(streampos)
istream& seekg(streamoff, seek_dir)
streampos tellg( )
int sync( )
istream& get(char*, int, char = '\n')
istream& get(signed char*, int, char = '\n')
istream& get(unsigned char*, int, char = '\n')
istream& read(char*, int)
istream& read(signed char*, int)
istream& read (unsigned char*, int)
istream& getline(char*, int, char = '\n')
istream& getline(signed char*, int, char = '\n')
istream& getline(unsigned char*, int, char = '\n')
istream& get(streambuf&, char = '\n')
istream& get(char&)
istream& get(signed char&)
istream& get(unsigned char&)
int get( )
int peek( )
int gcount( )
istream& putback(char)
istream& ignore(int = 1, int = EOF)
istream& operator>> (istream&)
istream& operator>> (ios&)
istream& operator>> (char*)
istream& operator>> (signed char*)
istream& operator>> (unsigned char*)
istream& operator>> (char&)
istream& operator>> (signed char&)
istream& operator>> (unsigned char&)
istream& operator>> (short&)
istream& operator>> (int&)
```

```
istream& operator>> (long&)

istream& operator>> (unsigned short&)

istream& operator>> (unsigned int&)

istream& operator>> (unsigned long&)

istream& operator>> (float&)

istream& operator>> (double&)

istream& operator>> (long double&)

istream& operator>> (streambuf*)
```

DESCRIPTION istream is a class that models the input stream. The **istream** class recognizes binary and text strings. The **istream** class has functionality that handles single characters and blocks of characters. The **istream** class has member functions that translate generic streams of bytes into objects that can be extracted from the input stream.

Stream Extraction and Object Translation

Objects are inserted into the output stream and extracted from the input stream. In order for an object to be extracted from the input stream, an object representing the input stream must first exist. A good example and much used input stream object is the predefined object *cin*, which is a specific instance of the class **istream**. The declaration:

```
istream cin; (simplified declaration)
```

has been made for the C++ programmer in the **iostream** header file. The **cin** instance of **istream** is an object not a *function* or a *keyword*! Because **cin** is an object, **cin** has a data component as well as operations that interact with its data component. In fact, the **cin** object has an **ios** object and a **streambuf** object encapsulated within its own structure. This means that everything that **ios** is and has, the **cin** object is and has. The **istream** class relation diagram is identical to the object relationship diagram for the **cin** object. Therefore, all the applicable **istream** data members and member functions can be accessed by a **cin** object. For instance:

```
cin.rdstate( );

cin.rdbuf( );

cin.width( );

cin.flags( );

cin.open("keyb", ios::in);

cin.rdbuf( )->sgetn( );

etc.
```

The **cin** object has been predefined. The C++ programmer is at liberty to define as many **istream** objects as are necessary.

The Extraction Operator >>

The operator >> is defined in C++ as the *right bitwise shift* operator. Normally, this operator takes two arguments, and shifts bits in one argument the number of times indicated in the second argument. This operator has been overloaded in the IOSTREAM classes so that it can be used for input operations. The operator takes on additional meaning when it is overloaded. While the >> operator retains its original meaning relative to bit shifting, it also has new responsibilities when used in conjunction with an **istream** object. Although the semantics of the operator is enhanced during overloading, the syntax of the operator's usage must remain the same. When the >> operator is overloaded in the IOSTREAM classes, it is called the *extraction* operator. It no longer only performs right bit shifts, but it also extracts data objects from a data stream. The data stream may be connected to any input device that is connected to the computer. The **cin istream** object is connected to the console.

The >> extraction operator gives the **istream** class its appearance of genericity and device-independence. This is accomplished through *polymorphism*. Because the >> operator has been overloaded for all the built-in data types, the programmer can extract any built-in data type from an **istream** object using the same syntax (Listing 3.2).

Listing 3.2

```
// This program demonstrates the polymorphic effect of overloading the
// << and >> operators.

#include <iostream.h>

void main (void)
{
    float PI;
    long double AvogadroNumber;
    int SpeedOfLight;
    double Planck;

    cout << "What is the value of pi ";
    cin >> PI;
    cout << "What is Avogadro Number? ";
    cin >> AvogadroNumber;
    cout << "What is the speed of Light? ";
    cin >> SpeedOfLight;
    cout << "What is Planck's constant? ";
    cin >> Planck;
}
```

The >> insertion operator is a good example of single interface, multiple implementation.

Translation and Conversion

The extraction operator does more than just extract objects from a stream (*technically, the* **streambuf** *component does the extraction*). The extraction operator also calls a function that does data conversion or translation. Operators in C++ are really just function names that invoke functions. When the programmer specifies:

```
cin >> object - form 1
```

it is equivalent to calling the function:

```
>>(cin,object) - form 2
```

The function name is in infix notation in the first form. In the second form, the function name is in prefix notation. The prefix function notation has the name **>>**, and it is passed two arguments: an **istream** object, and an object. The function's purpose is to take a generic stream of bytes and convert it into the specified data type during extraction. Put more simply, the **>>** function converts a generic stream of bytes into objects. This conversion process is sometimes called *translation* or *conversion*. The **>>** operator or function is said to translate a stream of bytes into a built-in object or a user-defined object. It is this facility that gives the C++ environment the ability to handle user-defined data types and data structures easily. If the **>>** operator is defined for the user-defined data type or data structure, then the **>>** operator is responsible for translating the generic stream of bytes into the user-defined object. This is how the stream concept is connected to object orientation.

Formatted stream extraction achieves its goal first through polymorphism, by defining the **>>** operator for all fundamental built-in data types and allowing the operator to be defined for user-defined data types. Second, formatted stream extraction achieves its goal by obtaining (translating) objects from generic streams of bytes. A more detailed discussion of overloading the **>>** operator is presented in Chapter 5.

Unformatted Extractions

The **>>** operator performs formatted extractions. The objects that are extracted from the **istream** class originate as generic streams of bytes. They are converted from simpler data types into more complex data objects during the translation process. In many circumstances, it is desirable to extract the data from the input stream without formatting or translation.

The **istream** class has several member functions that extract information from the stream without translation. These member functions are the **get( )**, **getline( )**, **and read( )** member functions.

The get( ) Member Functions

The **get( )** member function has been overloaded and can be used to get data from the attached **streambuf** type and store it into input objects. The **get( )** member function takes on three basic forms. The first form:

```
istream& get(char* Destination, int Len, char Delim)
istream& get(signed char* Destination, int Len, char Delim)
istream& get(unsigned char* Destination, int Len, char Delim)
```

extracts a number of characters from the attached buffer, and stores those characters into a character array pointed to by **Destination.** This form of the get( ) member function will extract characters from the attached buffer until either **Len–1** number of characters has been extracted, the **Delim** is reached, or some error condition is caused—whichever happens first. The error condition could be the get( ) member function trying to extract beyond the EOF. **Len–1** is the most characters that will be extracted from the input stream. **Delim** is a character that will cause the extraction process to terminate. The default Delimiter is the **\n** new line character. Obviously, if the extraction process does not encounter the **Delim**, then it will attempt to extract **Len–1** characters. An error condition occurs if the source of the extraction does not contain **Len–1** characters. This form of the get( ) member function will always store **\0** the NULL character at the end of **Destination**, even if there were no character extracted. In Listing 3.3 a string of characters is assigned to a **strstreambuf**.

Listing 3.3

```
// This program demonstrates the use of get( ) member function.
// The program also shows how to declare all istream object and its
// associated buffer.

#include <iostream.h>
#include <strstrea.h>
#include <string.h>
void main(void)
{
    const char Word[] = "speed of light";
    char Dest[81] = "";
    strstreambuf Buffer(81);
    Buffer.sputn(Word,strlen(Word));
    istream InputStream(&Buffer);
    if(!InputStream){
        cerr << "Error Setting up stream";
    }
    InputStream.get(Dest,81,'e');
    cout << Dest << endl;
    InputStream.seekg(0,ios::beg);
    InputStream.get(Dest,InputStream.rdbuf( )->in_avail( ),'\n');
    cout << Dest << endl;
    InputStream.seekg(0,ios::beg);
    InputStream.get(Dest,5,'\n');
    cout << Dest << endl;

}
```

Output from Listing 3.3

```
sp
speed of ligh
spee
```

In Listing 3.3, the first **get( )** will extract the characters *sp* and stop extraction when it encounters *e.* The second **get( )** will extract the entire string and stop extraction at the value of ***InputStream.rdbuf( )->in_*** avail( ). The third **get( )** will extract up to *d* and the extraction will terminate.

This form of the **get( )** member function will leave the delimiter *Delim* in the stream. It will not extract *Delim* and store it in *Destination.* This means that in some cases there will be an unwanted character in the input stream that must be dealt with. The **istream& ignore(int N, int Delim)** member function can solve this problem. The **ignore( )** member function discards *N* number of characters or up to the *Delim*, whichever comes first. The program in Listing 3.3 contains four **iostream** objects. **Buffer** and **InputStream** are user-declared objects. The other objects, **cout** and **cerr**, are predefined objects. The **cerr** object is an **ostream** object that is connected to the standard **err** stream. The **istream** object is connected to the **Buffer** object. This connection specifies that the source of **InputStream** object's extraction will be the **Buffer** object. The **istream** object's constructor requires a pointer to a **streambuf** class. The **streambuf** class used should be one of **streambuf**'s derived classes, such as **ststreambuf** or **filebuf.**

One important aspect of processing input streams is the separation from the stream and the destination of the data. Although the destination may require only three characters, the stream may contain 10 characters. When one of the **get( )** member functions is used to extract the three characters into the destination, the stream still contains seven characters. These characters will be processed by the next extraction operation. The programmer must make provisions for the behavior of stream extraction. The **ignore( )** member function is appropriate if the data isn't needed.

The second form of the **get( )** member function:

```
istream& get(streambuf& Buffer, char Delim)
```

extracts a number of characters from a **streambuf** and stores them into another **streambuf.** The first form extracted characters from a **streambuf** and stored them into a character array. The second form goes from **streambuf** to **streambuf.** However, the second form does not specify how many characters to extract. It will extract characters until *Delim* is reached, **EOF** is reached, or until an error condition occurs.

The third form of the **get( )** member function:

```
istream& get(char& Character)
istream& get(signed char& Character)
istream& get(unsigned char& Character)
int get( )
```

extracts a single character from the stream and stores it in *Character.*

getline( ) Member Functions

The **getline( )** member function has been overloaded and can be used to extract data from the attached stream and store it into input objects.

```
istream& getline(char* Destination, int, char Delim)
istream& getline(signed char* Destination, int, char Delim)
istream& getline(unsigned char* Destination, int, char Delim)
```

The **getline( )** member function extracts a number of characters from the attached buffer, and stores those characters into a character array pointed to by **Destination.** The **getline( )** member function will extract characters from the attached buffer until either **Len–1** number of characters has been extracted, the **Delim** is reached, or some error condition is caused, whichever happens first. The error condition could be the **getline( )** member function trying to extract beyond EOF. **Len–1** is the most characters that will be extracted from the input stream. **Delim** is a character that will cause the extraction process to terminate. The default **Delimiter** is the **\n** new line character. Obviously, if the extraction process does not encounter the **Delim**, then it will attempt to extract **Len–1** characters. If the source of the extraction does not contain **Len–1** characters, then an error condition occurs. The **getline( )** member function will always store **\0**, the NULL character, at the end of **Destination**, even if there are no characters extracted.

Whereas the **get( )** member function did not extract the delimiter from the stream, the **getline( )** member function does extract the delimiter from the stream. Neither member function stores the delimiter in **Destination.**

read( ) Member Function

The **read( )** member function has been overloaded and can be used to extract data from the attached stream buffer, and store it into a character array.

```
istream& read(char* Destination, int Len)
istream& read(signed char* Destination, int Len)
istream& read(unsigned char* Destination, int Len)
```

The **read( )** member function extracts **Len** characters from the stream buffer and stores them in the character array pointed to by **Destination.** The **read( )** member function does not store a **\0 NULL** character at the end of **Destination.** The **read( )** member function extracts **Len** characters, as opposed to the **Len–1** that the **get( )** and **getline( )** member functions extract.

Checking the State of the Stream

The **gcount( )** member function returns the number of bytes that were extracted for the last unformatted extraction performed. The **gcount( )** member function can be used immediately after the **get( )**, **getline( )**, and **read( )** member functions to determine how many characters were extracted. Although the **gcount( )** member function is useful for counting characters, the buffer state functions:

- **good( )**
- **bad( )**
- **fail( )**
- **eof( )**

should be used constantly while working with the IOSTREAMS. These member functions provide the programmer with a snapshot of the stream state at any given point.

The Prefix and Suffix Functions ipfx( ) and isfx( )

These two functions perform precondition and postcondition processing for the **>>** extraction operator, and precondition processing for some of the unformatted extraction member functions. The **>>** member function calls the precondition function **ipfx( )** before extracting characters from the input stream, and calls the postcondition **isfx( )** member function after extracting characters from the input stream. Some of the unformatted extraction member functions call **ipfx(1).** The prefix or precondition member function will have a slightly different behavior, depending on whether the operation is dealing with formatted or unformatted extraction. The **ipfx( )** and **isfx( )** member functions can also have implementation-specific processing responsibilities. The precondition function **ipfx( )** checks the buffer state of the attached **streambuf** object. If the buffer is in an error state, the precondition function **ipfx( )** returns a zero. If this function returns a zero, the insertion operation will fail. Nothing can be extracted from the stream until the **error** state is cleared. If the buffer is not in an error state, the **ipfx( )** member function will flush the attached buffer and return a nonzero value.

The **ipfx( )** member function and the **isfx( )** member function are part of the object-oriented mechanism that helps to propagate errors throughout the IOSTREAM class hierarchy. With these member functions in place, once a stream enters an error state, it remains in that error state in a do-nothing mode until the error state is cleared. The error state can be cleared by calling the **clear( )** member function.

peek( ) and putback( ) Member Functions

The **peek( )** member function returns the next character in the stream without extracting the character from the stream. The **peek( )** member function will call **ipfx(1)** to determine if it can return a character from the stream.

The **putback( )** member function takes a *char* argument:

```
istream & putback(char Character)
```

It attempts to put this character back into the stream. The character must equal the character that the get pointer is at. If *Character* does not equal the character get pointer is at, then the **putback( )** function fails.

ostream Class—An Object-Oriented Model of Output

The **ostream** class is the foundation for the object-oriented output stream in the C++ environment. The object-oriented facilities in the C++ language bring the added power of I/O modeling, user-defined I/O structures, and uniformity of expression to the stream concept. The **ostream** class is derived from the **ios** class. This means that the power of expression and representation that is contained in the **ios** class is also contained in the **ostream** class and its derived classes. All the member functions that are callable from an **ios** class are callable from an **ostream** class. All the protected and public data members that are contained in the **ios** class are contained in the **ostream** class.

The **ios** class contains a pointer to a **streambuf** class. The **ostream** class inherits this pointer to the **streambuf** class. This means that the **ostream** class has full access to the functionality of the **streambuf** class and the services that it provides. The class relationship diagram in Figure 3.5 shows the relationship between the **ostream** class, **ios** class, and **streambuf** class. The relationship between **ostream** and **ios** is an inheritance relationship. This inheritance relationship means that **ios** is a subset of the **ostream** class. The class relationship diagram in Figure 3.5 shows that **ostream** will contain a pointer to a **streambuf** class. This means that the **ostream** class can access the functionality of the **streambuf** class only through its public members.

Through encapsulation and inheritance, the **ios** class and **streambuf** classes are combined with the **ostream** protoclass to form the **ostream** class. The **ostream** class

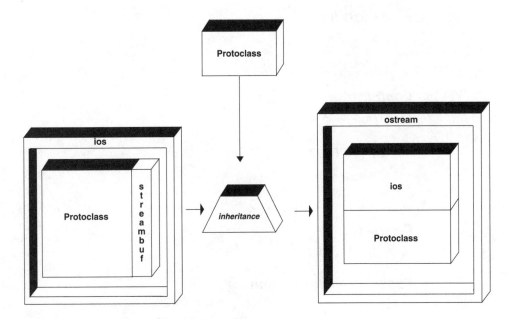

Figure 3.5 *Class relationship of the **ostream** class.*

implements the notion of the *object-oriented output* stream. This object-oriented output stream can be a **binary stream** or a **text stream.** The object-oriented stream can be buffered or unbuffered. The **ostream** class has facilities to process single characters or blocks of characters. When characters or blocks of characters are sent to an **ostream** object, the operation is referred to as *insertion*. A C++ program can contain multiple **ostream** objects. There can be an **ostream** object for every output device and output file in the program. This gives the programmer maximum flexibility in I/O design.

The **ostream** class is the fundamental base class for the **ofstream** class and the **ostrstream** class. These two classes are a specialization of **ostream** that deal with files and memory areas, respectively. Familiarity with the structure and operations of the **ostream** class will shed light on the entire IOSTREAM class hierarchy.

Class Interface Specification:

```
ostream
```

Declared in:

```
<iostream.h>
```

Derived from:

```
ios
```

Base Class for:

```
ofstream
ostrstream
```

Contains:

```
streambuf *
```

Constructors:

```
ostream(streambuf*)
ostream( )
```

Destructor:

```
virtual ~ostream( )
```

Public Member Functions:

```
int opfx( )
void osfx( )
```

```
ostream& flush( )
ostream& seekp(streampos)
ostream& seekp(streamoff, seek_dir)
streampos tellp( )
ostream& put(char)
ostream& put(signed char)
ostream& put(unsigned char)
ostream& write(const char*, int)
ostream& write(const signed char*, int)
ostream& write(const unsigned char*, int)
ostream& operator<< (char)
ostream& operator<< (signed char)
ostream& operator<< (unsigned char)
ostream& operator<< (short)
ostream& operator<< (unsigned short)
ostream& operator<< (int)
ostream& operator<< (unsigned int)
ostream& operator<< (long)
ostream& operator<< (unsigned long)
ostream& operator<< (float)
ostream& operator<< (double)
ostream& operator<< (long double)
ostream& operator<< (const char*)
ostream& operator<< (const signed char*)
ostream& operator<< (const unsigned char*)
ostream& operator<< (void*)
ostream& operator<< (streambuf*)
```

DESCRIPTION ostream provides formatted and unformatted output to a **streambuf**.

Stream Insertion and Object Translation

Objects are inserted into the output stream and extracted from the input stream. In order for an object to get inserted into the output stream, an object representing the output stream must first exist. A good example and much used output stream object is the predefined object **cout**, which is a specific instance of the class **ostream**. The declaration:

```
ostream cout; (simplified declaration)
```

has been made for the C++ programmer in the IOSTREAM header file. The **cout** instance of **ostream** is an object, not a *function* or a *keyword*! Because **cout** is an object, **cout** has a data component as well as operations that interact with its data component. In fact, the **cout** object has an **ios** object and a **streambuf** object encapsulated within its own structure. This means that everything that **ios** is and has, the **cout** object is and has. The **ostream** class relationship diagram is identical to the object relationship diagram for the **cout** object. Therefore, all the applicable **ostream** data members and member functions can be accessed by a **cout** object. For instance:

```
cout.rdstate( );
cout.rdbuf( )
cout.flush( );
cout.width( );
cout.precision( );
cout.width( );
cout.flags( );
cout.fill( );
cout.open("con",ios::out);
cout.rdbuf( )->sputn( );
etc.
```

The **cout** object has been predefined. The C++ programmer is at liberty to define as many **ostream** objects as necessary.

The Insertion Operator <<

The operator << is defined in C++ as the *left bitwise shift* operator. This operator has been overloaded in the IOSTREAM classes so that it can be used for output operations. When an operator is overloaded, the operator takes on additional meaning. While the << operator retains its original meaning relative to bit shifting, it also has new responsibilities when used in conjunction with an **ostream** object. Although the semantics of the operator are enhanced during overloading, the syntax of the operator's usage must remain the same. When the << operator is overloaded in the IOSTREAM classes, it is called the *insertion operator*. It no longer only performs left bit shifts, but it also inserts objects into a data stream. The data stream may be connected to any output device that is connected to the computer. The **cout ostream** object is connected to the console.

When objects are inserted into the **cout ostream**, they are sent to the console (monitor). For example, the program in Listing 3.4 sends a string to the console.

Listing 3.4

```
// This program demonstrates the insertion of a string into the
// cout object.
#include <iostream.h>
void main(void)
{
    cout << "The speed of light is 3.00e8 m/sec";
}
```

Output from Listing 3.4

The speed of light is 3.00e8 m/sec

The << insertion operator gives the **ostream** class its appearance of genericity, and device-independence. This is accomplished through polymorphism. Because the << operator has been overloaded for all the built-in data types, the programmer can insert any built-in data type into an **ostream** object using the same syntax. For example, the program in Listing 3.5 uses the << insertion operator with four different data types.

Listing 3.5

```
// This program demonstrates the usage of << operator with
// different built-in data types.
#include <iostream.h>
void main(void)
{
    float PI = 3.159;
    double AvogadrosNumber = 6.023E23;
    int SpeedOfLight = 3.00E8;
    char Word[] = "Planck's Constant";

    cout << PI << endl;
    cout << AvogadrosNumber << endl;
    cout << SpeedOfLight << endl;
    cout << Word;
}
```

Output from Listing 3.5

3.159
6.023e+23
300000000
Planck's Constant

The << insertion operator is a good example of single interface, multiple implementation.

Translation and Conversion

The insertion operator does more than just insert objects into a stream. Overloading the insertion operator shall be discussed in greater detail in Chapter 5, but for now, let it suffice to say that operators in C++ are really just function names, and simply invoke functions. When the programmer specifies:

```
cout << object;
```

it is equivalent to calling the function:

```
<<(cout,object);
```

In the first form, the function name is in infix notation. In the second form, the function name is in prefix notation. The prefix function notation has the name << and it is passed two arguments: an **ostream** object, and object. The function's purpose is to take the object and convert it into a stream of bytes that will be inserted into the stream and inevitably sent to the output device that is connected to the stream. Put more simply, the << function converts objects into a generic stream of bytes. This conversion process is sometimes called *translation*. The << operator or function is said to translate an object into a stream of bytes. It is this facility that gives the C++ environment the ability to handle user-defined data types and data structures easily. If the << operator is defined for the user-defined data type or data structure, then the << operator is responsible for translating the user's object into a generic stream of bytes. This is how the stream concept is connected to object orientation.

Formatted stream insertion achieves its goal first through polymorphism, by defining the << operator for all the built-in data types and allowing the operator to be defined for user-defined data types. Second, formatted stream insertion achieves its goal by converting (translating) objects into generic streams of bytes.

Unformatted Insertions: put( ) and write( ) Member Functions

The << operator performs formatted insertions. The objects that are inserted into the **ostream** class are not sent to the output as they are. They are first translated into simpler data types (streams of bytes). In many circumstances, it is desirable to insert the data into the stream without formatting or translation. The **ostream** class has two member functions that send information to the stream as is. The first member function **put( )** inserts either a character, unsigned character, or signed character into the output stream.

Listing 3.6

```
// This program shows how the put( ) member function is called by an
// ostream object.
#include <iostream.h>
void main(void)
```

```
{
    cout.put('A');
}
```

The program in Listing 3.6 sends the character *A* to the output. The second member function, **write( )**, inserts from one character to a block of characters into the output stream. This member function does not do any translation; it is used to write unformatted binary blocks to files and output devices. This member function takes a pointer to a *char*, signed *char*, or unsigned *char*, along with the number of bytes to write as an argument, and then sends the data to its stream.

Listing 3.7

```
// This program uses the write( ) member function to insert a double
// into the streambuf of the cout object.

#include <iostream.h>

void main(void)
{
    double SpeedOfLight = 3.00E8;
    cout.write((unsigned char*)&SpeedOfLight,sizeof(double));
}
```

When the program in Listing 3.7 is executed, it will write the value of *Speed-OfLight* in its unformatted form to the stream that the **cout** object is connected to. **cout**'s stream is connected to the console; therefore, a series of bytes appears on the console that represent an unformatted double.

The Prefix and Suffix Functions opfx( ) and osfx( )

These two functions perform precondition and postcondition processing for the << insertion operator. The << member function calls the precondition function **opfx( )** prior to inserting characters into the output stream, and calls the postcondition **osfx( )** member function after inserting characters into the output stream. The precondition function **opfx( )** checks the buffer state of the attached **streambuf** object. If the buffer is in an error state, the precondition function **opfx( )** returns a zero. If this function returns a zero, the insertion operation will fail. Nothing can be inserted into the stream until the error state is cleared. If the buffer is not in an error state, the **opfx( )** member function will flush the attached buffer and return a nonzero value.

The postcondition function **osfx( )** is called before the << member function returns. The **osfx( )** member function will flush the buffer that is attached to the **ostream** object. The **opfx( )** member function and the **osfx( )** member function are part of the object-oriented mechanism that helps to propagate errors throughout the IOSTREAM class hierarchy. With these member functions in place, once a stream enters an error state, it remains in that error state in a do-nothing mode until the error state is cleared. The error state can be cleared by calling the **clear( )** member function.

We discuss the positioning member functions under our discussion of **ofstream.** These functions are best understood when they are working with a **filebuf** component.

ifstream Class—The Object-Oriented Input File

The **ifstream** class is derived from the **istream** class. The **ifstream** class models the *input file* stream. Whereas the **istream** class focuses on an input stream normally attached to the console, the **ifstream** focuses on a stream normally attached to a file. The **ifstream** is a specialized **istream** class. The **ifstream** class is an important class in the operating system environments that implement devices as files. UNIX, OS/2, and MS-DOS are good examples of operating systems that see devices as specialized files. In these operating system environments, **ifstream** classes can be used to access any device that is recognized as a file by the operating system. The **ifstream** class adds member functions and an important data member that are specifically designed to deal with files. The class relationship diagram in Figure 3.6 shows the relationship between the **ifstream** protoclass and the **istream** class. It shows the relationship as an inheritance relationship. Figure 3.7 compares the **ifstream** class and the **istream** class. Notice that in Figure 3.7, **ifstream** has a **filebuf** component, as opposed to a **streambuf** component.

The **filebuf** component is a specialized **streambuf.** Refer to the **filebuf** description earlier in this chapter. Through the **filebuf** component, the **ifstream** class has access to the file descriptor. The file descriptor can be accessed through the **fd( )** member function of the **filebuf** component. The file descriptor gives the C++ programmer access to the low-level nonobject-oriented I/O functions that require file descriptor arguments. Because **ifstream** is a descendent of **istream**, it has the same capacity to deal with formatted and unformatted operations. Any protected or public member function that can be called in an **istream** class can be called in an **ifstream** class. Extraction has basically the same semantics in an **ifstream** class. The **ifstream** class is said to extend the services of the **istream** class to include files.

Class Interface Specification:

ifstream

Declared in:

<fstream.h>

Derived from:

istream

Base Class for:

fstream

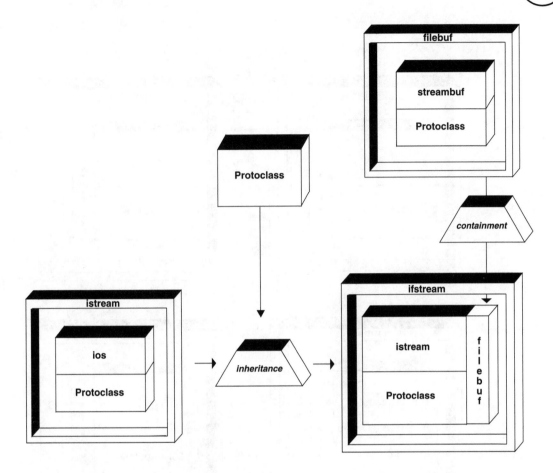

Figure 3.6   *Class relationship of the **ifstream** class.*

Contains:

```
filebuf
```

Constructors:

```
ifstream( )
ifstream(const char *,int = ios::in,int = filebuf::openprot)
ifstream(int)
ifstream(int, char *, int)
```

Destructor:

```
~ifstream( )
```

A.

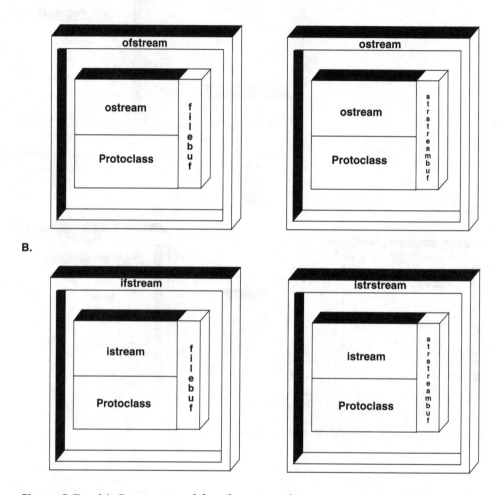

B.

Figure 3.7 *(a) Comparison of the **ofstream** and **ostrstream** classes. (b) Comparison of the **ifstream** and **istrstream** classes.*

Public Member Functions:

```
void attach(int)
void close( )
void setbuf(char *, int)
filebuf* rdbuf( )
void open(const char *, int = ios::in,int = filebuf::openprot)
```

DESCRIPTION **ifstream** is a class that models the input file stream. The **ifstream** class recognizes binary and text file sequences. The **ifstream** class has functionality that handles single characters and blocks of characters. The **ifstream** class has member functions that translate sequences of bytes from files into objects that can be extracted from the input stream. The **ifstream** class has facilities that handle formatted and unformatted extraction.

Opening Files in the ifstream Class

Files can be opened in an **ifstream** class using two methods. The first method uses the constructor:

```
ifstream(const char * FileName ,int OpenMode,int ProtectMode);
```

An **ifstream** object can be declared, and the file to be attached to the object can be specified in the constructor:

```
ifstream Source("myfile.dat",ios::in | ios::binary);
```

The constructor opens the file specified by *FileName.* If the file cannot be opened, the buffer state will contain the error condition. The second method uses a member function:

```
open(const char *FileName, int OpenMode,int ProtectMode);
```

This member function can be called after the **ifstream** object has been declared.

Listing 3.8

```
// This program opens a file for binary input.
#include <fstream.h>
void main(void)
{
   unsigned char Byte;
   ifstream Source;

   Source.open("pic1.pcx",ios::in | ios::binary);
   Source >> Byte;
   Source.close( );
}
```

The **close( )** member function closes the file attached to the **ifstream** class.

Attaching Files to an ifstream Object

Open files may be attached to an **ifstream** object using two methods. The first method uses constructors:

```
ifstream(int FileDescriptor);
ifstream(int FileDescriptor, char *Pos, int Len);
```

Using the constructor method of attaching files requires that the file already be open. The opened file could have been opened by one of the IOSTREAM classes or by one of the standard nonobject-oriented functions. Listing 3.9 shows the **Source1 ifstream** object opening a file using the **open( )** member function, and the constructor for the **Source2** object accepting the file descriptor that belongs to the **Source1** file.

Listing 3.9

```
// This program demonstrates the attachment of a file descriptor
// through the constructor for an ifstream object. The descriptor
// is accessed through the fd( ) member function of the contained
// buffer.

#include <fstream.h>

void main(void)
{
    ifstream Source1;
    ifstream Source2(Source1.rdbuf( )->fd( ));

    Source1.open("file1.txt");
    cout << Source2.rdbuf( );
    Source1.close( );
    Source2.close( );
}
```

Contents of file1.txt in Listing 3.9

9.11e-31
1.3806e-23
1.60e-19
1.67e-27
6.63e-34
6.667e-11
8.314
9.0e9
3.00e8
6.023e23

Output from Listing 3.9

9.11e-31
1.3806e-23
1.60e-19
1.67e-27
6.63e-34

6.667e-11

8.314

9.0e9

3.00e8

6.023e23

The program in Listing 3.9 inserts the entire contents of the file connecting to **Source1** into **cout**. Notice that **Source2.rdbuf( )** is inserted into **cout**, not **Source1.rdbuf( )**. This is possible because the constructor for **Source2** received the file handle, or file descriptor, belonging to the file attached to **Source1**. Once **Source2** has this file descriptor, it can then access **Source1**'s file as though it were **Source2**'s open facility. The **cout<<Source2.rdbuf( )** displays the contents of the file connected to **Source2** (in this case, **Source1**'s file) to the console.

The second form of **ifstream** constructor that accepts a file descriptor also accepts *Length* and *Pos* as arguments. *Length* specifies how big the associated **filebuf**'s reserved area will be, and *Pos* specifies where in the buffer to begin extraction. The second method of attaching an open file to an **ifstream** class object uses a member function:

```
void attach(int FileDescriptor)
```

The program in Listing 3.10 shows an example of a call to the **attach( )** member function.

Listing 3.10

```
// This program demonstrates the attach( ) member function. The
// attach( ) member function, accepts a file descriptor, and connects
// to a file that is open.

#include <fstream.h>

void main(void)
{
    ifstream Source1;
    ifstream Source2;

    Source1.open("file1.txt");
    Source2.attach(Source1.rdbuf( )->fd( ));
    if(Source2.good( )){
        cout << Source2.rdbuf( );
    }
    Source1.close( );
    Source2.close( );
}
```

Output from Listing 3.10

9.11e-31

1.3806e-23

1.60e-19

1.67e-27

6.63e-34

6.667e-11

8.314

9.0e9

3.00e8

6.023e23

In the program in Listing 3.10, the **attach( )** member function accepts a file descriptor of an open file as an argument. If the file is not open, or if the **ifstream** class object is already attached to a file, an error condition is created. It is advisable to check the state of the buffer after a call to the **attach( )** member function. The state of the buffer can be checked by calling:

bad( )

good( )

fail( )

eof( )

Once the file is attached, the **ifstream** class object can use the file as if it had originally opened the file. By attaching a file descriptor, or file handle, as it is sometimes called, the programmer can access files that were opened with the low-level UNIX-style I/O functions. For example, the function **open( )** in the standard I/O library returns a file handle. This file handle can be passed to the **attach( )** member function to allow an **ifstream** class object to access this file. This is another method that allows the C++ programmer to use the IOSTREAM facilities in C environments.

Buffer Access for the ifstream Class

The **ifstream** class declares two member functions that handle buffers; **rdbuf( )** and **setbuf( )**. The **rdbuf( )** member function returns a pointer to the **filebuf** component that the **ifstream** class contains. This is a powerful and often overlooked facility in the IOSTREAMS. Through the pointer to **ifstream**'s **filebuf**, the **ifstream** class has access to all the functionality of a **filebuf** (**streambuf**) class. This means, given the declaration:

```
ifstream Source("File1.txt);
```

the **filebuf** component member functions may be accessed as follows:

```
Source.rdbuf( )->sgetn( )
Source.rdbuf( )->sbumpc( )
Source.rdbuf( )->snextc( )
Source.rdbuf( )->sgetc( );
```

```
Source.rdbuf( )->in_avail( );
Source.rdbuf( )->stossc( );
Source.rdbuf( )->sputbackc( ) etc.
```

This gives the C++ programmer total control of the buffer area that is connected to the **ifstream** class object. The **setbuf( )** member function allows the programmer to specify both the size of the buffer attached to the **filebuf** object, and the position in the buffer where the extraction will start. The **setbuf( )** member function should be called before a file is assigned to the **ifstream** class.

The IOSTREAM class hierarchy is built on inheritance, encapsulation, and polymorphism. In order for the C++ programmer to get the maximum benefit from the IOSTREAM classes, the programmer must be constantly aware of the hierarchy and components of all the IOSTREAM classes. In object-oriented programming, the emphasis is on relationships between classes and objects. The knowledge of what a class contains determines what member functions can be called. It must be remembered that an object is considered as a type in the C++ environment and can be used in expressions, put in array declarations, written to files, sorted, added, printed, read, created, destroyed, and so on. The program in Listing 3.11 creates an array of **ifstream** objects. Two of the **ifstream** objects are connected to text files that will be extracted from the input stream. The program in Listing 3.11 extracts numeric values from the two files (**List1.txt & List2.txt**) and performs a merge sort on the values. As the program is performing the merge sort, it inserts the values into the predefined **cout** stream. The program in Listing 3.11 is an example of using multiple streams within one program.

Listing 3.11

```
// This program reads in two files and performs a merge sort
// to the predefined stream cout.

#include <fstream.h>
#include <strstrea.h>
#include <stdlib.h>

ifstream Stream[2];

void main(void)
{

  double Object[2];

    Stream[0].open("list1.txt");
    if(!Stream[0].good()){
      cerr << "could Not open file 1";
      exit(0);
    }
    Stream[1].open("list2.txt");
    if(!Stream[1].good()){
      cerr << "could not open file 2 ";
      exit(0);
    }
```

```
Stream[0] >> Object[0];
Stream[1] >> Object[1];
while(!Stream[0].eof() && !Stream[0].fail() &&
      !Stream[1].eof() && !Stream[1].fail())
{
  if(Object[0] < Object[1]){
    cout << Object[0] << endl;
    Stream[0] >> Object[0];
  }
  else
    if(Object[1] < Object[0]){
        cout << Object[1] << endl;
        Stream[1] >> Object[1];
    }
     else{
        cout << Object[0] << endl << Object[1] << endl;
        Stream[0] >> Object[0];
        Stream[1] >> Object[1];
    }
}
while(!Stream[0].eof() && !Stream[0].fail())
{
  Stream[0] >> Object[0];
  cout << Object[0] << endl;
}
while(!Stream[1].eof() && !Stream[1].fail())
{
  Stream[1] >> Object[1];
  cout << Object[1] << endl;
}
Stream[0].close();
Stream[1].close();
}
```

Input Files for Listing 3.11

File1.txt	*File2.txt*
9.11e-31	9.0e10
1.3806e-23	4e-7
1.60e-19	9.81
1.67e-27	5.98e24
6.63e-34	6.38e6
6.667e-11	5570
8.314	3.84e8
9.0e9	1.496e11
3.00e8	1.99e30
6.023e23	7.0e8

Output from Listing 3.11

```
6.63e-34
9.11e-31
1.67e-27
1.3806e-23
1.6e-19
6.667e-11
4e-07
8.314
9.81
5570
6380000
3e+08
3.84e+08
7e+08
9e+09
9e+10
1.496e+11
6.023e+23
1.99e+30
1.99e+30
```

The program in Listing 3.11 contains four streams. The first and second streams are **ifstreams** and have been attached to **List1.txt** and **List2.txt**, respectively. The third and fourth streams, **cerr** and **cout**, are **ostreams.** These are predefined streams. Error messages can be inserted into the **cerr** object. Notice that the **ifstream** objects are contained within the array named *Stream.* This is another advantage of object-oriented I/O. The streams are objects just as any other object in the C++ environment, and can be used in expressions, array declarations, and so on. The program in Listing 3.11 does not do any serious error checking. The **good( )**, **fail( )**, and **eof( )** member functions are called for demonstration purposes.

ofstream Class—The Object-Oriented Output File

The **ofstream** class is derived from the **ostream** class. The **ofstream** class models the **output file** stream. The **ofstream** class can be used whenever the C++ programmer has to deal with files. Whereas the **cout ostream** class focuses on an output stream normally attached to the console, the **ofstream** focuses on a stream normally attached to a file. The **ofstream** is a specialized **ostream** class. Some operating systems, such as UNIX, OS/2, and MS-DOS, see devices as specialized files. In these operating system environments, **ofstream** classes can be used to access any device that is recognized as a file. The **ofstream** class adds member functions and important data members that are specifically designed to deal with files. The class relationship diagram in Figure 3.8 shows the relationship between the **ofstream** protoclass and the **ostream** class. It shows the relationship as an inheritance relationship. Figure 3.7 compares the **ofstream** class and the **ostream** class. Notice that in Figure 3.7, **ofstream** has a **filebuf** component, as opposed to a **streambuf** component.

The **filebuf** class is derived from the **streambuf** class. It is the **filebuf** class that is ultimately connected to the device or file that has been opened. The **filebuf** component gives the **ofstream** class access to the file descriptor. The **fd( )** member function

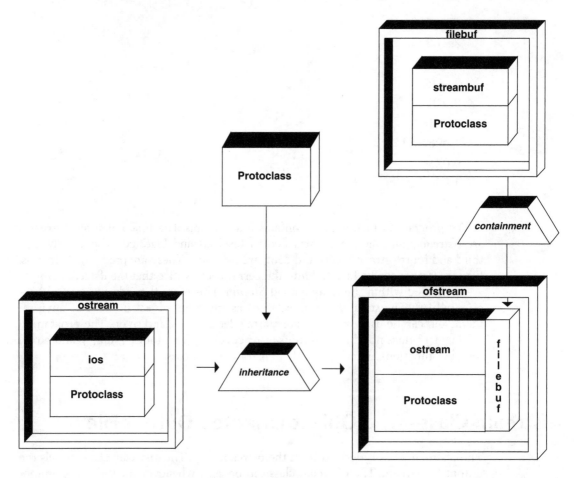

Figure 3.8   *Class relationship of the **ofstream** class.*

returns the file descriptor or file handle of the file that the **filebuf** component is attached to. Through the file descriptor, the C++ programmer has access to the low-level nonobject-oriented I/O functions that require file descriptor arguments. The inheritance relationship shown in Figure 3.8 shows that the entire **ostream** class is a component of the **ofstream** class. This means that any protected or public members that are in **ostream** are accessible in an **ofstream** class. The **ofstream** class has formatted and unformatted extraction functionality. The **ofstream** class indirectly inherits the **ios** class through the **ostream** class. This gives the **ofstream** class a **format** state, a **buffer** state, and an **open** state. The **ofstream** class extends the capabilities of the **ostream** class to deal with output files.

Class Interface Specification:

```
ofstream
```

Declared in:

```
<fstream.h>
```

Derived from:

```
ostream
```

Base Class for:

```
fstream
```

Contains:

```
filebuf
```

Constructors:

```
ofstream( )
ofstream(const char *,int = ios::in,int = filebuf::openprot)
ofstream(int)
ofstream(int, char *, int)
```

Destructor:

```
~ifstream( )
```

Public Member Functions:

```
void attach(int)
void close( )
void setbuf(char *, int)
```

```
filebuf* rdbuf( )
void open(const char *, int = ios::in,int = filebuf::openprot)
```

DESCRIPTION ofstream is a class that models the output file stream The **ofstream** class recognizes binary and text file sequences. The **ofstream** class has functionality that handles single characters and blocks of characters. The **ofstream** class has member functions that translate objects into sequences of bytes in an output stream. The **ofstream** class has facilities that handle formatted and unformatted insertion.

Opening Files in the ofstream Class

Files can be opened in an **ifstream** class using two methods. The first method uses the constructor:

```
ofstream(const char * FileName ,int OpenMode,int ProtectMode);
```

An **ofstream** object can be declared, and the file to be attached to the object can be specified in the constructor:

ofstream Source("myfile.dat",ios::out I ios::app);

The constructor opens the file specified by *FileName.* If the file cannot be opened, the **buffer** state will contain the error condition. The second method uses a member function:

open(const char *FileName,int OpenMode,int ProtectMode);

This member function can be called after the **ofstream** object has been declared. Listing 3.12 demonstrates a use of the **open( )** and **close( )** member functions.

Listing 3.12

```
// This program demonstrates the open( ) and close( ) member functions.
#include <fstream.h>
void main(void)
{
    unsigned char Byte;
    ofstream Destination;
    Destination.open("myfile.dat",ios::noreplace | ios::binary);
    Destination << Byte;
    Destination.close( );
}
```

The **close( )** member function closes the file attached to the **ifstream** class.

Attaching Files to an ofstream Object

Open files may be attached to an **ofstream** object using two methods. The first method uses constructors:

```
ofstream(int FileDescriptor);
ofstream(int FileDescriptor, char *Pos, int Len);
```

Using the constructor method of attaching files requires that the file already be open. The opened file could have been opened by one of the IOSTREAM classes or by one of the standard nonobject-oriented functions. Listing 3.13 shows the *Source* **ifstream** object opening a file using the **open( )** member function, and the constructor for the *Destination* object accepting the file descriptor that belongs to the **Source1** file.

Listing 3.13

```
// This program demonstrates how to attach a file descriptor of a
// already open file to an ofstream object using a constructor
// and the fd( ) member function of the filebuf object.

#include <fstream.h>

void main(void)
{
    ifstream Source;
    Source.open("file1.txt");

    ofstream Destination(Source.rdbuf( )->fd( ));
    cout << Destination.rdbuf( );
    Source.close( );
    Destination.close( );
}
```

The program in Listing 3.13 inserts the entire contents of the file connecting to **Source1** into **cout**. Notice that **Destination.rdbuf( )** is inserted into cout, not **Source.rdbuf( )**. This is possible because the constructor for *Destination* received the file handle or file descriptor belonging to the file attached to *Source*. Once *Destination* has this file descriptor, it then can access **Source1**'s file as though it were opened with *Destination*'s open facility. The **cout << Destination.rdbuf( )** displays the contents of the file connected to *Destination* (in this case, *Source*'s file) to the console.

The second form of **ofstream** constructor that accepts a file descriptor also accepts *Length* and *Pos* as arguments. *Length* specifies how big the associated **filebuf**'s reserved area will be, and *Pos* specifies where in the buffer to begin insertion. The second method of attaching an open file to an **ofstream** class object uses a member function:

```
void attach(int FileDescriptor)
```

The program in Listing 3.14 shows an example of a call to the **attach( )** member function.

Listing 3.14

```
// This program demonstrates how to attach a file descriptor or file
// handle of an already open file to an ofstream object using the
// attach( ) member function and the fd( ) member function of the
```

```
// filebuf object.
#include <fstream.h>
void main(void)
{
    ifstream Source;
    ofstream Destination
    Source.open("file1.txt");

    Destination.attach(Source.rdbuf( )->fd( ));
    if(Destination.good( )){
    cout << Destination.rdbuf( );
    }
    Source.close( );
    Destination.close( );
}
```

In the program in Listing 3.14, the **attach( )** member function accepts a file descriptor of an open file as an argument. If the file is not open, or if the **ofstream** class object is already attached to a file, an error condition is created. It is advisable to check the state of the buffer after a call to the **attach( )** member function. The state of the buffer can be checked by calling:

bad( )

good( )

fail( )

eof( )

Once the file is attached, the **ofstream** class object can use the file as if it had originally opened the file. By attaching a file descriptor, or file handle, as it is sometimes called, the programmer can access files that were opened with the low-level UNIX-style I/O functions. For example, the function **open( )** in the standard I/O library returns a file handle. This file handle can be passed to the **attach( )** member function to allow all **ofstream** class object to access this file. This is another method that allows the C++ programmer to mix the IOSTREAM facilities in C environments.

Buffer Access for the ofstream Class

The **ofstream** class declares two member functions that handle buffers: **rdbuf( )** and **setbuf( )**. The **rdbuf( )** member function returns a pointer to the **filebuf** component that the **ofstream** class contains. This is a powerful and often overlooked facility in the IOSTREAMS. Through the pointer to **ofstream**'s **filebuf**, the **ofstream** class has access to all the functionality of a **filebuf** (**streambuf**) class. This means that, given the declaration:

```
ofstream Destination("File1.txt);
```

the **filebuf** component member functions may be accessed as follows:

```
Destination.rdbuf( )->sputn( );
Destination.rdbuf( )->sbumpc( );
Destination.rdbuf( )->snextc( );
Destination.rdbuf( )->sputc( );
Destination.rdbuf( )->out_waiting( );
Destination.rdbuf( )->stossc( ) etc.
```

This gives the C++ programmer total control of the buffer area that is connected to the **ofstream** class object. The **setbuf( )** member function allows the programmer to specify both the size of the buffer attached to the **filebuf** object, and the position in the buffer where the insertion will start. The **setbuf( )** member function should be called before a file is assigned to the **ofstream** class.

istrstream Class—Input Memory Device

The **istrstream** class implements the functionality of an object-oriented input memory device; whereas the **cin**-type **istream** object is normally tied to the console, and the **ifstream** class is connected to a file or a device that is recognized as a file. The **istrstream** class is connected to a block of memory or a character array. The **istrstream** class is a model of a character or byte array.

The **istrstream** class is derived from the **istream** class. Figure 3.9 shows the relationship between the **istrstream** class and the **istream** class as inheritance. This means that the protected and public data members and member functions of **istream** are all inherited and accessible by the **istrstream** class. The inheritance relationship allows the **istrstream** class to apply the extraction >> operator to a memory device. The programmer can use the **read( )** member function and the **get( )** member functions to extract characters from the block of memory that the **istrstream** class object is connected to. Because the **istrstream** class is derived from **istream**, it also is indirectly derived from the **ios** class. This means that **istrstream** has a **format** state, **buffer** state, and **open** state!

Whereas the **istream** class has a **streambuf** component, and the **ifstream** has a **filebuf** component, the **istrstream** class has a **strstreambuf** component. The **strstreambuf** component is a specialized **streambuf**. It is derived from **streambuf**. The **strstreambuf** component is connected to a character array, as opposed to a file. The source of a **strstreambuf** is intended to be a memory device. The programmer can have direct access to the **istrstream** memory device through the **strstreambuf** component. The **strstreambuf** component can be reached by the **rdbuf( )** member function.

In the nonobject-oriented standard library, the C++ programmer has access to memory buffers and a set of functions that manipulate character arrays and strings. However, these facilities do not offer the advantages of object orientation. The

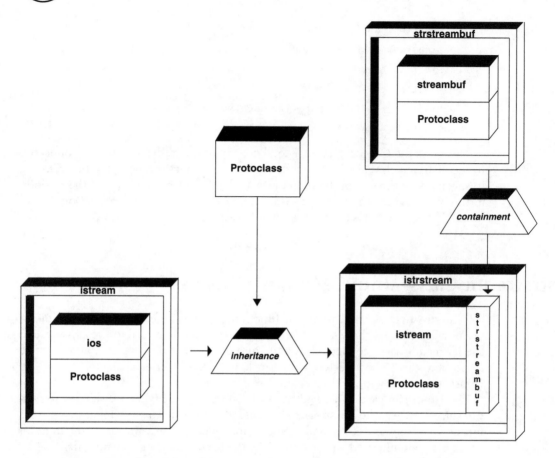

Figure 3.9 *Class relationship of the **istrstream** class.*

istrstream class brings object orientation to the character array or memory block. The memory block or memory object can represent buffered or unbuffered data, formatted or unformatted data.

Class Interface Specification:

istrstream

Declared in:

<strstrea.h>

Derived from:

istream

Base Class for:

None

Contains:

```
strstreambuf
```

Constructors:

```
istrstream(char* str);
istrstream(signed char* str);
istrstream(unsigned char* str);
istrstream(char* str, int size );
istrstream(signed char* str, int size);
istrstream(unsigned char* str, int size);
istrstream(const char* str);
istrstream(const signed char* str);
istrstream(const unsigned char* str);
istrstream(const char* str, int size );
istrstream(const signed char* str, int size);
istrstream(const unsigned char* str, int size);
```

Destructor:

```
~istrstream( )
```

Public Member Functions:

```
strstreambuf* rdbuf( )
```

DESCRIPTION **istrstream** is a class that models the input memory stream or character array. The **istrstream** class recognizes binary and text strings. The **istrstream** class has functionality that handles single characters and blocks of characters. The **istrstream** class has member functions that translate generic streams of bytes into objects that can be extracted from the input stream.

The Buffer Component of the istrstream Class

The **istrstream** buffer component is accessed by the **rdbuf( )** member function. The **rdbuf( )** member function returns a pointer to the **strstreambuf** component of the **istrstream** class. Through this component, the C++ programmer has access to all the public member functions of the **strstreambuf** class. The actual reserved area used by the **strstreambuf** component can either be dynamically allocated by the system, or can be provided by the programmer.

The constructor that is used with **istrstream** object will determine whether the **istrstream** object is attached to a string (character array with NULL terminator) or to a regular character array. The **istrstream** constructors:

```
istrstream(char* Str);
istrstream(signed char* Str);
istrstream(unsigned char* Str);
istrstream(const char* Str);
istrstream(const signed char* Str);
istrstream(const unsigned char* Str);
```

will cause the **istrstream** class object to be attached to a null-terminated string pointed to by *Str.*

The **istrstream** constructors:

```
istrstream(signed char* str, int size);
istrstream(unsigned char* str, int size);
istrstream(const char* str, int size );
istrstream(const signed char* str, int size);
istrstream(const unsigned char* str, int size);
```

will cause the **istrstream** class object to be attached to a character array, not a string.

ostrstream Class—Output Memory Device

The **ostrstream** class implements the functionality of an object-oriented output memory device, whereas the **cout**-type **ostream** object is normally tied to the console, and the **ofstream** class is connected to a file or a device that is recognized as a file. The **ostrstream** class is connected to a block of memory or a character array. The **ostrstream** class is a model of a character or byte array.

The **ostrstream** class is derived from the **ostream** class. Figure 3.10 shows the relationship between the **ostrstream** class and the **ostream** class as inheritance. This means that the protected and public data members and member functions of **ostream** are all inherited and accessible by the **ostrstream** class. The inheritance relationship allows the **ostrstream** class to apply the insertion << operators to a memory device. The programmer can use the **write( )** member function to insert characters into the block of memory that the **ostrstream** class object is connected to. Because the **ostrstream** class is derived from **ostream**, it is also indirectly derived from the **ios** class. This means that **ostrstream** has a **format** state, **buffer** state, and **open** state!

Whereas the **ostream** class has a **streambuf** component, and the **ofstream** has a **filebuf** component, the **ostrstream** class has a **strstreambuf** component. The

strstreambuf component is a specialized **streambuf**; it is derived from **streambuf**. The **strstreambuf** component is connected to a character array, as opposed to a file. The source and target of a **strstreambuf** are intended to be a memory device. The programmer can have direct access to the **ostrstream** memory device through the **strstreambuf** component. The **strstreambuf** component can be reached by the **rdbuf( )** member function.

The C++ program has access to memory buffers and a set of functions that manipulate character arrays and strings in the nonobject-oriented standard library. However, these facilities do not offer the advantages of object orientation. The **ostrstream** class brings object orientation to the character array or memory block. The memory block or memory object can represent buffered or unbuffered data, formatted or unformatted data.

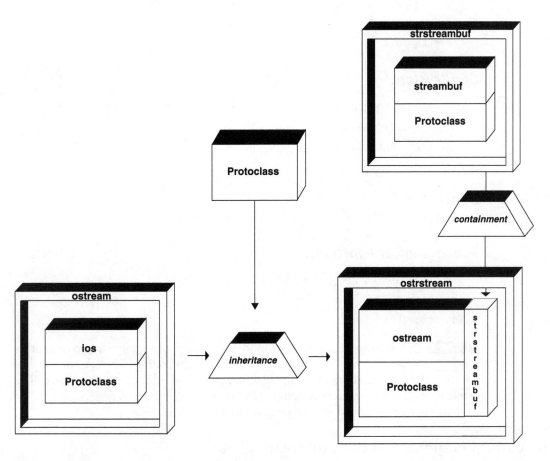

Figure 3.10 *Class relationship of the **ostrstream** class.*

Class Interface Specification:

ostrstream

Declared in:

<strstrea.h>

Derived from:

ostream

Base Class for:

None

Contains:

strstreambuf

Constructors:

```
ostrstream(char *, int, int = ios::out)
ostrstream(signed char *, int, int = ios::out)
ostrstream(unsigned char *, int, int = ios::out)
ostrstream( )
```

Destructor:

~ostrstream( )

Public Member Functions:

```
strstreambuf* rdbuf( )
char * str( )
int pcount( )
```

DESCRIPTION **ostrstream** is a class that models the output memory stream or character array. The **ostrstream** class recognizes binary and text strings. The ostrstream class has functionality that handles single characters and blocks of characters. The **ostrstream** class has member functions that translate objects into generic streams of bytes that can be inserted into an output stream.

The Buffer Component of the ostrstream Class

The **ostrstream** buffer component is accessed by the **rdbuf( )** member function. The **rdbuf( )** member function returns a pointer to the **strstreambuf** component of the istrstream class. Through this component, the C++ programmer has access to all the public member functions of the **strstreambuf** class.

ostrstream Construction

The actual reserved area used by the **strstreambuf** component can either be dynamically allocated by the system or can be provided by the programmer. The constructor that is used with the **ostrstream** object will determine whether the **ostrstream** object is attached to a string (character array with NULL terminator) or a regular character array. The **ostrstream** constructor that takes no arguments:

```
ostrstream( )
```

will designate a dynamically allocated buffer for the **ostrstream** class.

The **ostrsream** constructors:

```
ostrstream(char *Pos, int Len, int OpenMode)
ostrstream(char *Pos, int Len, int OpenMode)
ostrstream(signed char *Pos, int Len, int OpenMode)
```

will cause the **ostrstream** class object to be constructed and connected to a buffer that is *Len* in size. The insertions for the buffer will start at the location pointed to by *Pos*. If the *OpenMode* specifies **ios::app** or **ios::ate**, *Pos* points to a null-terminated string and insertion begins at the null character.

Accessing ostrstream's Character Array

The character array that is attached to the **ostrstream** object can be accessed using the **str( )** member function. The **str( )** member function returns a pointer to the array that the **ostrstream** object is using. The **ostrstream** object will either be attached to a user-declared character array, or the **ostrstream** object will be attached to a dynamically allocated array that the **ostrstream** allocates. It is the responsibility of the **ostrstream** destructor to take care of the space that has been dynamically allocated if the **str( )** member function has not been called. However, once the **str( )** member function has been called, the ostrstream object calls the **freeze( )** member function, and it is the programmer's responsibility to deal with memory deallocation from that point on. The **pcount( )** member function returns the number of bytes that have been stored in the character array. The number of bytes returned will include the NULL terminator if any.

iostream, fstream, and strstream I/O Classes

iostream, fstream, and **strstream** are bidirectional classes. Each class is derived from an input class and output class. The ANSI C++ draft has eliminated these classes.

iostream Class = istream + ostream

The **iostream** class is derived from the **istream** class and the **ostream** class. The class relationship diagram in Figure 3.11 shows the relationship as an inheritance relationship. The type of inheritance that is depicted in Figure 3.11 is multiple inheritance. Since the **iostream** class has an **istream** component and an **ostream** component, the **iostream** class can be used for input and for output modeling.

The protected and public data members and member functions that are contained in **istream** and **ostream** are components of the **iostream** class. The **iostream** class is a combination of **istream** and **ostream.**

fstream Class = ifstream + ofstream

Like the **iostream** class, the **fstream** class is an input class and output class. When the programmer needs to do simultaneous input and output to a file or a device that has been opened as a file, the programmer can declare an object of type **fstream.** The **fstream** object will have all the combined protected and public data members and member functions of the **ifstream** and **ofstream** classes. The class relationship diagram in Figure 3.12 shows the components that make up the **fstream** class. Keep in mind the notion of inheritance. The **fstream** class will contain **ios, istream, ostream, ifstream, ofstream,** and **filebuf** classes. The **fstream** represents a culmination of practically the entire IOSTREAM hierarchy.

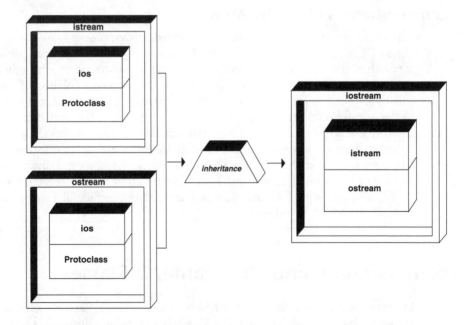

Figure 3.11   *Class relationship of the **iostream** class.*

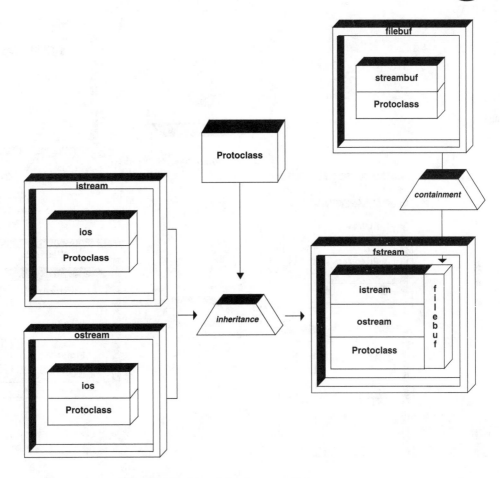

Figure 3.12 *Class relationship of the **fstream** class.*

strstream Class = istrstream + ostrstream

The **strstream** class is another bidirectional (input/output) class. Figure 3.13 shows the components that make up the **strstream** class. The **strstream** object will have a character array or character string as the source and target of its operations. The **strstream** class is often overlooked but proves to be one of the most important classes when tying the IOSTREAM family of classes to the new breed of operating system. We will have much to say about **istrstream**, **ostrstream**, and **strstream** in Chapters 8, 9, and 10. Because the **strstream** class and its base classes are models of a memory device, insertion and extraction can take place in a device-independent manner. The **strstream** classes have an important place in the Windows and Presentation Manager environments.

The program in Listing 3.15 is an example of using multiple I/O object streams in a program. This program has **fstream** objects and the predefined **ostream** objects

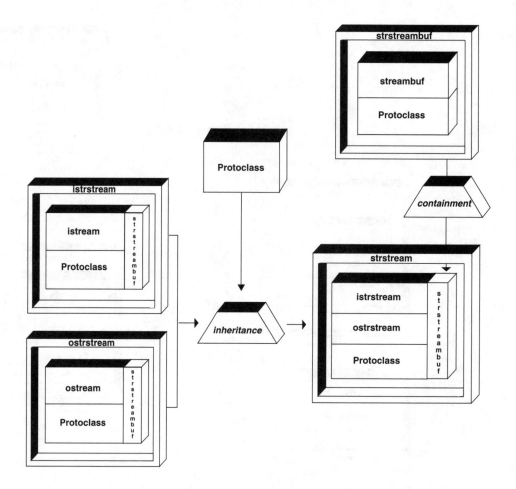

Figure 3.13   *Class relationship of the **strstream** class.*

cerr and **cout.** The program in Listing 3.15 opens two **fstream** objects for input, and two **fstream** objects for output. This program reads in two lists of numbers and merges those numbers into the **cout** object, an **ofstream** object that is connected to a file (**List3.txt**) and an **ofstream** object connected to a printer. The program has two input stream objects and four output stream objects. The number of I/O objects is limited only by the operating system and hardware resources.

Listing 3.15

```
#include <fstream.h>
#include <strstrea.h>
#include <stdlib.h>

fstream Stream[4];
```

```cpp
void main(void)
{
  double Object[2];

  Stream[0].open("list1.txt",ios::in);
  if(!Stream[0].good()){
    cerr << "could Not open file 1";
    exit(0);
  }
  Stream[1].open("list2.txt",ios::in);
  if(!Stream[1].good()){
    cerr << "could not open file 2 ";
    exit(0);
  }

  Stream[2].open("list3.txt",ios::out);
  if(!Stream[2]){
    cerr << "could not open file 3";
    exit(0);
  }
  Stream[3].open("prn",ios::out);
  if(!Stream[3]){
    cerr << "could not open printer";
    exit(0);
  }
  Stream[0] >> Object[0];
  Stream[1] >> Object[1];
  while(!Stream[0].eof() && !Stream[0].fail() &&
        !Stream[1].eof() && !Stream[1].fail())
  {
    if(Object[0] < Object[1]){
      cout << Object[0] << endl;
      Stream[2] << Object[0] << endl;
      Stream[3] << Object[0] << endl;
      Stream[0] >> Object[0];
    }
    else
     if(Object[1] < Object[0]){
      cout << Object[1] << endl;
      Stream[2] << Object[1] << endl;
      Stream[3] << Object[1] << endl;
      Stream[1] >> Object[1];
    }
    else{
      cout << Object[0] << endl << Object[1] << endl;
      Stream[2] << Object[0] << endl;
      Stream[3] << Object[0] << endl;
      Stream[2] << Object[1] << endl;
      Stream[3] << Object[1] << endl;
      Stream[0] >> Object[0];
      Stream[1] >> Object[1];
    }
  }
  while(!Stream[0].eof() && !Stream[0].fail())
```

```
  {
    Stream[0] >> Object[0];
    cout << Object[0] << endl;
    Stream[2] << Object[0] << endl;
    Stream[3] << Object[0] << endl;
  }
  while(!Stream[1].eof( ) && !Stream[1].fail( ))
  {
    Stream[1] >> Object[1];
    cout << Object[1] << endl;
    Stream[2] << Object[1] << endl;
    Stream[3] << Object[1] << endl;
  }
  Stream[0].close();
  Stream[1].close();
  Stream[2].close();
  Stream[3].close();

}
```

Output Sent to Printer in Listing 3.15

6.63e-34

9.11e-31

1.67e-27

1.3806e-23

1.6e-19

6.667e-11

4e-07

8.314

9.81

5570

6380000

3e+08

3.84e+08

7e+08

9e+09

9e+10

1.496e+11

6.023e+23

1.99e+30

CHAPTER 4

Extraction and Insertion of User-Defined Objects

It is important first to obtain an overall quantitative picture of the operation under study. One must first see what is similar in operations of a given kind before it will be worthwhile seeing how they differ from each other. In order to make a start in so complex a subject, one must ruthlessly strip away details . . .

PHILLIP M. MORSE AND GEORGE E. KIMBALL
—*HOW TO HUNT A SUBMARINE*

There are four essential advantages of implementing object-oriented input and output using the IOSTREAM facility:

1. Ease of creation of input/output facility for user-defined objects
2. Single interface, multiple implementations
3. Type safeness
4. Reusability and extensibility

The IOSTREAMS extensibility gives the programmer the ability to create facilities that allow the inputting and outputting of user-defined objects. The programmer can create overloaded functions and operators specifically defined to handle input and output for these complex data types. These facilities help to establish the user-defined objects as fully functioning elements of the C++ language in the same manner as built-in data types function. The syntax of inputting and outputting will not have to be altered to accommodate user-defined types. The input and output facilities for built-in types are extended to user-defined objects.

One interface, multiple implementation means that *there is one way to ask and many ways to perform*. In the IOSTREAM facility, when a message is sent to an object to perform a task, the data is sent to the object, then the object determines which implementation (which of its member functions) will actually be activated. The correct implementation is not determined by the programmer, but by the object that carries out the behavior.

The IOSTREAMS have strong type checking or are type safe. Because the IOSTREAMS do not use format conversion specifiers to represent the data, mismatches between conversion specifiers and data types that can cause runtime errors do not occur. The correct implementation to display or scan in that data type will automatically be executed. This occurs because the IOSTREAM has one interface, multiple implementations. Although the programmer specifies only the << insertion operator, the environment picks the correct object to insert into the stream.

The measure of reusability is based on the software or program's ability to be reused. Programs or software should be designed and written so that aspects of commonality among them are exploited to avoid reproducing the same code repeatedly. Reusability leads to extensibility, the ability of software or a program to be adapted without major changes. If a program or software is reusable, it is likely that it can be extended. This extensibility allows the programmer to keep the same syntax used for the insertion and extraction of built-in data types to be extended to user-defined objects.

Insertion and Extraction of User-Defined Objects

There are two methods for insertion and extraction of user-defined objects. Insertion places data into the output stream associated with an output device, and extraction removes data from an input stream for assignment. The data can be formatted or unformatted. When data is formatted, some type of translation or conversion of the data takes place. When the data is unformatted, no translations occur. The formatting method of insertion and extraction for user-defined objects overloads the insertion and extraction operators. The left shift operator (<<) is overloaded to insert built-in data types into an output stream. The right shift operator (>>) is overloaded to extract built-in data types from an input stream for assignment. Both of these operators can be overloaded again to insert and extract user-defined classes to and from output and input streams. The operator function that overloads the insertion operator is called an *inserter*, and the operator function that overloads the extraction operator is called an *extractor*. The unformatted method of insertion and extraction for user-defined objects utilizes the **sputn( )** and **write( )** member functions for insertion, and the **get( )** and **read( )** member functions for extraction.

Formatted Insertion and Extraction of User-Defined Objects

When an insertion operator or extraction operator is overloaded, the programmer defines what that operation will do relative to a user-defined class. This definition of the extractor or inserter should essentially maintain the semantics of the operator and should be consistent with expected syntax normally associated with the operator. The inserter or extractor is declared in the header file of the class for which the operator is created. In the header file of the class, the inserter or extractor should be declared as a *friend* operator. An operator declared as a friend of a class has the advantage of having access to the private elements without being a member of the class.

To create an inserter for a user-defined object, this prototype is listed as part of the declaration for the class:

```
friend ostream& operator<<(ostream&, &class_object)
```

The first parameter in the parameter list is a reference to an **ostream.** This is a reference because the stream will be altered once the *class_object* has been inserted into the stream. The **ostream** appears on the left side of the inserter operator. The second parameter in the list is the *class_object* that appears on the right side of the inserter operator. This is the user-defined object that will be inserted into the stream. It should be a reference to the object for the sake of efficiency if the object is very large. It returns a reference to the **ostream** to allow numerous inserters to be strung along into one message. The operator is a friend operator; therefore, the keyword precedes the prototype declaration.

To create an extractor for a user-defined object, this prototype is listed as part of the declaration for the class:

```
friend istream& operator>>(istream&, class_object&)
```

The first parameter in the parameter list is a reference to an **istream.** The second parameter in the list is a reference to the *class_object*. This object has to be a reference because the object will be altered when data is assigned. The **istream** appears on the left side of the operator, and the *class_object* appears on the right side of the operator. It returns a reference to the **istream** to allow numerous extractors to be strung along into one message. It is also a friend operator.

Listing 4.1 is an example of a user-defined class called *rational*. This class converts two *long int* into a rational number. The class is capable of addition (+), subtraction (−), division (/), multiplication (*), and reduction of rational objects. It can also input and output the rational type.

Listing 4.1

```
// This is the declaration for the rational class.

#include <iostream.h>
#include "rational.h"
```

```
class rational{
protected:
      long Numerator;
      long Denominator;
public:
      rational (long Num = 0,long Den = 1);
      void assign(long X, long Y);
      rational operator*(rational X);
      rational operator+(rational X);
      rational operator=(rational X);
      rational operator-(rational X);
      rational operator/(rational X);
      boolean operator==(rational X);
      long numerator(void);
      long denominator(void);
      void reduce(void);
      friend ostream &operator<<(ostream &Out, rational &X);
      friend istream &operator>>(ostream &In, rational &X);
};
```

In Listing 4.1, the insertion and extraction operator prototypes are declared as friend operators. The **friend** keyword precedes the prototypes for both operators. The insertion operator returns a reference to an **ostream**. In the parameter list, the first parameter is a reference to an **ostream** object, *Out*, and the second parameter is a reference to an object of type rational, *X*. The extraction operator returns a reference to an **istream**. In its parameter list, the first parameter is a reference to an istream object, *In*, and the second parameter is a reference to an object of type rational, *X*.

Defining the Inserter and Extractor

The insertion and extraction operators not only insert or extract data to and from a stream, but before the data is inserted or extracted, the data is also translated (Figure 4.1). The insertion operator converts built-in data types or user-defined objects to a generic stream of bytes that is directed to some output device. The extraction operator converts a generic stream of bytes into built-in data types or user-defined objects that are then assigned to a variable. The inserter and extractor for user-defined objects performs two levels of conversion: the conversion of the user-defined objects to or from built-in type, and the conversion of built-in types to or from a generic stream of bytes.

Defining the Inserter   The user-defined object is composed of built-in data types. The inserter must translate the user-defined object into the simpler built-in data types. The following is an example of the definition of the inserter for the rational object.

```
ostream &operator<<(ostream& Out, rational &X)
{
  if(X.Denominator < 0){
```

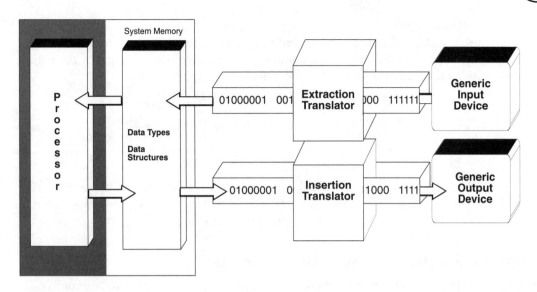

Figure 4.1 *Generic sequence of bytes going into an extraction translator from a generic input device, and coming from an insertion translator to a generic output device connected to a computer.*

```
      X.Denominator *= -1;
      X.Numerator *= -1;
   }
   if(X.Numerator == X.Denominator){
      out << 1;
      return Out;
   }
   else
      if(X.Denominator == 1){
         out << X.Numerator;
         return Out;
   }
   else
      if(X.Numerator != X.Denominator){
         out << X.Numerator << "/" << X.Denominator;
         return Out;
      }
}
```

In this definition of an inserter, the appropriate output is selected that accurately represents the data as a rational number. The inserters insert built-in data types into the stream that represents the rational object. The **X.Numerator** and **X.Denominator** are declared as **long int** in the private part of the rational object. After the data has been inserted into the **ostream** object, **Out**, the stream is returned.

Defining the Extractor   The extractor must translate the simpler built-in data types into the user-defined object. The built-in data types are extracted from the **istream** and assigned to the user-defined object. The following is an example of the definition of the extractor for the rational object.

```
istream& operator>>(istream &In, rational &X)
{
   In >> X.Numerator;
   In >> Y.Denominator;
   return(In);
}
```

In this definition, the extractor assigns built-in data types extracted from the stream to the appropriate elements of the rational object. The ***X.Numerator*** and ***X.Denominator*** are assigned numeric values from the **istream**, ***In***; then the stream is returned.

Unformatted Insertion for User-Defined Objects

As mentioned earlier, unformatted insertion performs no translation. With unformatted insertion, the user-defined object is inserted into a stream object directly without translating into simpler built-in data types. This method of insertion of unformatted data can be performed by using the **sputn( )** and **write( )** member functions. The **sputn( )** is a member function of the **streambuf** class and its derivatives, and the **write( )** is a member function of the **ofstream** class and its derivatives. The **sputn( )** or **write( )** member function can be used to insert from a character, an unsigned character, or a signed character to a block of characters into the stream object.

The **sputn( )** member function has two parameters. The first parameter is a pointer to the class object, and the second parameter is the size of the object. The data is inserted into the stream that is associated with a file or some output device. Listing 4.2 is an example of a rational object, unformatted, inserted into a file.

Listing 4.2

```
// This program demonstrates how a user-defined type can be inserted
// directly into the streambuf component of an ofstream object, using
// the sputn( ) member function.

#include <ofstream.h>

void main(void)
{
   ofstream OutFile;
   streambuf *X;
   OutFile.open("Rational.dat");
   rational Delta(355,113);

   X = OutFile.rdbuf( );
   X-> sputn((char *) &Delta, sizeof(rational))
   OutFile.close( );
}
```

This program declares an object of type **ofstream** called *OutFile*; a pointer, *X*, to **streambuf**; and an object of type rational, *Delta.* It opens an **ofstream** file called *Rational.dat.* The *OutFile* object sends a message to the **rdbuf( )** member function that returns the pointer to the buffer of the *OutFile* object. That value is stored in the pointer *X.* Since the *X* pointer is a pointer of the **streambuf** class, a message is sent to the **sputn( )** member function. The **sputn( )** member function inserts a specified number of characters from a string into an output buffer. In this case, the output buffer is for the file, **Rational.dat.** The call to **sputn( )** has two arguments: The first argument supplies the source of the data to be inserted, and the second argument supplies the number of characters. The source, in this case, is a rational object. The reference to the object is typecast as a pointer to *char.* The second argument will return the size of the rational object. The **sputn( )** member function will insert the rational object up to the size of the object, and insert it into the buffer.

The **write( )** member function is also used to insert from a single character to a block of characters. The **write( )** member function has two parameters: The first parameter is a pointer to the class object, and the second parameter is the size of the object. The data is inserted into the stream that is associated with a file or some output device. The **write( )** member function of the **ostream** class is a simpler and more widely used method of inserting unformatted data to a stream. The **write( )** member function could be used instead of the **sputn( )** member function. The program in Listing 4.3 shows how the **write( )** member function can be used to write the rational object to a file.

Listing 4.3

```
// This program demonstrates how a user-defined type can be inserted
// into the streambuf component of an ofstream object, using
// the write( ) member function.

#include <ofstream.h>

void main(void)
   {
   ofstream OutFile;
   OutFile.open("Rational.dat");
   rational Delta(355/113);

   write((char *) &Delta, sizeof(rational))

   }
```

Unformatted Extraction of User-Defined Objects

The method of extraction of unformatted data can be performed by using the **get( )** and **read( )** member functions of the **ifstream** class. The **get( )** or **read( )** member function can be used to extract from a character, an unsigned character, or a signed character to a block of characters from the **ifstream** object.

The **get( )** member function will extract a certain number of characters, or up to a delimiter, whichever comes first. The first parameter of this member function is a character array pointer. The second parameter is the number of characters to be extracted; the third parameter is the delimiter. The default delimiter is a new line character.

The **read( )** member function can also be used to extract characters from a stream to be stored to a destination. The **read( )** member function works similarly to the **get( )** member function, and has the same parameters except that it does not use a delimiter. It will extract a specified number of characters determined by the second parameter, and will store them in the first parameter. For a more detailed description of **put( )**, **write( )**, **get( )**, and **read( )** member functions, refer to Chapter 3 **streambuf**, **istream**, and **ostream** class discussions.

The program in Listing 4.4 demonstrates the use of extractors and inserters on the user-defined class, **rational**.

Listing 4.4

```
// This program reads in a list of doubles from a file and prints
// them out as fractions in symbolic form using the overloaded
// inserters.

#include <fstream.h>
#include <r_approx.h>
#include <stdlib.h>
#include <iomanip.h>

void main(void)
{
    double NValue;
    ifstream In("file5.txt");
    ofstream Out[2];

    Out[0].open("file5-1.txt");
    Out[1].open("prn");
    if(!In.good( )){
        cout << "could not open file";
        exit (0);
    }
    rational_approximation Value(4.2);
    while(!In.eof( ) && !In.fail( ))
    {
        In >> NValue;
        Value = NValue;
    if(!In.eof( )){
        cout << setw(10) << NValue << "\t" << Value << endl;
    Out[0].write((char *) &NValue,sizeof(rational_approximation));
    Out[1] << setw(10) << NValue << "\t" << Value << endl;
    }
    }
    In.close( );
}
```

Contents of file5.txt from Listing 4.4

```
0.25
0.33
0.75
1.25
0.10
0.50
0.40
0.60
0.20
-0.25
```

Output from Listing 4.4

0.25	1/4
0.33	33/100
0.75	3/4
1.25	5/4
0.1	1/10
0.5	1/2
0.4	2/5
0.6	3/5
0.2	1/5
-0.25	-1/4

This program uses a class derived from the **rational** class. The **rational_approximation** class uses the same **<<** insertion operator that its base class uses. This program inserts the user-defined object *Value* into a **cout** object and two *Out* objects. The first *Out* object is directed to a file. The second *Out* object is directed to a printer. Note that although the object has been inserted into three different streams with different destinations, the syntax is the same. This is another example of single interface, multiple implementations.

CHAPTER 5

Manipulators

The essential operating characteristic of the automaton consists of describing how it is caused to change its state, that is, to go over from state i into a state j.

JOHN VON NEUMAN—*THE GENERAL AND LOGICAL THEORY OF AUTOMATA*

What Are Manipulators?

Manipulators are functions or objects that are inserted into or extracted from a stream and affect the format state of the stream. The format state of the stream is represented by the **ios** component of the stream object under consideration. The **ios** component has a state variable that specifies the base in which numeric objects are represented, such as decimal, octal, or hexadecimal. The **ios** component has width, precision, and fill character components. Manipulators can change the state of these components.

The manipulators provide a level of convenience and expressional elegance. Since the **ios** class has member functions that can set, unset, or instantiate the format variables that it contains, the manipulators technically are not necessary. However, they help make program more readable. The syntax of manipulators allows them to be inserted into a stream just like any other object in the C++ environment.

The Predefined Manipulators

Table 5.1 lists the 13 predefined manipulators. To use the manipulators **dec**, **endl**, **ends**, **flush**, **hex**, and **ws**, the programmer must include **iostream.h**. To use

Table 5.1   List Manipulators—Their Type and Purpose

Manipulator	Purpose	Type
endl	Outputs a new line character and flushes the stream.	Output
ends	Outputs a null character.	Output
flush	Flushes a stream.	Output
dec	Converts numeric values to decimal.	I/O
hex	Converts numeric values to hexadecimal.	I/O
oct	Converts numeric values to octal.	I/O
resetiosflags(long int)	Turns off flags specified by **long int**.	I/O
setbase(int)	Sets the number base to **int**.	Output
setfill(int)	Sets the fill character to **int**.	I/O
setiosflags(long int)	Turns on flags specified by **long int**.	I/O
setprecision(int)	Sets the precision to **int**.	I/O
setw(int)	Sets the field width to **int**.	I/O
ws	Skips white-space characters.	Input

setbase( ), **setprecision( )**, **setfill( )**, **setiosflags( )**, **resetiosflags( )**, and **setw( )**, the programmer must include **iomanip.h**.

The New Line Manipulator endl

The manipulator **endl** is inserted into an **ostream** class object or one of its derived classes. The **endl** manipulator causes a new line character, **\n**, to be inserted into the output stream. The **endl** manipulator also flushes the stream after the **\n** has been inserted. The program in Listing 5.1 inserts a string into **cout**'s stream, and then inserts the **endl** manipulator.

Listing 5.1

```
// This program demonstrates the use
// of the endl manipulator.

#include <iostream.h>

void main(void)
{
   double Speed-3.00e8;

   cout << "The speed of light is " << endl;
   cout << Speed << " m/sec";
}
```

The program in Listing 5.1 then prints the value of **Speed** and the succeeding string on the next line. Although inserting the **\n** character into the stream will cause the output to look the same, the stream is not immediately flushed after inserting an \n character. The **endl** manipulator is used only on output streams.

The NULL Manipulator ends

The **ends** manipulator causes a **NULL** to be inserted into an **ostream** class object or one of its derived classes. This manipulator can be used to convert character arrays to character strings upon insertion into an output stream. The manipulator can be inserted into the stream like any other object:

```
cout << CharacterArray << ends;
```

The **ends** manipulator is used only with an output stream.

Flushing a Stream with the Flush Manipulator

The **flush** manipulator is inserted into an **ostream** object or one of its derived objects. The **flush** manipulator will flush the buffer component of the **ostream** object. The manipulator has the same effect on the stream as if **setf(ios::unitbuf)** had been called prior to inserting values into the stream.

Numeric Formatting Manipulators

The manipulators that change the format state of numeric bases have member function counterparts in the **ios** class. The **hex** manipulator sets the format state to translate numbers that are inserted or extracted to the hexadecimal base. The **oct** manipulator sets the format state to translate numbers that are inserted or extracted to the octal or base 8. The **dec** manipulator sets the format state to translate numbers to base 10. These manipulators are mutually exclusive. If they are inserted or extracted from the stream at the same time, the results are unpredictable. The **setbase( )** member function takes an *int* argument and must be either 0, 8, 10, or 16. The **setbase(int X)** member function changes the state of the format stream to represent numbers in base **X**.

The program in Listing 5.2 shows how the numeric manipulators contrast with the **setf( )** member function method of setting the format state of the stream.

Listing 5.2

```
// This program shows how the numeric manipulators can be used.
#include <iostream.h>
#include <iomanip.h>

void main(void)
{
    int AvgDensity = 5570;
    double Speed = 300000000.00;

    cout.setf(ios::hex);
    cout << " Earth Density in hexadecimal " << AvgDensity
```

```
            << " kg/m " << endl;
    cout.unsetf(ios::hex);
    cout << oct << " Earth Density in octal " << AvgDensity
            << " kg/m " << endl;
    cout << resetiosflags(ios::oct) << dec
            << " Earth Density in decimal ";
    cout << AvgDensity << endl;
    cout << " Speed of Light "
            << setiosflags(ios::scientific | ios::showpoint)
            << setprecision(2) << Speed << resetiosflags(ios::hex)
            << setbase(8) << endl << " Earth Density in octal "
            << AvgDensity;
}
```

Output from Listing 5.2

Earth Density in hexadecimal 15c2 kg/m

Earth Density in octal 12702 kg/m

Earth Density in decimal 5570

Speed of Light 3.00e+08

Earth Density in octal 12702

The program in Listing 5.2 uses the manipulators **hex**, **oct**, and **setbase( )** to change the state of the format stream. The manipulators are inserted into the stream just like any other object in the C++ programming environment. The **hex**, **oct**, and **dec** manipulators can be used for insertion and extraction operations.

Skipping White Spaces with the ws Manipulator

The **ws** manipulator skips leading white-space characters on input. White spaces are tabs, spaces, and new line characters. The **ws** manipulator is used only with an **istream** class object or one of its derived classes. The **ws** manipulator extracts the white-space characters from the input stream. This creates the effect of skipping white spaces. The same effect can be achieved by calling the **setf(ios::skipws)** member function.

setiosflags( ) and resetiosflags( ) Flag Manipulators

The **setiosflags( )** and **resetiosflags( )** manipulators change the format state variable of the **ios** component. The flags that these manipulators can turn on and off are the same flags that the **ios::setf( )** and **ios::unsetf( )** member functions access:

```
enum{
  skipws = 0x0001,
  left = 0x0002,
```

```
right = 0x0004,
internal = 0x0008,
dec = 0x0010,
oct = 0x0020,
hex = 0x0040,
showbase = 0x0080,
showpoint = 0x0100,
uppercase = 0x0200,
showpos = 0x0400,
scientific = 0x0800,
fixed = 0x1000,
unitbuf = 0x2000,
stdio = 0x4000
}
```

When these flags are passed to the **setiosflags( )** and **resetiosflags( )** manipulators they use the full-scope resolved name. For example, **ios::showpoint** would be passed to **setiosflags( )** using the following syntax: **setiosflags(ios::showpoint)**. Through the use of these manipulators, the programmer can control the format state of the stream.

When the **skipws** flag is set, the format state of the stream specifies that whitespace characters will be ignored for input. When the **left** format flag is set, the format state of the stream specifies that padding used to meet a field width is placed after the actual data value. If the **right** format flag is set, the format state of the stream specifies that padding used to meet a field width is placed before the actual data value. A set **internal** format flag describes a format state of the stream that pads a field width between any sign type (base information or integer sign) and the actual data value. The data will appear to be right-justified. By default, the **right** format flag is set.

When the **showbase** format flag is set, the format state of the stream specifies that numeric data will display its base convention for output. The default is numeric data absent of the base conventions. The base convention for hexadecimal numbers is *0x* and the base convention for octal numbers is *0* placed before the number. There is no base convention for decimal numbers. Setting a **showpoint** format flag describes the format state of the stream in which floating point numbers will display a decimal point and trailing zeros for output. The decimal point and trailing zeros will be displayed only with a floating point number with precision greater than 0. There will be as many trailing zeros as needed to meet precision. If this flag is set and precision is zero, there will be no decimal point or trailing zeros. The **showpos** format flag when set specifies a format state of the stream that displays a plus sign for positive integers for output. Negative integers will automatically display a minus sign regardless of the setting of this flag. The other bases are unsigned. The **uppercase** format flag when set specifies a format state in which numeric data represented with hexadecimal digits will display the **hex** base indicator when the **showbase** format flag is set and hexadecimal digits *A-F* are in uppercase. The floating point numbers represented in scientific notation will display an uppercase *E* for output. The default is lowercase.

Setting the **unitbuf** format flag causes the format state of the stream to specify that output is flushed after each output operation. When the **stdio** format flag is set, the format state of the stream specifies that the **stout** and **sterr** are flushed after an insertion operation when a program uses both the IOSTREAMS and the **stdio** functions for output. This flag is used by **sync_with_stdio( )** and should not be set directly. Therefore, if the IOSTREAMS and the **stdio** library are to be combined for output, the **sync_with_stdio( )** should be used.

The **hex**, **oct**, or **dec** format flags can be set in order for integer data inserted or extracted from or to the stream to be represented in these various bases. If the **dec** format flag is set, integers will be represented in the decimal base. If the **hex** format flag is set, integers will be represented in the hexadecimal base. If the **oct** format flag is set, integers will be represented in the octal base. By default, numeric values retain their original base.

Floating point numbers can be represented in scientific or fixed notation by setting the **scientific** or **fixed** format flags. If the **scientific** format flag is set, the format state of the stream will represent floating point data in scientific notation. Scientific notation expresses floating point numbers with the decimal placed behind the first digit. The *e* represents exponentiation of 10 to a power. Floating point data will be represented in scientific notation if the exponent after the conversion is less than –4 or greater than or equal to the current precision. When the **fixed** format flag is set, the format state of the stream specifies that floating point numbers will be displayed in decimal notation with a set number of digits after the decimal. The number of digits after the decimal is determined by the precision currently set.

The **setiosflags( )** turns on the flags specified in its argument. The programmer can specify a single flag to be turned on, or a combination of flags to be turned on. If more than one flag is specified in the **setiosflags( )** argument list, they must be *or*ed together; for example:

```
setiosflags(ios::scientific | ios::showpoint | ios::unitbuf);
```

The **resetiosflags( )** manipulator turns off whichever flag bit is specified. The argument to **resetiosflags( )** may be a single flag or a combination of flags *or*ed together. The program in Listing 5.2 demonstrates the use of the **setiosflags( )** and **resetiosflags( )** manipulators. These manipulators can be used on input and output streams, for extraction and insertion.

The Padding and Fill Manipulators setw( ) and setfill( )

The **setw( )** manipulator sets the width of positions that will be inserted or extracted from a stream. The **setw( )** member function takes an *int* argument. The *int* argument represents the field width size to pad the object with on insertion. The **setw( )** manipulator cannot reduce the required size of an object. For instance, if:

```
char CharacterArray[80];
```

is declared, specifying **setw(60)** will not truncate the *CharacterArray* when it is inserted into the output stream. Instead, all the characters necessary to represent the *CharacterArray* will be inserted into the output stream. The **setw( )** manipulator can increase only the field width of the object to be inserted. The **setfill( )** manipulator accepts an *int* that represents a character to be used in padding the output. If the actual field width of the object is less than the **x_width** data member specifies, then the remaining positions will pad with the character passed to the **setfill( )** manipulator, and will be either left- or right-justified.

User-Defined Manipulators

The programmer is not restricted to the 13 built-in manipulators. The C++ environment provides facilities that allow the programmer to design custom manipulators. There are two kinds of manipulators: those that do not take arguments and those that do. The manipulators that do not take arguments are the simplest to implement.

The manipulators that do not require arguments will have the general form:

```
Xstream &manipulator (Xstream &Stream)
{
    // User Code
    return Stream;
}
```

where *Xstream* is either from the **ostream** family of classes or from the **istream** family of classes. If we wanted to define a manipulator that would change the state of the stream to represent numbers that are inserted in scientific notation with decimal point and a certain precision, we could define a manipulator called **scientific** as follows:

```
ostream &scientific(ostream &Mystream)
{
    Mystream << setiosflags(ios::showpoint | ios::scientific);
    Mystream << setprecision(2);
    return(Mystream);
}
```

The program in Listing 5.3 shows how this manipulator would be used.

Listing 5.3

```
// This program demonstrates the definition and usage of a user-defined
// manipulator.

#include <iostream.h>
#include <iomanip.h>

ostream &scientific(ostream &Mystream)
```

```
{
    Mystream << setiosflags(ios::showpoint | ios::scientific);
    Mystream << setprecision(2);
    return(Mystream);
}

void main(void)
{

    int AvgDensity = 5570;
    double Speed = 300000000.00;

    cout << oct << " Earth Density" << AvgDensity << " kg/m";
    cout << endl;
    cout << resetiosflags(ios::oct) << hex << " Earth Density ";
    cout << AvgDensity << endl;
    cout << "Speed Of Light " << scientific << Speed;
}
```

Output from Listing 5.3

Earth Density 12702 kg/m

Earth Density 15c2

Speed Of Light 3.00e+08

This manipulator could have also been defined to work with extraction and an **istream** class object:

```
istream &scientific(istream &Mystream)
{
    Mystream >> setiosflags(ios::showpoint | ios::scientific);
    Mystream >> setprecision(2);
    return(Mystream);
}
        .
        .
        .
    cin >> scientific >> Number;
```

The manipulators that take an argument require two basic functions: The first function actually defines the manipulator. The second function is a call to a template that has been defined in the **iomanip.h** file. There are three templates defined:

   imanip for the **istream** and its derived classes

   omanip for the **ostream** and its derived classes

   smanip a combination of **istream** and **ostream**

Note: Some implementations define **imanip**, **omanip**, and **smanip** as macros, and to use them, the programmer must specify them as **IMANIP**, **OMANIP**, or **SMANIP**, (***int***).

The program in Listing 5.4 demonstrates the definition and usage of a user-defined manipulator that takes an ***int*** argument.

Listing 5.4

```
// This program demonstrates the definition and usage of user-defined
// manipulators with arguments and user-defined manipulators without
// arguments. The scientific manipulator is an example of a user-
// defined manipulator without an argument, and the spaces(N)
// manipulator is an example of a user-defined manipulator that
// takes an argument.

#include <fstream.h>
#include <iomanip.h>

ostream &scientific(ostream &Mystream)
{
   Mystream << setiosflags(ios::showpoint | ios::scientific);
   Mystream << setprecision(2);
   return(Mystream);
}
ostream &setspaces(ostream &MyStream, int N)
{
   int CurrentWidth;

   CurrentWidth = MyStream.width( );
   MyStream << setw(N) << " ";
   MyStream << setw(CurrentWidth);
   return(MyStream);
}

omanip<int> spaces(int N)
{
   return omanip<int>(&setspaces,N);
}
void main(void)
{
   ofstream Out;
   Out.open("prn");
   int AvgDensity = 5570;
   double Speed = 300000000.00;

   Out << " Earth Density" << spaces(2) << AvgDensity << " kg/m";
   Out << spaces(10) << "Speed Of Light" << spaces(2);
   Out << scientific << Speed;
   Out.close( );
}
```

Output from Listing 5.4

Earth Density 5570 kg/m

Speed Of Light 3.00e+08

The program in Listing 5.4 sends a formatted line to the printer. The **spaces(N)** manipulator determines how many white spaces to print between inserted objects. The manipulators can help reduce program code and make programs more readable.

CHAPTER 6

Extending the IOSTREAM Classes

> *. . . we simply find that we can see and imagine innumerable discrete locations existing simultaneously: things in other places. With our eyes and in our mind's eye, we can see innumerable paths and routes between locations; we see that most objects retain their identity as they move from one place to another.*
>
> MICHAEL BENEDIKT—*CYBERSPACE: SOME PROPOSALS*

IOSTREAMS—Specialization, Extension, Evolution

In Chapter 1, we talked about the advantages of the C++ IOSTREAMS over the nonobject-oriented I/O routines contained in the **stdio** library. *Extensibility* is one of the IOSTREAM's major advantages. When an I/O library is being designed, the implementer tries to consider the environment(s) that the library will have to perform in, and how the I/O will be used. This is a gargantuan task! If that library is not object-oriented, the final design is usually fixed and the library will be capable only of what it is capable of! If the environment that the I/O library operates in changes radically from the original environment, the I/O library becomes useless. If the way I/O is approached changes radically from the implementer's original plan, the I/O library becomes useless. Well-thought-out designs can prolong the usefulness of an I/O library but they cannot resist radical change unless extensibility has been built into the architecture of the library.

Normally, an I/O library or I/O model does not dissolve overnight; instead, it is slowly eroded by new ideas and subtle changes in nuance until it no longer serves its purpose. Whether the library fails because of radical change or because of slow and gradual erosion, the net result is still the same—*uselessness*. Object-oriented input and output using the C++ IOSTREAMS challenges the mortality rate for I/O design and programming. With encapsulation, inheritance, polymorphism, and operator overloading, the C++ IOSTREAMS can be constantly adapted to work in new environments, with different demands. Because the IOSTREAMS are composed of classes (not functions!), the classes can be augmented with other classes, new classes that are well suited for new environments. The IOSTREAM classes themselves can be specialized through *inheritance* to deal with subtle changes in nuance, or gradual changes in I/O philosophy. One of the original models that the IOSTREAMS was designed to address was the line of text. This line of text could be sent to a file, printer, or to the console. Characters follow in a position by position horizontal succession until a **\b**, **\t**, **\n** or **<< endl** occurs. The idea of positioning and formatting text for a screen display, printer, or file in a nonsequential or horizontal fashion did not receive much attention in the original design of the **<<** insertion operator, or the **write( )**, **sputn( )**, and **put( )** member functions. However, the IOSTREAM classes can be extended to deal with spatial formatting. The program in Listing 6.1 shows a simple example of extending the IOSTREAM classes to deal with spatial formatting. Because the IOSTREAM classes are not a set of functions depending on accessing some global data structures, the IOSTREAMS can be separated into discrete useful components. The programmer may need the functionality of a **streambuf** without any conversion or translation. The programmer may need the functionality of the **ios** as a formatting class while incorporating a specialized **streambuf** that handles audio devices. In some situations, an overloaded **<< insertion** or **>> extraction** operator is all that is called for to adapt to a totally different or new environment. The C++ IOSTREAMS support this kind of evolution. C++ supports *specialization*. Specialization is used to customize an already existing class to meet demands that it was not originally designed to meet. However, the existing class should be conceptually similar to the new class, or it should have something in common with the new class. A class called **consolestream** can be derived from an **ostream** to handle spatial movement on a display unit. In this instance, the **ostream** class is given a little more functionality through inheritance to meet the programmer's requirements.

Specialization through inheritance is *additive*. The specialization process does not take away characteristics or attributes from a class, but rather adds characteristics, attributes, and functionality to deal with some specific set of requirements. The IOSTREAM classes can be specialized through inheritance by adding new data members and member functions. The data members can describe new or different I/O attributes of connected devices. The member functions can add new or different functionality to the IOSTREAM classes to deal with radical change or subtle change. In Chapters 7, 8, and 9, we talk about how various IOSTREAM classes can be adapted to work in the new multimedia environments.

By adding new classes to the IOSTREAM family of classes, the IOSTREAMS can be extended to work in any imaginable I/O environment. New object-oriented I/O classes can be built upon any or all the components in the IOSTREAM hierarchy. This leads to productivity through reuse. If the existing I/O model can be extended, or specialized to adapt to a new I/O model, then productivity gains follow.

The core components of the IOSTREAM classes encapsulate three aspects of I/O:

- Buffering
- Formatting
- Conversion(Translation)

These components have been described in the broadest sense, and must be specialized or extended to handle other I/O components, such as timing. Good object-oriented programming and design are the results of insight, talent, and experience. There are no concrete rules on how to model a concept. The decisions to choose one object-oriented design over another is usually made through an aesthetic eye. We cannot offer ironclad rules for knowing when, how, or to what extent to specialize or extend the IOSTREAMS. We can only offer some very general guidelines.

The prerequisite to extending or specializing any of the IOSTREAM classes in any meaningful way is a thorough understanding of all the components and the relationships between the components of the IOSTREAM classes. This requires an initial extra investment in time, but will pay for itself through solid extensible and reusable designs.

General Guidelines for Extending the IOSTREAM Classes

IOSTREAM Class Extension Evaluation Checklist

1. Classify your extension as input, output, or bidirectional.
2. Determine whether your extension requires buffering.
3. Determine whether your extension requires specialized formatting.
4. Determine whether your extension is intended for a block device, character device, or some hybrid.
5. Attempt to classify your extension as either a buffer, translator, or format. If your extension cannot be classified as one of these, you will probably have to add a fundamentally new class to the IOSTREAMS.
6. Determine if you need to add a new class or classes that are not fundamentally different but add some new functionality to the IOSTREAMS.
7. Determine if you need to add only member functions to existing classes, or member functions *and* data members.

8. Understand the relationships between your extension and the existing classes.

9. Do the IOSTREAM classes have virtual member functions that can be overridden to meet your requirements?

10. Are the I/O areas that your extension needs to access private, protected, or public? Are there any overflow and underflow concerns?

11. Will your extension require overloading, overriding, or both?

12. If the extension involves displayed output, is the display in graphics mode or text mode?

13. Does the extension really require specializing or extending the IOSTREAMS, or does it require defining a user-defined object that cannot really be described as an object-oriented stream?

Once this checklist is taken under consideration, the programmer should find where in the IOSTREAM class relationships the new class or manipulator will fit. The core IOSTREAMS can be extended by deriving a new class from an existing class, and adding either new data members or member functions to the new class. The core IOSTREAM classes can be extended by adding manipulators. The core IOSTREAM classes can be extended by overriding virtual member functions in existing classes. New IOSTREAM classes can be added that do not retain anything from the core IOSTREAM classes other than the consumer interface. If every component of the IOSTREAM classes proves to be awkward for specialization, then the programmer can start from scratch but retain the insertion and extraction operators, function names, and concepts. Although this is unlikely, it can happen; and in this instance the programmer will be maintaining the single interface, multiple implementation advantage of object-oriented programming. Even if the I/O class is designed from scratch, it will have the benefit of looking the same as the rest of the IOSTREAM classes, thus reducing program complexity, consumer learning curve, and I/O ambiguity.

Extending ios Class

The **ios** class contains the *format state*, the *buffer state* (sometimes referred to as the **error state**), and the *open mode state* of the IOSTREAM classes. When deciding whether to extend the **ios** class, consider if the new class, data members, or member functions to be added can be described as part of the format state, buffer state, or open mode state. For instance, if a new *graphicsstream* is to be added to the IOSTREAM classes, the **ios** class should be extended to represent the state of the palette, and the display mode format. Foreground color and background color data members could be added. Member functions to set the current line width and font choice could be added. However, member functions that paint polygons, or draw pixels on the display unit should be saved for the translator classes. There is a temptation to add functionality to the **ios** class because it is a component of the majority of the IOSTREAMS, and an easy way to add functionality to all the IOSTREAMS in one swoop. Avoid these temptations; they lead to ambiguous and poorly defined classes.

An **ios** class can be constructed using a pointer to any class that has been derived from the **streambuf** class. Therefore, another subtle way to extend the functionality of the **ios** class is to construct it using a derivative of the **streambuf** class. In fact, to declare an object of type **ios**, the programmer must construct it using a pointer to **streambuf** or some derivative:

```
#include <iostream.h>
#include <strstrea.h>

ostrstream LightStream;
ios LightIos (LightStream->rdbuf( ));
```

Most implementations of the IOSTREAMS in current use do not virtualize any member functions for the **ios** class, and, therefore, the member functions of the **ios** class cannot be overridden in a derived class. The **xalloc( )**, **bitalloc( )**, **iword( )**, and **pword( )** member functions can be used to extend the format state of the **ios** class. Through these member functions, the programmer can add new numeric base (i.e., a binary base) or new format flags (i.e., for bolding) to the **ios** class. If the format state has been extended, then the programmer can set the format state through user-defined manipulators, such as:

```
long int GravitationalPull;
cout << bolded << binary << GravitationalPull;
```

Extensions to the **ios** class should be restricted to representations of stream or device state. The **ios** class is used to describe the persistent components of the object-oriented stream. To maintain the conceptual semantics of the IOSTREAM hierarchy, extensions to the **ios** class should involve only format and state data members or member functions.

Extending the Conversion Classes

The conversion classes, also known as the translator classes, are *istream, ostream, iostream, istrstream, ostrstream, strstream, ifstream, ofstream,* and *fstream*. These classes give the entire IOSTREAM class hierarchy its object-oriented look and feel. These classes are responsible for translating or converting user-defined or built-in types to generic sequences of bytes, and for translating generic sequences of bytes into user-defined or built-in types. These classes encapsulate the actual output and input of objects to and from the devices to which they are connected. When deciding whether to extend the conversion classes, determine whether the extension actually involves a translation from a user-defined or built-in type to an output, or a translation from an input to a user-defined or built-in type. For example, an operation that translates hexadecimal values to pixels on a display unit would represent an extension of a translator class. A data structure that was represented as a file on disk, and a set of bitplanes when in memory, would make a good candidate for translation.

Any extension of the translator classes, especially with respect to the insertion and extraction operators and functions, must take special care to preserve the functionality of the prefix and suffix functions of the **ostream** and **istream** classes. The **opfx( )** and **osfx( )** functions for the **ostream** class are integral components of error propagation for the **ostream** classes. The **ipfx( )** and **isfx( )** functions perform the same function for the **istream** family of classes. These functions perform precondition and postcondition processing and checking on the object-oriented stream. If the stream is okay, then a go-ahead signal is propagated. If the processing failed or the checking encountered an error condition, then the appropriate error state is set within the **ios** component of the stream. This is why it is important to keep the functional semantics of the **iostream** classes intact. Although the IOSTREAM components can be used individually, they work together to achieve the object-oriented stream metaphor. When overloading the inserter or extractor operators, calling the prefix and suffix functions helps to maintain the semantic integrity of the IOSTREAMS. Refer to our discussion of inserters and extractors in Chapter 3.

Overloading the << insertion operator or the >> extraction operator represents the easiest way to extend to the IOSTREAM classes to put and get user-defined classes. When these operators are overloaded, unless the programmer is absolutely sure that the prefix and suffix functions are not necessary, they should be called. For example:

```
ostream &operator<<(mystream &Out,userobject &Object)
{
    if(Out.opfx( ))
    {
        Out << Object;
        Out.osfx( );
    }
    return(Out);
}
```

If the **ostream** or **istream** base classes are completely replaced, the new stream class should be derived from a virtual **ios** or **ios** derivation to keep the stream relationship intact. In most implementations of the IOSTREAMS, the **ios** component is a virtual base class. This is necessary because of the multiple instances of classes that would occur during the multiple inheritance process. If class *c* inherits class *a* and class *b*, and class *a* and class *b* both contain class *m*, then class *c* would contain multiple instances of class *m*. By declaring the base class *m* to be virtual, the duplication of class *m* in the inheritance process does not occur. Virtual base classes play an important role in the design, use, and specialization of the IOSTREAM classes. *The C++ Programming Language* by Bjorne Stroustrup contains a discussion of the need for virtual base classes.

streambuf Extension and Virtuals

The **streambuf** class and its derivatives represent the buffer component of the IOSTREAM classes. This buffer component is at the core of the IOSTREAM functionality. Every IOSTREAM component, except for the buffer component, has a **streambuf** or derivative data member. Proper extension or specialization of the **streambuf** component requires advanced knowledge of the **underflow( )** and **overflow( )** member functions, and thorough knowledge of the entire IOSTREAM hierarchy. The programmer must have a command of the hardware that is being addressed, as well as the virtual member functions that the **streambuf** family contains:

```
virtual ~streambuf( )
virtual streambuf* setbuf(char*, int)
virtual int do_sgetn(char*, int)
virtual int underflow( )
virtual int pbackfail(int)
virtual int do_sputn(const char* s, int n)
virtual int overflow(int = EOF)
virtual streampos seekoff(streamoff, ios::seek_dir,int = (ios::in |
    ios::out))
virtual streampos seekpos(streampos, int = (ios::in | ios::out))
virtual int sync( )
virtual void lock( );
virtual void unlock( );
virtual int doallocate( );
```

Be aware that many of these member functions are implementation-defined. There is still much ambiguity in the latest ANSI draft in the area of specializing **streambufs**. When considering whether to specialize the buffer component, the extension to be added should clearly be recognized as either data for a buffer component or functionality for a buffer component. Unless this is the case, the extension or specialization could change the entire meaning of the IOSTREAM classes. (For more information on specializing a **streambuf** class, see Teale, 191.)

The program in Listing 6.1 demonstrates simple ways to extend IOSTREAM classes to handle new demands. In this case, the demand was to be able to send text the display unit at any *X,Y* location, as well as to control the display mode and cursor format. The program extends the **ios** class by deriving a class called **conios**. The **conios** class maintains the cursor format and the device mode format of the console. This specialization is another way to extend the format component of the **ios** class. The program also defines a new translator class called **consolestream**. The class relationship diagram in Figure 6.1 shows the relationship between **ios**, **conios**, **ostream_with-assign**, and the **consolestream** classes. The **consolestream** class overloads the =

assignment operator to allow stream assignment with **cout**. The **consolestream** class also defines the **setX( )** and **setY( )** member functions. These functions control the spatial (two-dimensional) position of the cursor in the **consolestream.**

Listing 6.1

```
// This program demonstrates how iostream classes can be extended
// to handle spatial two-dimensional output, as opposed to linear
// one-dimensional output to a display unit.

#include <iostream.h>
#include <strstrea.h>
#include <iomanip.h>

class conios : virtual public ios{
protected:
    char TopCursor;
    char BotCursor;
    char VideoMode;

public:
    conios(streambuf *Buffer);
    void setVideoMode(char Mode);
    void setCursorSize(char Bot,char Top);

};

conios::conios(streambuf *Buffer) : ios(Buffer)
```

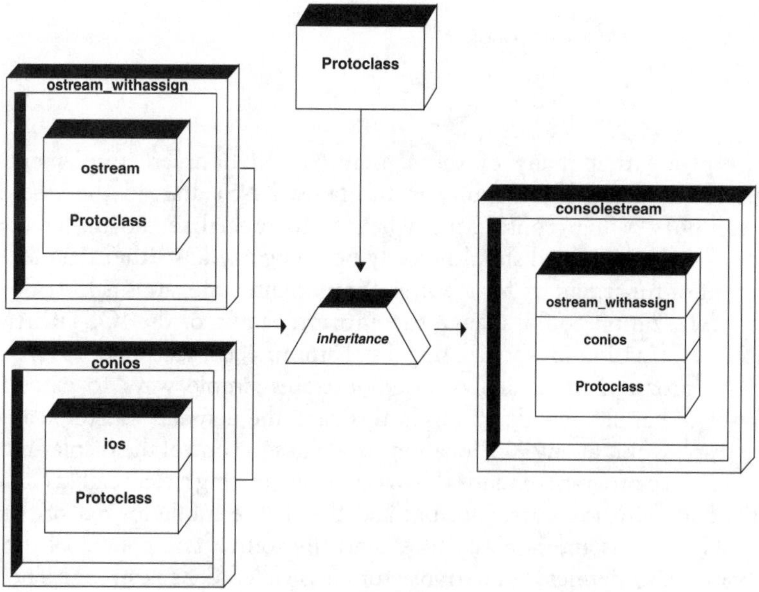

Figure 6.1 *Class relationship diagram showing the relationship between **ios, conios, ostream_withassign**, and **consolestream** objects*

```
{
    TopCursor = 0;
    BotCursor = 0;
}
void conios::setVideoMode(char Mode)
{
    asm}
        mov ah,00
        mov al,Mode
        int 10h
    }
}

void conios::setCursorSize(char Bot,char Top)
{
    asm{
        mov ah,01h
        mov ch,Top
        mov cl,Bot
    }
}

class consolestream : public ostream_withassign,public conios{
protected:
    char X;
    char Y;
public:
    consolestream(streambuf *Buffer);
    void setX(char XX);
    void setY(char YY);
    consolestream &operator=(ostream &Out);
};

void consolestream::setX(char XX)
{
    X = XX;
    char y = Y;
    asm{
    mov ah, 0x02;
    mov bh, 0;
    mov dh,y;
    mov dl,XX;
    int 10h
    }
}
void consolestream::setY(char YY)
{
    Y = YY;
    char x = X;
    asm{
        mov ah, 0x02;
        mov bh, 0;
        mov dh, YY;
        mov dl,x;
```

```
        int 10h
        }
    }

consolestream &consolestream::operator=(ostream &Out)
{
    ios::init(Out.rdbuf( ));
    return(*this);
}

consolestream::consolestream(streambuf *Buffer) : conios(Buffer)
{
    X = 1;
    Y = 1;
}

ostream &setspaces(ostream &MyStream, int N)
{
    int CurrentWidth;
    CurrentWidth = MyStream.width( );
    MyStream << setw(N) << " ";
    MyStream << setw(CurrentWidth);
    return(MyStream);
}

OMANIP(int) spaces(int N)
{
    return OMANIP(int) (setspaces,N);
}

void main(void)
{
    double Speed = 3.00e8;
    consolestream Out(cout.rdbuf( ));

    Out = cout;
    Out.setVideoMode(0x01);
    Out.setY(5);
    Out.setX(20);
    Out.setCursorSize(0,3);
    Out << "The speed of light is " << spaces(10) << Speed;
    cin.get( );
}
```

The program in Listing 6.1 maintains the semantic integrity of the IOSTREAMS by restricting specialization to the proper classes. Since the cursor format and the device mode have to do with the format state of the display unit, and the display unit is connected to our **consolestream** object, the **ios** class was specialized. The **ios** class is specialized in the **conios** class. The **conios** class has three data members and three member functions that access the format state of the display unit. Obviously, this is a scaled-down version of the display unit, and is meant only to facilitate a clear understanding of how to specialize an **ios** class object. The declaration of the **consolestream** class is an example of how to combine two IOSTREAM classes through multiple inheritance into a new user-defined translator class. This class declaration is a skeleton for a translator class based on an **ostream_withassign** object. The **ostream_withassign** is an **ostream** object that has the assignment operator defined. This allows the assignment of any **ostream** object to another **ostream** object. The **istream** class also has an **istream_withassign**. The *cout* object is an **ostream_withassign** object. The **cin** object is an **istream_withassign** object. The **consolestream** class has member functions that control the *X,Y* position of the cursor in the **consolestream.** Because *X,Y* position control is a form of *coordinate translation*, the **consolestream** is a specialized translator class. Although the class is simple, it demonstrates the power of inheritance and operator overloading to adapt the IOSTREAM classes to do work they were not originally designed to do. The **setX( )** and **setY( )** member functions make use of standard inline assembly to call the MS-DOS video API.

The two classes **conios** and **consolestream** are specializations of **ios** and **ostream**, respectively. They extend **ios** and **ostream.** The other form of IOSTREAM extension that this program demonstrates is the use of the **spaces(N)** manipulator. User-defined manipulators are also means to modify the original functionality of the IOSTREAMS. In this case, the **spaces(N)** manipulator moves the cursor *N* spaces from its current position. For those who are formatting screens, printer, or text file output, advancing *N* spaces is a normal routine that must be accomplished repeatedly. The core IOSTREAMS do not come with this functionality built in. However, the notion of the object-oriented stream allowed us to implement the space's manipulator with only a few lines of code.

The program in Listing 6.1 declares a variable *Out* of type **consolestream**. This variable is constructed with the **streambuf** component from the **cout** object. The *Out* object could have been constructed using other methods; however, we chose this method for simplicity. A **streambuf** component is necessary for the constructor of the **consolestream** object, because the **consolestream** inherited **conios**, and **conios** needs to know which buffer it is working with. Next, the program assigns **cout** to **consolestream.** This is a bit like aliasing. Now **cout** and **consolestream** both refer to the display unit. The advantage is that **consolestream** has been specialized to deal with spatial output. The **Out.setVideoMode( )** message sets the video mode to 40 × 25. Now the state of the display unit is 40 × 25 until it is changed by another call to the **setVideoMode( )** member function. The **setY( )** and **setX( )** position the cursor at the *X,Y* location specified by the arguments to those member functions. The **setCursorSize( )** member function is used to set the cursor format for the display unit. Both the **setVideoMode( )** and **setCursorSize( )** are persistent states of the display unit, and will not be changed unless these member functions are called again. The program in Listing 6.1 demonstrates several straightforward methods to extend the IOSTREAMS. We have not included any exception handling or error trapping so as not to confuse the issue. The classes **conios** and **consolestream** are skeleton classes that can be further developed and used in real-world applications. This program represents an extension of the IOSTREAM classes in text mode, the same text-mode environment that it was designed for. For the remainder of this book, we shall show examples of adaptations and uses of the IOSTREAMS in graphics mode and multimedia environments.

CHAPTER 7

The New Breed of Operating Systems

Imagine a vast sheet of paper on which straight Lines, Triangles, Squares, Pentagons, Hexagons, and other figures, instead of remaining fixed in their places, move freely about on or in the surface . . . you will then have a pretty correct notion of my country and countrymen.

EDWIN ABBOTT—*FLATLAND*

Any operating system will perform at least two functions:

1. Provide a virtual machine for programmers to work with.
2. Manage the I/O devices that are connected to the computer.

Providing a virtual machine interface to the programmer makes programming the devices connected to the computer simpler. The programmer does not have to be concerned with specific addresses for peripherals, blocking factors for tape drives, intersector gap spacing, disk drive interleaves, timer specifics for adapter cards, or device-specific status codes. Instead, the operating system furnishes the programmer with a set of system services that exchange the device-specific details for higher-level abstractions. These higher-level abstractions come in the form of generic open and close commands, generic read, write, and seek commands. The programmer uses these higher-level constructs to access hardware that is connected to the computer. These abstractions that the operating system provides to the programmer are usually packaged in libraries called an operating system *API* (Application Programmers Interface), or in a library referred to as *system services*.

The operating system is also responsible for managing the input and output devices that are connected to the computer system. It is the operating system

181

that coordinates the I/O activity in a computer system. The operating system determines whether to get the next block of data from a CD-ROM, or deal with a keyboard request. The operating system helps to synchronize the full motion video sequences that appear on our monitors with the sound sequences that come from sound-card adapters. The operating system designates which program has access to which I/O device, and when a program has access to any given I/O device.

Early operating systems had only to provide virtual interfaces for and to manage the basic computer I/O devices:

> *Punched card readers*
> *Punched paper tape readers*
> *Cathode ray tube devices*
> *Consoles*
> *Line printers*
> *Magnetic tape drives*
> *Magnetic ink character recognition devices*

The next generation of operating systems had to support a wider array of peripherals:

> *Disk drives*
> *Monitors that supported simple graphics*
> *Keyboards*
> *Dot matrix printers*
> *Line printers*
> *Plotters*
> *Synch/async modems*
> *Microfilm devices*
> *Optical character recognition devices*
> *Magnetic tape drives*

However, the current generation operating systems, known as 5th generation, must support a much larger spectrum of I/O devices. The following is a partial listing:

> | | |
> |---|---|
> | *Joysticks* | *Gamesticks* |
> | *Mice* | *Magnetic optical drives* |
> | *Trackballs* | *Digital audio tapes* |
> | *Pen input devices* | *Worm drives* |
> | *Scanners* | *Digitizers* |
> | *CD-ROMs* | *Optical drives* |
> | *Video capture cards* | *Large-screen monitors* |

High-speed memory chips	*Sound-card technology*
24-bit graphics technology	*Voice acquisition*
Facsimile devices	*Voice mail adapters*
Color laser printers	*Color InkJet printers*
High-speed modems	

This new spectrum of devices plays a major role in the implementation of multimedia I/O. Originally, these devices were considered occasional add-ons to the desktop computer. Today, the vast majority of these devices are considered standard components of the desktop computer. Multimedia was born when software began to integrate text with graphics. Now multimedia has been extended to include the integration of text, graphics, sound, video, music, and voice in any combination. Each of these components has its own type of hardware device. The modern operating system must have built-in support for these devices. The modern operating system must provide a virtual machine interface, a set of system services, or an API to this new set of I/O devices.

Some operating systems, such as UNIX and MS-DOS have evolved to support multimedia I/O. Other operating systems, such as Windows NT, System 7, and OS/2, were designed from the beginning to be flexible enough to support the new peripherals as they are introduced. Windows NT, System 7, and OS/2 are examples of the new breed of operating systems. This new breed of operating systems supports the multimedia metaphor. These operating systems have built-in support for high-resolution graphics, sound technology, and CD-ROM technology. They support voice acquisition devices and pointing devices of all sorts. These operating systems provide the programmer with a virtual machine that abstracts the reading and writing of bitmaps to video memory, and sound files to sound cards. Two good examples of the multimedia component are in Windows for the NT operating system, and Presentation Manager for the OS/2 operating system. Both the Windows API and the Presentation Manager's API give the programmer access to animation, sound, graphics, full motion video, pointing devices, high-resolution monitors, and voice acquisition. Windows and Presentation Manager furnish the programmer with a virtual interface to the multimedia I/O devices.

The new breed of operating systems are multimedia operating systems that support a multimedia environment and give the programmer a multimedia API to access the new spectrum of I/O devices that are connected to the computer. The change in I/O processing in the new operating systems calls for emphasizing different components in the IOSTREAM classes than are emphasized under the UNIX or MS-DOS model of I/O.

A New Default Mode of Operation

One of the most striking changes in desktop operating systems is the move from text mode as the default startup mode to graphics mode as the default startup mode.

Operating systems, such as UNIX and MS-DOS, were born before graphics technology became widely available. The I/O model in these operating systems is character driven. The alphanumeric mode or teletype mode is the fundamental model for the console and the printer; it is the default startup mode for these operating systems. These environments have built-in support for the text-based **con** device, and the text-based **prn** or **lpt** device. Applications written in C++ can redirect files to **con**, **prn**, or **lpt1** and send streams of characters to these devices. The **stdin** and **stdout** in these environments default to text devices.

This has an enormous impact on basic I/O programming assumptions in C++. The **ostream** object **cout** is tied to **stdout**. The **istream** object **cin** is tied to **stdin**. This means that the default I/O processing in the C++ IOSTREAMS is done in the text mode. This poses a small dilemma for the C++ programmer using the IOSTREAM classes in an environment that starts up automatically in the graphics mode. The **cin** and **cout** objects are connected to text devices that don't have any meaning in the graphics driven environment. Operating systems, such as UNIX and MS-DOS, have several default devices that are opened as files and are available to programmers immediately:

```
con

keyb

prn

lpt1

lpt2

aux

com1

com2
```

These devices are essentially character devices. The **con** and **prn** devices are looking for something like an ASCII code. The programmer might ask why a new graphics device, such as **graphdev**, can be added, and then connect **stdin** and **stdout** to the new graphics device. This solution turns out to be impracticable and inefficient. The wide range of new graphics technology, pointing devices, and high-resolution graphics printers makes it virtually impossible to make a simple built-in **graphdev** as a generic default source and destination for data.

Instead, the new breed of operating system has totally reworked the I/O model for the desktop computer. The character-based alphanumeric mode and the familiar **con** and **prn** text devices are still available for those applications that require them; however, the character mode is now only a subset of the I/O model in the new operating systems. Furthermore, the character mode is no longer the default mode of operation. It has given place to high-resolution graphical display units and pointing devices. In the new breed of operating system, the graphics mode has taken center stage. The printing capabilities are assumed to include graphics, and the display unit must have graphics capabilities. Some sort of pointing device is assumed or highly recommended. The software that runs on these new operating systems will most likely be full of colors, icons, and multiple types of fonts; and will be logically grouped together in one or more windows. The window is another hallmark of the new breed of operating system.

Windows and Windowing

In the software arena, the term *windows* can refer to several very different things. First, there is the software product called **Windows**, produced by Microsoft Inc. This product is a software environment that adds a graphical user interface with multitasking capabilities to the MS-DOS operating system. Second, there is the concept of *windowing*. Windowing is one among many techniques employed in user-interface design and development. Windowing creates logical groups of input areas and output areas on a display unit. These logical groups are separated by frames, colors, location, size, and sometimes level. Designers and developers refer to these visual segregations of data as *windows*. The logical groupings can represent different functional parts within one application, or different applications sharing the same display unit in which each window represents a different application. Finally, there is the notion of *virtual device windows*, where the display unit is divided into several virtual devices. The virtual devices can range from hardware windows to workstations on a network. These virtual devices are capable of communication with each other through messaging. The physical area of the display unit is divided among these virtual devices, and each device controls its area of the screen. In this window model, the display unit becomes a visual meeting place for virtual devices.

The C++ IOSTREAMS have application in all three window contexts; however, we shall focus our discussion of a connection between the C++ IOSTREAMS, the window I/O model in Microsoft Windows, and the window I/O model that is found in the Multimedia Presentation Manager (MMPM/2) for OS/2. Although the C++ IOSTREAMS are object-oriented, they can be successfully mixed in nonobject-oriented environments. Strictly speaking, the Windows API and the MMPM/2 API are not object-oriented, even though they do support the object metaphor at the user level. The C++ programmer can bring the advantages of the IOSTREAMS to these environments by interfacing the Windows API or MMPM/2 API with member functions of the IOSTREAMS. This interfacing forms a hybrid approach to I/O, giving the C++ programmer the best of both worlds.

In this chapter, we shall explore the fundamental concepts behind input and output in the Windows environment and the Presentation Manager environment. We will discuss the device context and the presentation space. Finally, we will show examples of the C++ IOSTREAMS used in conjunction with Windows device contexts and OS/2 Presentation Manager Presentation Spaces.

The Windows I/O Model

In the Windows environment, a window is a rectangular space on a display unit that represents a logical output area, a logical input area, or combination of output and input. The display unit will be in the *graphics mode*. Although logically the window can represent an input area, physically a window is an output area on the display unit. Any output programming to the window will have to use *graphics mode programming techniques*. For instance, while the display unit is in graphics mode, the ASCII control sequences, such as \n, \f, \t, or \b, do not have the same meaning as they do in text mode. The distances between rows are measured in pixels, as opposed to characters. The distances between columns are measure in pixels, as opposed to characters. The output coordinates are represented as world coordinates, device coordinates, client coordinates, page coordinates, or model coordinates. Text, character, and numeric output sent to the display unit must first be converted to strings or bitmaps. Output going to a device that is in graphics mode is considerably slower than output going to a device in text mode, and, finally, font selection, font width, and font height become major programming issues.

The Space Metaphor

In the Windows I/O model, the stream metaphor is joined by the space or area metaphor. In the stream metaphor, data is seen as moving to and from generic sequences or streams of bytes where the streams are connected to an input or output device. The programmer achieves a level of device-independence by conceptualizing the output as a stream. In the space metaphor, data is seen as moving to and from a generic canvas that supports painting, drawing, scaling, pens, brushes, and palettes. The data is not conceptualized as sequences of bytes, but rather as sequences of objects. Whereas the stream metaphor can be applied to almost any I/O device, the space metaphor is applied only to display units, printers, memory, and sometimes files. In the Windows environment, the I/O model includes both *streams* and *spaces*. Figure 7.1 shows the relationship between the Windows applications, the stream metaphor, the space metaphor, and their connection to I/O devices. In the C++ environment under Windows, the programmer can freely mix the stream, object-oriented stream, and space metaphors while doing I/O programming and design.

The Pseudo Object and the Pseudo Method

The window concept is a *pseudo object*. It has a physical representation, logical representation, data structures, and a computer program assigned to it. The computer program assigned to the window is a *pseudo method*. The computer program is like a member function that can access a data member in C++. In this analogy, the *window* is the data member, and the *computer program* assigned to the window is the member function. In this sense, it is like an object in the C++ environment. The window

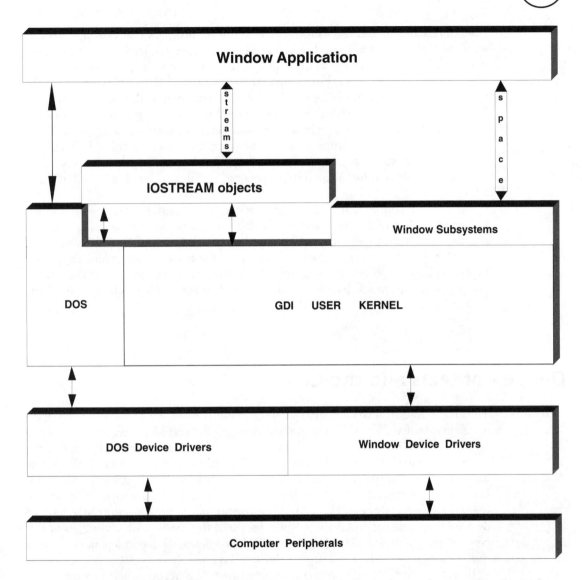

Figure 7.1 *The stream and space metaphors and their relationship with an application and connected I/O devices.*

concept supports a minimal level of encapsulation. However, the window concept does not support inheritance or polymorphism, so in the truest sense, the window is not a complete object.

How the window appears and what appears in the window at any given time is determined in part by the Windows environment and in part by the *computer pro-*

gram that is assigned to the window. The computer program that is assigned to the window (rectangular area on the screen) is sometimes referred to as the *window procedure*. The Windows environment captures input from the pointing device and the keyboard. When this input occurs while the area of the display unit that the window occupies has the *focus*, the Windows environment calls the computer program that is associated with the window. The Windows environment passes a parameter to this computer program. This parameter is called a *message* or an *event*. The parameter will determine whether the computer program should change the window in any way. Depending on the parameter or message, the computer program may do only internal nonvisible processing, such as writing information to a file.

The physical component of the window is the display unit. It is the high-resolution and rich color set of the wide array of available graphics monitors and adapters that give the window its representational power. It is also the availability of this wide array of graphics adapters and monitors that prompted the device-independence approach that is used in the Windows environment. One of the main concepts in the device-independence approach that the Windows environment employs is that of the *device context*.

Device Contexts and the GDI

The *GDI* (Graphical Display Interface) is a major component of the Windows operating environment. The GDI component manages the graphics-intensive output and input. In the Windows I/O model, the programmer does not write directly to the hardware. Instead, the programmer calls GDI functions from the GDI API. These functions then call the appropriate device driver, and the device driver finally translates any commands it receives to device-dependent data and commands. By accessing the hardware through the GDI, the programmer is programming at a level of device-independence. In Chapter 1, we discussed the merits and advantages of this type of programming. The Windows GDI promotes device-independence as it relates to display devices and printer devices (Figure 7.2).

To access the GDI, the programmer must first gain access to a *device context*. A device context is a data structure that contains the description and state of a device. In the Windows environment, graphic displays and printers will have an assigned device context. This device context is a method of maintaining information about the display or printer that is connected to the computer. The programmer can also create a memory device context that simulates either a graphic display or a printer. The programmer interacts with the actual device through the GDI. The GDI uses the device context as a common ground between the device driver and the application. Figure 7.3 shows the relationship between an application, the GDI, the device context, the device driver, and the actual output device.

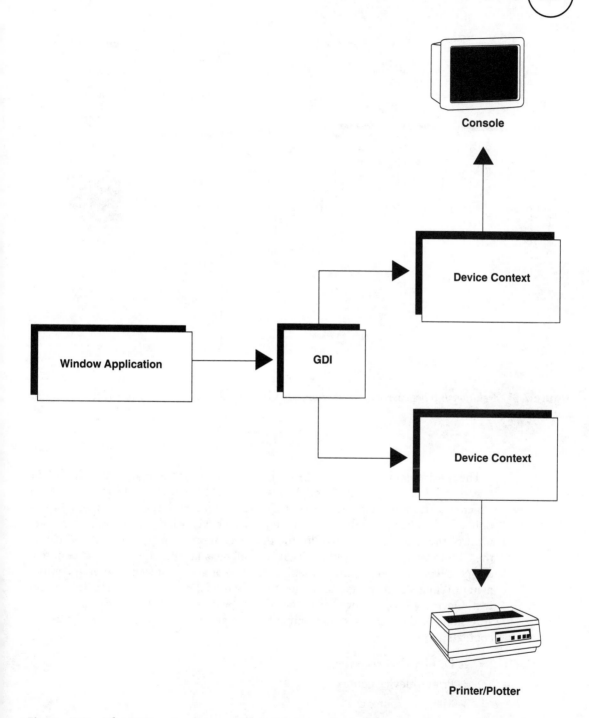

Figure 7.2 *The GDI as it relates to an application, a display device, and a printer device.*

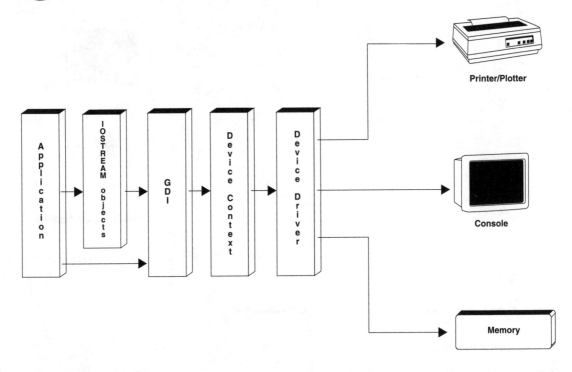

Figure 7.3   *Relationship between an application, the GDI, the device context, device drivers, and the output devices.*

The programmer can get a handle to the device context through two methods: The first method uses the **BeginPaint( )** function, which returns the device context for whichever window handle it is passed. The second method uses the **GetDC( )** function, which returns the device context for whichever window handle it is passed. Most of the GDI functions require the device context as an argument. This enables the GDI to know what type of device it is handling, and what the current state of that device is. For the programmer to send output to or get input from the GDI component of Windows, the programmer must supply the GDI functions with a device context. Once the programmer has obtained the device context, the GDI functions are accessible. In the Windows environment, there are essentially three kinds of device contexts:

1. Display device context
2. Printer device context
3. Memory context

The memory device must be compatible either with a display device or a printer device.

Device Contexts for Displays

A handle for a display device is returned by **BeginPaint( )** and **GetDC( )**. Begin-Paint( ) is normally called during a **WM_PAINT** message. The excerpt in Listing 7.1 demonstrates the **WM_PAINT** message and the use of the **BeginPaint( )** function.

Listing 7.1

```
// This excerpt demonstrates how to get the handle to a device
// context using the BeginPaint( ) GDI function

long FAR PASCAL export WINDOWPROCEDURE(HWND hwnd,
                                       UNIT message,
                                       UNIT wParam,LONG 1Param)
{
   HDC hdc;
   PAINTSTRUCT Ps;
   RECT Area;
   int X,Y;
   X = 100;
   Y = 100;

   switch(message)
   {
         .
         .
         .
      case WM PAINT :
          hdc = BeginPaint(hwnd,&ps);
          TextOut(hdc,X,Y,"Speed Of Light",14);
          EndPaint(hwnd,&ps);
   }
   return 0;
}
```

The code excerpt in Listing 7.1 declares *hdc* to be of type **HDC**. **HDC** is a **typdef** that is defined in **windows.h**. The *hdc* variable is used to hold the handle that is returned from the **BeginPaint( )** function. Once the handle is obtained, then the GDI function **TextOut( )** is called to send the string *"Speed Of Light"* to the display. After the device context is used, it is released by the **Endpaint( )** function.

Listing 7.2

```
// This excerpt demonstrates how to get the handle
// to a device context using the GetDC( ) GDI function

long FAR PASCAL _export WINDOWPROCEDURE(HWND hwnd, UNIT message,
                                        UNIT wParam,
                                        LONG 1Param)

{
   HDC hdc;
   int X,Y;
   X = 100;
   Y = 100;
```

```
    .
    .
    .
  switch(message)
  {
    case IDM SHOW ;
      hdc = GetDC(hwnd);
      TextOut(hdc,X, Y,"Speed Of Light",14);
      ReleaseDC(hWnd,hdc);
  }
  return 0;
}
```

The code excerpt in Listing 7.2 gets a handle to the device context using the **GetDC( )** function. Once the handle to the device context is obtained, then the **TextOut( )** GDI function is called to send the string *"Speed Of Light"* to the display at location *X, Y.* Although the **TextOut( )** function sends text to the display, the coordinates are graphics mode coordinates that represent distances in pixels. After the device context has been used, it is released using the **ReleaseDC( )** GDI function.

Printer Device Contexts

To obtain a device context for a printer, the **CreateDC( )** function must be used. The **CreateDC( )** function creates a device context for the printer and returns a handle to the device context. The **DeleteDC( )** is called to release the context. The **CreateDC( )** function must be passed the name of the device driver; the name of the specific printer (if the driver supports more than one); the name of the filename that specifies the port that the printer is connected to; and some device initialization parameters. Usually, the device driver name and specific printer information are obtained from the **win.ini** file using the **GetProfileString( )** function.

Once a device context is created for the printer, the GDI functions can be called to send output to that printer. The functions are the same functions that would be used to send output to the display. This means that whether the output is going to a screen or to a printer, the programmer can use the same GDI functions. The device context technique increases reusability and extensibility.

Listing 7.3

```
// This program excerpt demonstrates how to create a device
// context for a printer using the CreateDC( ) function.
long FAR PASCAL _export WINDOWPROCEDURE(HWND hwnd, UNIT message,
                                        UNIT wParam,
                                        LONG lParam)

{
  HDC hdc;
  char PInfo[80] = "";
  char DriverName[20];
  char DeviceName[40];
  char Other[20];
  int X,Y;
```

```
        X = 100;
        Y = 100;
            .
            .
            .
        switch(message)
        {
          case IDM PRINT :
            GetProfileString("windows","device","",PInfo.80);
            istrstream In(PInfo);
            In.getline(DeviceName,80,",");
            In.getline(DriverName,80,",");
            In.getline(Other,80,",");
            hdc = CreateDC(DriverName,DeviceName,Other,NULL);
            Escape(hdc,STARTDOC,8,(LPSTR) "EXAMPLE",01);
            TextOut(hdc,X, Y,"Speed Of Light",14);
            Escape(hdc,NEWFRAME,0,OL,OL);
            Escape(hdc,ENDDOC,0,OL,OL);
            DeleteDC(hdc);
        }
        return 0;
    }
```

The program excerpt in Listing 7.3 uses the **GetProfileString( )** function to get specific information about the printer device driver. Next, the profile string is passed as an argument to an **istrstream** object, and the **getline( )** member function is used to parse the profile string into its component parts. The excerpt then creates a printer device context and uses the **TextOut( )** GDI function to send a string to the printer. After the string is sent, the **DeleteDC( )** function is called to release the device context and its associated memory.

Memory Device Contexts

The memory device context must be created with the **CreateCompatibleDC( )** function. A memory device context treats a section of memory as a virtual device. The device is assigned the same attributes as the device for which it was created. Once the handle is obtained, the programmer can use the same GDI functions that were used to send output to the display or to a printer. The output is sent to a bitmap that has been selected into the memory device. The bitmap can be copied to any device that supports *raster* operations. We discuss memory device contexts farther in Chapter 9.

IOSTREAM Classes and the Windows Programming Environment

In the Windows programming environment, the GDI functions work together with the device context to present the programmer with the *space metaphor*. The objects sent to the generic space can be polygons or bitmaps. When the programmer needs to send text, characters, or numeric data to the display, that data must first be converted to strings and then sent to the display. This can involve calling **sprintf( )**, **wsprintf( )**, **atoi( )**, **ltoa( )**, **gcvt( )**, or any number of conversion formatting routines. Using members of the IOSTREAM classes can simplify the programmers I/O routines in the Windows environment.

The **cout**, **cin**, and **cerr** objects are usually the first IOSTREAM components that the programmer encounters when initially introduced to C++. These objects are normally tied to the console, and the console is assumed to be in text mode. Because the Windows environment supports the console only in graphics mode, the **cout**, **cin**, and **cerr** objects have no use unless they are redirected.

As a rule of thumb, any **iostream** object that is connected to **stdin**, **stdout**, and **stderr** will not behave as expected in the Windows environment unless **stdin**, **stdout**, and **stderr** are redirected to something other than the text mode console. The IOSTREAM family of classes can be used for *file I/O, memory formatting, buffering, data conversion, state formatting*, and *bitmaps* in the Windows environment. Figure 7.4 shows the relationship between the Windows application, IOSTREAMS classes, the GDI, MS-DOS, device contexts, device drivers, and the output devices.

For example, the **ostrstream** class can work with the GDI functions **TextOut( )** and **DrawText( )**, or **MessageBox( )**, to send formatted text to the display unit. The **ostrstream** class has all the functionality of the **ios** class, **ostream** class, and **strstreambuf** class. Using the **ostrstream** class, the programmer can insert numeric and text data into an **ostrstream** object-oriented stream, and then pass the formatted information to the GDI functions. This simplifies Windows display output programming when much text or numeric data must be displayed.

The program in Listing 7.4 uses two **ifstream** objects to access **list1.txt** and **list2.txt**. It then uses an **ostrstream** object to format text to the **MessageBox( )** function. The program then does a merge sort on the two lists and inserts the output into an **ostrstream** object. The GDI **DrawText( )** function then accesses the **str( )** member function of the **ostrstream** object to paint the sorted list to the display unit.

Listing 7.4

```
// This program demonstrates the use of ifstream. and ostrstream
// objects in combination with GDI functions and the Windows
// environment

#include <windows.h>
#include <stdlib.h>
#include <stdio.h>
#define IDM QUIT 102
#define Example 101
#include <fstream.h>
#include <strstrea.h>
#include <string.h>

long FAR PASCAL export exampleMain(HWND hWnd,UNIT wMessage,UNIT
                                wParam,LONG lParam):
```

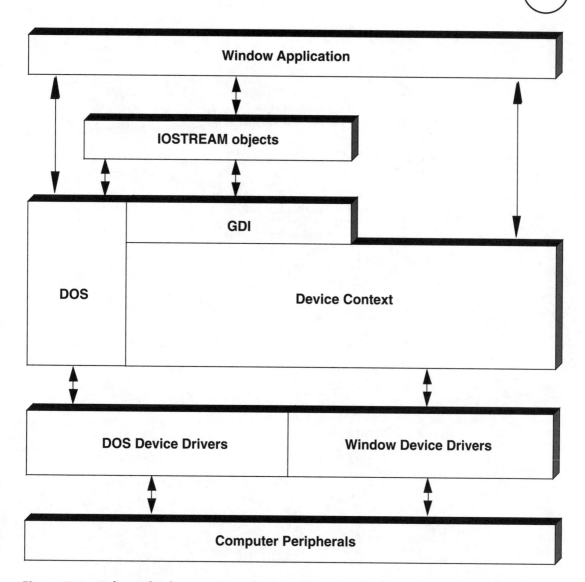

Figure 7.4 *Relationship between a Windows application, IOSTREAM classes, the GDI, MS-DOS, the device context, device drivers, and the output devices.*

```
long FAR PASCAL export exampleMain(HWND hWnd,UNIT wMessage,UNIT
                                        wParam,LONG lParam)
{
    HDC DeviceContext;
    PAINTSTRUCT PresentationSpace;
    static char Area[1000] = "";
    RECT box;
```

```cpp
double Object[2];
ifstream Stream[2];

switch(wMessage)
{
  case WM PAINT :
    BeginPaint(hWnd,&PresentationSpace);
    EndPaint(hWnd,&PresentationSpace);
    break;

  case WM COMMAND:
    switch(wParam)
    {
      case Example:
        SetRect(&box,10,10,200,300);
        DeviceContext = GetDC(hWnd);
        ostrstream Out(Area,999);
        ostrstream Cerr;
        Stream[0].open("list1.txt");
        if(!Stream[0].good( )){
          Cerr << "could Not open file 1";
          MessageBox(hWnd,Cerr.str( ),"Error",MB_OK);
          ReleaseDC(hWnd,DeviceContext);
          break;

        }
        Stream[1].open("list2.txt");
        if(!Stream[1].good( )){
          Cerr << "could not open file 2 ";
          MessageBox(hWnd,Cerr.str( ),"Error",MB_OK);
          ReleaseDC(hWnd,DeviceContext);
          break;

        }
        Stream[0] >> Object[0];
        Stream[1] >> Object[1];
        while(!Stream[0].eof( ) && !Stream[0].fail( ) &&
              !Stream[1].eof( ) && !Stream[1].fail( ))

        {
        if(Object[0] < Object[1]){
          Out << Object[0] << endl;
          Stream[0] >> Object[0];
        }
        else
          if(Object[1] < Object[0]){
            Out << Object[1] << endl;
            Stream[1] >> Object[1];
          }
          else
          {
            Out << Object[0] << endl << Object[1] << endl;
            Stream[0] >> Object[0];
            Stream[1] >> Object[1];
          }
```

```
        }
        while(!Stream[0].eof( ) && !Stream[0].fail( ))
        {
          Stream[0] >> Object[0];
          Out << Object[0] << endl;

        }
        while(!Stream[1].eof( ) && !Stream[1].fail( ))
        {
          Stream[1] >> Object[1];
          Out << Object[1] << endl;
        }
        Stream[0].close( );
        Stream[1].close( );
        DrawText(DeviceContext,Out.str( ),-1,&box,DT WORDBREAK);
        ReleaseDC(hWnd,DeviceContext):
        break;

      case IDM QUIT :
        DestroyWindow(hWnd);
        break;
    }
    break;
    case WM DESTROY:
      PostQuitMessage(0);
      break;

    default:
      return DefWindowProc(hWnd,wMessage,wParam,1Param);
    }
    return(0L);
}

int PASCAL WinMain(HANDLE hInstance, HANDLE hPrevInstance, LPSTR
                   1pszCmdLine, int nCmdShow)

{
    HWND hWnd;
    MSG msg;
    WNDCLASS wndclass;

    if(!hPrevInstance){
      wndclass.style = CS HREDRAW : CS VREDRAW;
      wndclass.lpfnWndProc = (WNDPROC) exampleMain;
      wndclass.cbClsExtra = 0;
      wndclass.cbWndExtra = 0;
      wndclass.hInstance = hInstance:
      wndclass.hIcon = LoadIcon(NULL,IDI ASTERISK);
      wndclass.hCursor = LoadCursor(NULL,IDC ARROW);
      wndclass.hbrBackground = GetStockObject(WHITE BRUSH);
      wndclass.lpszMenuName = "MENU 1";
      wndclass.lpszClassName = "example1";
      if(!RegisterClass(&wndclass)){
          return(0):
```

```
          }
        }
        hWnd = CreateWindow("example1","iostreams in Windows
                            example",WS_OVERLAPPEDWINDOW,
                            CW_USEDEFAULT,CW_USEDEFAULT,
                            CW USEDEFAULT,CW USEDEFAULT,
                            NULL,NULL,hInstance,NULL);
        ShowWindow(hWnd,nCmdShow);
        while(GetMessage(&msg,NULL,NULL,NULL))
        {
          TranslateMessage(&msg);
          DispatchMessage(&msg);
        }
        return(msg.wParam);
      }
```

The program in Listing 7.5 uses an **istrstream** object as a parse buffer for the printer profile string. The **GetProfileString( )** GDI function returns the profile string in the *PInfo* variable. The **getline( )** member functions of the *In* istrstream object then parse the profile string into its component parts. The parts are then passed to the **CreateDC( )** GDI function to create a device context for the attached printer. This program obtains two device contexts, one for the display and one for the attached printer. The program uses two **ifstream** objects that are stored in the array *Stream* to extract two lists of numeric data. The lists are sorted using a simple merge sort, and the resulting list is sent to a printer using the **TextOut( )** function, and also sent to the display using the **DrawText( )** function. This program is a simplistic example of combining **IOSTREAM** objects with GDI functions in the Windows environment.

Listing 7.5

```
// This program demonstrates how an istrstream and ostrstream
// object can be used with the Windows GDI functions to send
// output to the display unit and to the printer.

#include <windows.h>
#include <stdlib.h>
#include <stdio.h>
#define IDM QUIT 103
#define PrintExample 102
#include <fstream.h>
#include <strstrea.h>
#include <string.h>

long FAR PASCAL export exampleMain(HWND hWnd.UNIT wMessage,UNIT
                                   wParam,LONG 1Param);
long FAR PASCAL export exampleMain(HWND hWnd,UNIT wMessage,UNIT
                                   wParam,LONG 1Param)

{
    HDC DeviceContext;
```

```
HDC hdc;
static char Area[1000] = "";
RECT box;
double Object[2];
ifstream Stream[2];
char PInfo[80] = "";
char DriverName[20];
char DeviceName[40];
char Other[20];
ostrstream Out(Area,999);
ostrstream Cerr;

switch(wMessage)
{
  case WM COMMAND:
    switch(wParam)
      {
        case PrintExample:
          GetProfileString("windows","device","",PInfo,80);
          istrstream In(PInfo);
          In.getline(DeviceName,80,',');
          In.getline(DriverName,80,',');
          In.getline(Other,80,',');
          hdc = CreateDC(DriverName,DeviceName,Other,NULL);
          Escape(hdc,STARTDOC,8,(LPSTR) "EXAMPLE",OL);
          SetRect(&box,10,10,200,300);
          DeviceContext = GetDC(hWnd);
          Stream[0].open("list1.txt");
          if(!Stream[0].good( )){
            Cerr << "could Not open file 1";
            MessageBox(hWnd,Cerr.str( ),"Error",MB_OK);
            ReleaseDC(hWnd,DeviceContext);
            break;
          }
          Stream[1].open("list2.txt");
          if(!Stream[1].good( )){
            Cerr << "could not open file 2 ";
            MessageBox(hWnd,Cerr.str( ),"Error",MB_OK);
            ReleaseDC(hWnd,DeviceContext);
            break;
          }
          Stream[0] >> Object[0];
          Stream[1] >> Object[1];
          while(!Stream[0].eof( ) && !Stream[0].fail( ) &&
                !Stream[1].eof( ) && !Stream[1].fail( ))
          {
            if(Object[0] < Object[1]){
              Out << Object[0] << endl;
              Stream[0] >> Object[0];
            }
            else
              if(Object[1] < Object[0]){
```

```
                         Out << Object[1] << endl;
                         Stream[1] >> Object[1];
                       }
                    else
                    {
                       Out << Object[0] << endl << Object[1];
                       Out << endl;
                       Stream[0] >> Object[0];
                       Stream[1] >> Object[1];
                    }
             }
             while(!Stream[0].eof( ) && !Stream[0].fail( ))
             {
                Stream[0] >> Object[0];
                Out << Object[0] << endl;

             }
             while(!Stream[1].eof( ) && !Stream[1].fail( ))
             {
                Stream[1] >> Object[1];
                Out << Object[1] << endl;
             }
             Stream[0].close( );
             Stream[1].close( );
             TextOut(hdc,1,1,Out.str( ),strlen(Out.str( )));
             Escape(hdc,NEWFRAME,0,0L,0L);
             Escape(hdc.ENDDOC,0,0L,0L);
             DeleteDC(hdc);
             DrawText(DeviceContext,Out.str( ),-1,&box,DT_WORDBREAK);
             ReleaseDC(hWnd,DeviceContext);
             break;
           case IDM QUIT :
             DestroyWindow(hWnd);
             break;
        }
       break;

    case WM DESTROY: PostQuitMessage(0);
       break;

    default:
       return DefWindowProc(hWnd,wMessage,wParam,lParam);
   }
   return(0L);
}
int PASCAL WinMain(HANDLE hInstance, HANDLE hPrevInstance, LPSTR
                 loszCmdLine, int nCmdShow)

{
   HWND hWnd;
   MSG msg;
   WNDCLASS wndclass;

   if(!hPrevInstance){
```

```
        wndclass.style = CS HREDRAW : CS VREDRAW;
        wndclass.lpfnWndProc = (WNDPROC) exampleMain;
        wndclass.cbClsExtra = 0;
        wndclass.cbWndExtra = 0;
        wndclass.hInstance = hInstance;
        wndclass.hIcon = LoadIcon(NULL.IDI ASTERISK);
        wndclass.hCursor = LoadCursor(NULL,IDC ARROW);
        wndclass.hbrBackground = GetStockObject(WHITE BRUSH);
        wndclass.lpszMenuName = "MENU 1";
        wndclass.lpszClassName = "List7-5";
        if(!RegisterClass(&wndclass)){
          return(0);
        }
    }
    hWnd = CreateWindow("List7-5","iostreams in Windows using the
                        printer", WS_OVERLAPPEDWINDOW, CW_USEDE-
                        FAULT,CW_USEDEFAULT, CW_USEDEFAULT,
                        CW_USEDEFAULT,NULL,NULL,hInstance,NULL);
    ShowWindow(hWnd,nCmdShow);
    while(GetMessage(&msg,NULL,NULL,NULL))
    {
      TranslateMessage(&msg);
      DispatchMessage(&msg);
    }
    return(msg.wParam);
}
```

Since C++ supports incremental object orientation, the C++ programmer can mix the object-oriented IOSTREAMS with the Windows GDI functions freely. The object-oriented metaphor is not forced on the Windows GDI access. The method of intermingling the IOSTREAM classes and the GDI functions discussed in this chapter offer the C++ programmer maximum flexibility in I/O programming design. The C++ programmer can use the Windows GDI API to take advantage of the high level of device-independence that it has for programming display units and printers. The programmer can incorporate the object-oriented IOSTREAMS to do all the file I/O, in-core memory formatting, buffering, and bitmap manipulation. By using the IOSTREAMS where feasible, the programmer increases the portability of the program. If the program needs to be moved between different versions of the same environment or to a different environment, the IOSTREAM portions of the program will go virtually unchanged.

The Windows API has upward of 600 function calls, and hundreds of messages. As Windows upgrades continue, the number of functions and messages increase. As the syntax complexities increase, the semantics of functions change. Any method that the programmer can use to simplify I/O programming in this rapidly growing environment provides a critical gain in productivity. Object-oriented input and output using the C++ IOSTREAM brings simplicity, single interface, and multiple implementation through polymorphism, reusability, and extensibility to the Windows I/O environment. The ANSI standard for the IOSTREAM classes offers a high degree of stability for I/O programming in any environment that supports the C++ language.

The OS/2 Presentation Manager I/O Model

The OS/2 Presentation Manager (PM) is the graphical interface API for the OS/2 operating system. The OS/2 operating system is one of the new breed of power-house operating systems that run on *cisc* as well as *risc* chip technologies. The Presentation Manager supports event-driven programming and the Windows I/O model. Presentation Manager programming is similar to Windows programming. This similarity is not a coincidence. Both environments evolved from a single ances-tor. At one point in history, IBM and Microsoft were partners working on a single operating system with a single graphical interface using new operating system tech-nologies. When the partnership disintegrated, the joint venture became two prod-ucts. At Microsoft, the product became the basis for the Windows operating environment, and the predecessor of the NT operating system. At IBM, the product became the basis for the Presentation Manager, the graphical front end for the OS/2 operating system. Both Windows for the NT and Presentation Manager for OS/2 have since taken separate development paths.

The Presentation Manager now supports multimedia I/O. It is the graphical foun-dation for the object-driven workplace shell. The Windows I/O model and the device context concept in Presentation Manager are very similar to the Windows I/O model and the device context concepts that are used in the Windows environ-ment. Yet, the Presentation Manager adds a level of abstraction above the device context. The Presentation Manager adds the *presentation space* to the I/O model. The presentation space takes the generic space metaphor to a higher degree of device-independence. Under the Microsoft Windows I/O model, the programmer must make a decision about the type of output device that will be written to before any GDI functions can be used. In Presentation Manager, the programmer can send output to a generic space that is not associated with any particular device. The pro-grammer is allowed to use the GPI (Graphic Programming Interface) functions without referring to any specific type of output device. This allows the programmer to defer the decision of the type of output device to a later time in the development. The extra layer of abstraction that the presentation space provides allows the Pre-sentation Manager program to be more device-independent than its Windows coun-terpart. Figure 7.5 shows the relationship between the presentation space, the device context, the GPI, the device driver, and the output device. Figure 7.6 con-trasts the Windows I/O model with the Presentation Manager I/O model. In Pre-sentation Manager, the application writes to a presentation space; the presentation space is then associated to a device context.

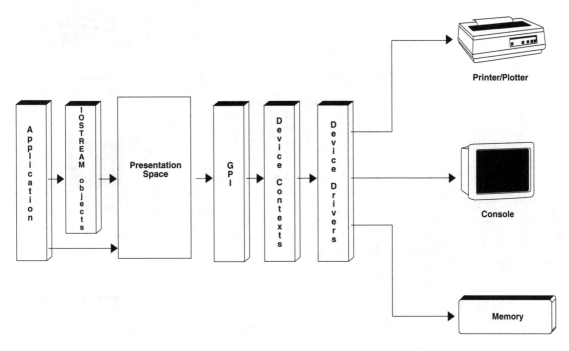

Figure 7.5 *Relationship between the presentation space, the device context, the GPI, device drivers, and the output devices.*

Presentation Spaces

The Presentation Manager has three types of presentation spaces:

- Micropresentation space
- Cached micropresentation space
- Normal presentation space

Micropresentation Spaces

The presentation spaces differ in memory usage, efficiency, and GPI access. The *micropresentation space* may be associated with any device. Once it is associated with a particular device, it cannot be associated to any other device. The micropresentation space cannot be used with retained graphics. That is, the presentation space cannot be in a retain or retain draw mode. The micropresentation space can be created using the **GpiCreatePS( )** function, or can be obtained using the **WinGetScreenPS( )** function. The presentation spaces that are created with the **GpiCreatePS( )** function can be deleted with the **GpiDestroyPS( )** function. The **GpiDestroyPS( )** function deletes the presentation space and all the resources owned by the space. Micropresentation

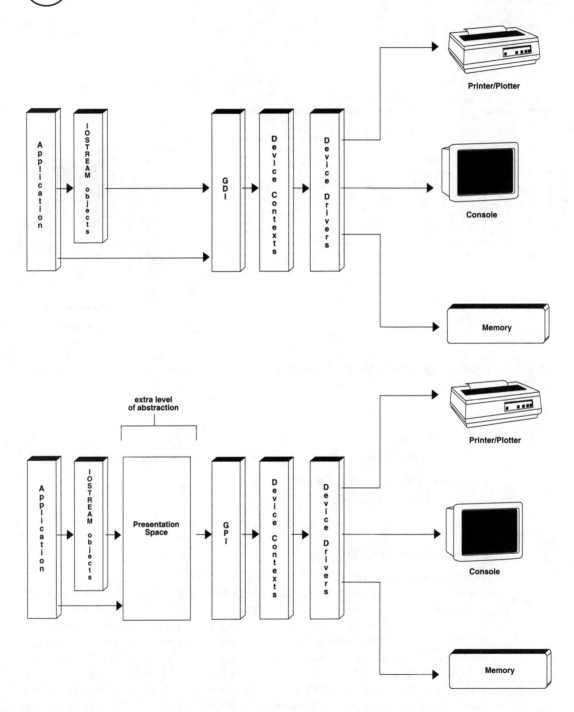

Figure 7.6   *Contrast between the Windows I/O model and the Presentation Manager I/O model.*

spaces are normally used when the drawing or screen output is simple, and if the application needs to create a separate space for each output device.

Cached Micropresentation Spaces

The *cached micropresentation spaces* can be used only in conjunction with the display. They cannot be associated to any other device. The cached micropresentation spaces are the most memory efficient and are used for simple output going to the screen. Cached micropresentation spaces are owned by the windowing system, not the programmer's application. Therefore, the programmer does not create cached spaces. The cached micropresentation space is obtained by either the **WinBeginPaint( )** function, the **WinGetScreenPS( )** function, or the **WinGetPS( )** function.

The cached spaces that are obtained by **WinBeginPaint( )** are released using **WinReleasePS( )**. The cached spaces that are obtained using **WinGetScreenPS( )** and **WinGetPS( )** are released using the **WinReleasePS( )** function. When a handle to a cached micro or micropresentation space is obtained using the **WinGetScreenPS( )** function, the programmer has access to the entire display screen. This can be both good and bad. If the programmer intends to take full responsibility for the display screen, then **WinGetScreenPS( )** accomplishes this.

Normal Presentation Spaces

Normal presentation spaces are the most flexible. A normal presentation space can be associated with multiple devices. Normal presentation spaces also require the most resources. The normal presentation space can be used when the presentation space is in a retained or retained-draw mode. If the drawings and output sent are complex, then normal presentation space should be used. A normal presentation space requires 114kb more space than a micropresentation space. The normal presentation space is created with the **GpiCreatePS( )** function, and destroyed with the **GpiDestroyPS( )** function. Both the micro and the normal presentation must be associated with a device context. Only the cached micropresentation space is automatically associated with a display. The normal presentation space is the only type of presentation space that supports retained graphics. The **GpiAssociate( )** function is used to associate the normal presentation space to a device context. The **GpiAssociate( )** function can also be used to reassociate the presentation space to another device context. Table 7.1 shows the features and restrictions of the normal, standard micro and cached micropresentation spaces.

Listing 7.6

```
// This excerpt shows how to obtain the handle to a presentation
// space using the WinBeginPaint( ) function and the WinGetPS( )
// function.

MRESULT EXPENTRY window func (HWND handle, ULONG mess, MPARAM
                             parm1, MPARAM parm2)
{
```

Table 7.1   Features and Restrictions of the Normal, Standard Micro, and the Cached Micropresentation Spaces

Feature/Restriction	Normal	Standard Micro	Cached Micro
Device Types Supported	Any device	Any device	Video display window only
Number of Supported Devices	Multiple	One	One
Available GPI Functions	All functions	All except segment functions	All except segment functions
Retained Graphics	Yes	No	No
Association	Associate and disassociate, as required	Associate at creation; cannot disassociate	Does not apply
Memory Considerations	Highest memory usage	Medium memory usage	Quickest allocation

```
HPS PSpace;
POINTL Coord;
CHAR ch;
CHAR str[80] = " ";
SHORT i;

switch(mess)
{
   case WM PAINT:
   PSpace = WinBeginPaint(handle,O,NULL);
   Coord.x = 0;
   Coord.v = 0;
   GpiSetColor(PSpace,CLR DARKCYAN);
   GpiCharStringAt(PSpace,&Coord,14,"Speed of Light");
   WinEndPaint(handle);
   break;
   case WM CHAR:
   if(SHORT1FROMMP(parm1) & KC KEYUP){
      break;
   }
   else
   {
      PSpace = WinGetPS(handle);
      Coord.x = 100;
      Coord.y = 0;
      GpiSetColor(PSpace,CLR DARKPINK);
      ch = CHAR4FROMMP(parm1);
      sprintf(str,"scan code %3d",ch);
      GpiCharStringAt(PSpace,&Coord,strlen(str),str);
      Coord.x = 300;
      Coord.v = 0;
      i = SHORT2FROMMP(parm2);
      sprintf(str."virtual code %3d",i);
```

```
                GpiCharStringAt(PSpace,&Coord,Strlen(str),str);
                WinReleasePS(PSpace):

            }
        break;
        case WM ERASEBACKGROUND:
            return(MRESULT) TRUE;
        default:
            return WinDefWindowProc(handle,mess,parm1,parm2);
    }
    return(MRESULT) FALSE:
}
```

The excerpt in Listing 7.6 uses the **WinBeginPaint( )** function to get the handle to a presentation space during a **WM_PAINT** message. Once the handle is obtained, GPI functions can be used to send output to the display. The excerpt also uses the **WinGetPS( )** function to get a handle to a presentation space during a **WM_CHAR** message. The **WinBeginPaint( )** function should be used only in response to a **WM_PAINT** message. Therefore, if a handle to a presentation space is required at any other time, the programmer must use one of the other functions that either creates a presentation space, or returns the handle to an already existing presentation space. Once a handle to a presentation space is obtained during the **WM_CHAR** message, output is then sent to the display using the **GpiCharStringAt( )** function. Although the vast majority of the GPI functions will require a handle to a presentation space, the functions do not need to know anything about the device context. The device context can be associated later. This is in contrast to Windows programming. The Windows GDI functions require the device context as an argument. Table 7.2 shows the primary presentation space functions.

All drawing in the Presentation Manager must be done in a presentation space. In a cached and micropresentation space, the space is automatically associated with the display. For micro and normal presentation spaces the programmer can use the **GpiAssociate( )** function to associate the presentation space to a device context.

The device context is one level of abstraction below the presentation space. It lies between the presentation space and the device drivers. The device context connects the presentation space to a type of output device. It converts the device-independent presentation space information into device-dependent information that is sent to the appropriate device drivers. Once a device context is created, it must be associated with a presentation space in order to display or print the graphic objects on the output device.

As there are three types of presentation spaces, there are three types of device contexts that are associated with the presentation spaces. The three types of device contexts are *cached, window,* and *normal.* The *cached device context* is a device context automatically associated with a cached presentation space when that space is acquired from the cache. The *window device context* is acquired by using the **WinOpenWindowDC( )** function. This type of device context represents a display window. The **WinOpenWindowDC( )** function accepts a handle to a window, and then returns the window device context handle. The window device context han-

Table 7.2   Primary Presentation Space Functions and Their Descriptions

Function Name	Description
GpliAssociate( )	Associates the current presentation space with a device context. Disassociates the current presentation space by passing a null device context.
GpiCreatePS( )	Creates the specified type of presentation space.
GpiDestroyPS( )	Deletes a normal presentation space or a standard micropresentation space.
GpiMove( )	Explicitly sets the current position.
GpiQueryPs( )	Determines the size, units, and other options of a presentation space.
GpiResetPS( )	Resets the presentation space.
GpiRestorePS( )	Pops the contents of a saved presentation space stack.
GpiSavePs( )	Saves items from the current presentation space onto an accessible stack.
GpiSetCurrentPosition( )	Explicitly updates the current position.
GpiSetPS( )	Sets the presentation space size, units, and format.
WinBeginPaint( )	Allocates a cached micropresentation space for **WM_PAINT** processing (if an existing presentation space is not being used) and establishes the update region for the paint.
WinEndPaint( )	Returns any cached micropresentation space to the cache, and signals completion of the processing.
WinGetPS( )	Allocates a cached micropresentation space from the cache.
WinOpenWindowDC( )	Creates a device context for a display window.

dle can be associated with a normal or a standard micropresentation space. The *normal device context* or standard device context connects a presentation space with any nonwindow output device. There are six types of normal device contexts. The **DevOpenDC( )** function will return a handle to only one of the six types of normal device context. Table 7.3 lists the six types of normal device contexts, their purpose, and usage. The **DevOpenDC( )** function is used to obtain a device context handle. The **DevCloseDC( )** function is used to close the device context.

IOSTREAMS and the Presentation Manager

The IOSTREAM classes can be used in the Presentation Manager environment in the same manner as they can be used in the Windows environment. The IOSTREAM

Table 7.3   The Six Types of Normal Device Contexts, Their Purpose and Their Usage

DC Type	Purpose	Usage
Queued	Links a presentation space with a printer or plotter shared by multiple applications sending spooled print jobs to the print queue. Queued device contexts store print jobs by using a program which keeps track of the order in which the jobs arrive at the printer and in which they are printed. This program is called the *print spooler*.	Applications use queued device contexts to offload printing from the application.
Information	Links the presentation space with a printer or a plotter directly enabling device information to be queried, but producing no output on the device.	An application can use an information device context with lower memory overhead, rather than use a direct device context, which could provide the same information.
Direct	Links the presentation space with a printer or a plotter, directly bypassing the spooler and the print queue. A direct device context is used by the spooler to process jobs as they are removed from the print queue.	An application normally does not use the direct device contexts, unless it is avoiding the queue (for security reasons) or going directly to a dedicated machine.
Memory	Links a presentation space with a bit map.	Applications use this type for drawing to a bit map and using it as a source or target of BitBlt operations.
Metafile	A special device context that enables a picture output to its associated presentation space to be recorded in a metafile for use in the future.	Only applications that use metafiles use metafile device contexts.
Metafile_NoQuery	Functionality the same as the metafile; however querying of presentation space attributes is not allowed.	If attributes of the presentation space are not to be queried, this device context offers improved performance.

classes can be used for all *file I/O, buffering, memory formatting,* and *bitmaps*. This can be accomplished without forcing the object-oriented paradigm on the Presentation Manager philosophy of I/O. The major point to remember here is that the Presentation Manager presents the **stdin** and the **stdout** in graphics mode. The normal type of text mode usage of the IOSTREAMS is not useful in the Presentation Manager philosophy. The streams must be redirected and the **istrstream**, **ostrstream**, and **strstream** classes play a larger role. Along with integrating the built-in IOSTREAM classes with the Presentation Manager, the programmer can encapsulate various components of the Presentation Manager as extensions to the IOSTREAM classes, thus adding new classes to the IOSTREAM family. This offers powerful opportunities for modeling presentation spaces, device contexts, pipes, queues, and subsystems. However, we can only begin to scratch the surface on this type of I/O modeling. Both the Presentation Manager and the Windows environments are enormous in terms of functionality and possibility. Volumes have been written about both environments, and the available information still falls short of what is required to implement serious applications. The ways that the IOSTREAM classes can be combined to encapsulate and extend the Presentation Manager or the Windows environment are no doubt endless. Even the IOSTREAM classes are just building blocks that can be combined, extended, and reused in a staggering number of combinations.

The program in Listing 7.8 demonstrates a basic approach to extending the IOSTREAM classes to include classes based on Presentation Manager components. One of the simplest methods of extending the IOSTREAM classes is to add a specialized translator class and overload the << insertion and >> extraction operators. The **textspace** class in Listing 7.7 is an example of this type of specialization.

Listing 7.7

```
// This is a simple extension to the iostream classes that adds
// a class that can be used in the Presentation Manager
// environment.
class textspace : public ostream{
protected:
    HPS PSpace;
    HWND WinHandle;
    POINTL Coord;
    long int Tab;
public:
    textspace(streambuf *Buffer, HWND Handle);
    ~textspace(void);
    HPS space(void);
    void setxy(long X, long Y);
    long int tab(void);
    void tab(long X);
    long getx(void);
    long gety(void);
    friend textspace &operator<<(textspace &Out,char *Text);
};
```

The class in Listing 7.7 is an extension of the **ostream** class and has been specialized to encapsulate a presentation space. In this case, the **textspace** class represents a cached microrepresentation space. This space will be used primarily as a space that contains text. It overloads the << insertion operator to insert a string into the text space. Upon insertion, the string is painted onto the device context that is connected to the presentation space. Figure 7.7 shows the class relationship diagram for the **textspace** class. This class encapsulates the presentation space. Since the class has a member function that returns the presentation space, it can interact with the entire GPI interface. This class has two data members that directly interface to the GPI: PSpace and WinHandle.

PSpace is the handle to the presentation space, and **WinHandle** is the handle to the window that contains the presentation space. By encapsulating these two components, the user-defined class **textspace** can access most of the windowing and GPI functions. The other two data members, **Coord** and **Tab**, represent some location on the space or distance within the space. This oversimplified object is enough to demonstrate how the programmer can extend the IOSTREAM classes to include the *graphic intensive* space or page metaphor found in the new breed of operating system. The program in Listing 7.8 has been condensed so that the basic concepts of object integration can be seen with minimal interference.

Listing 7.8

```
#define INCL WIN
#define INCL GPI

#include <os2.h>
#include <stdlib.h>
#include <stdio.h>
#include <string.h>
#include <fstream.h>
#include <strstrea.h>
#include <iomanip.h>

class textspace : public ostream{
protected:
```

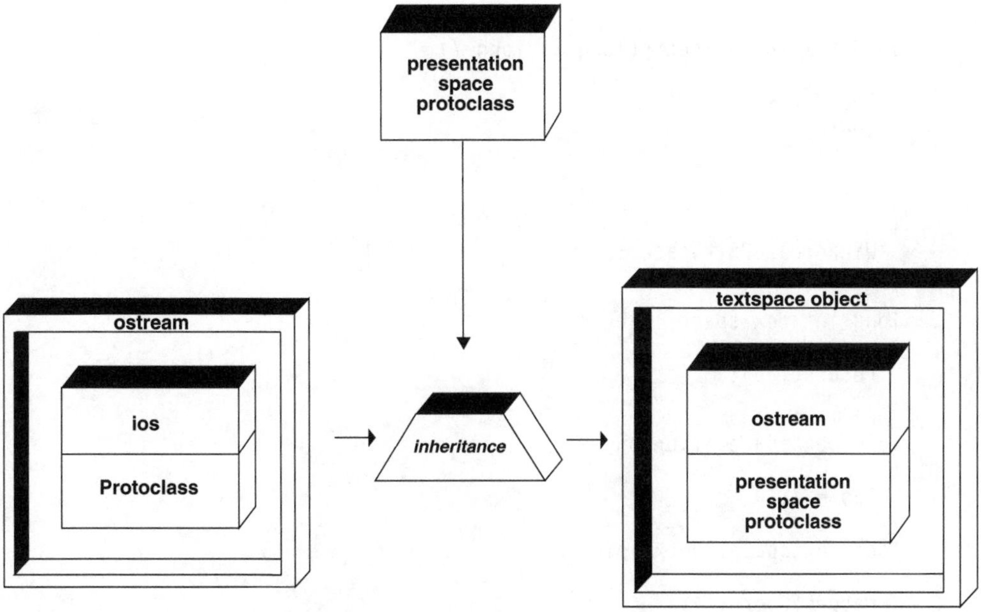

Figure 7.7 $\quad$ *Class relationship diagram of the **text space** object.*

```
        HPS PSpace;
        HWND WinHandle;
        POINTL Coord;
        long int Tab;
public:
        textspace(streambuf *Buffer, HWND Handle);
        ~textspace(void);
        HPS space(void);
        void setxy(long X, long Y);
        long int tab(void);
        void tab(long X);
        long getx(void);
        long gety(void);
        friend textspace &operator<<(textspace &Out,char *Text);
};

HPS textspace::space(void)
{
    return(PSpace);
}

textspace::textspace(streambuf *Buffer,HWND Handle) : ostream(Buffer)
{
  Coord.x = 10;
  Coord.y = 10;
  Tab = 5;
  PSpace = WinGetPS(Handle);
  WinHandle = Handle;
}

void textspace::setxy(long X, long Y)
{
  Coord.x = X;
  Coord.y = Y;
}

textspace::~textspace(void)
{
  WinReleasePS(PSpace);
}

long int textspace::tab(void)
{
  return(Tab);
}

void textspace::tab(long X)
{
  Tab = X;
}
long textspace::getx(void)
{
  return(Coord.x);
}

long textspace::getv(void)
```

```
{
   return(Coord.y);
}

textspace &operator<<(textspace &Out,char *Text)
{
   Out.rdbuf( )->sputn(Text,strlen(Text));
   GpiCharStringAt(Out.PSpace,&Out.Coord,strlen(Text),Text);
   return(Out);
}

textspace &tab(textspace &Mstream)
{
   Mstream.setxy(Mstream.getx( ),(Mstream.gety( ) + Mstream.tab( )));
   return(Mstream);
}

MRESULT EXPENTRY window_func(HWND,ULONG,MPARAM,MPARAM);

MRESULT EXPENTRY window_func(HWND handle, ULONG mess, MPARAM
                                 parm1, MPARAM parm2)

{
   HPS PSpace;
   POINTL Coord;
   CHAR ch;
   SHORT i;
   static char List[400] = "";
   char Number[25] = "";

   switch(mess)
   {
     case WM COMMAND:
       switch(SHORT1FROMMP(parm1))
       {
         case 101 :
           ifstream In("file1.txt");
           double Value;
           int N = 0;
           ostrstream Area(List,399);
           textspace Canvas(Area.rdbuf( ),handle);

           Canvas.setxy(10,300);
           Coord.y = 400;
           GpiSetColor(Canvas.space( ),CLR DARKCYAN);
           while(!In.eof( ) && !In.fail( ) && N < 10)
           {
             ostrstream Out(Number,24,ios::trunc);
             In >> Value;
             if(!In.eof( )){
               Out << Value;
             }
             Coord.y -= 15;
             Canvas.setxy(10,Coord.y);
             Canvas << Out.str( );
           }
```

```
            In.close( );
            break;
        }
    case WM ERASEBACKGROUND:
      return(MRESULT) TRUE;
    default:
      return WinDefWindowProc(handle,mess,parm1,parm2);
  }
  return(MRESULT) FALSE;
}

void main(void)
{
   HAB hand_ab;
   HMQ hand_mq;
   HWND hand_frame;
   QMSG q_mess;
   ULONG f1Flags;
   unsigned char Class[] = "MYCLASS";
   f1Flags = FCF MENU :
             FCF TITLEBAR :
             FCF SIZEBORDER :
             FCF MINMAX :
             FCF SYSMENU :
             FCF VERTSCROLL :
             FCF HORZSCROLL :
             FCF SHELLPOSITION;

   hand_ab = WinInitialize(0);
   hand_mq = WinCreateMsqQueue(hand_ab.0);
   if(!WinRegisterClass(hand_ab,
                        (PSZ) Class,
                        (PFNWP) window_func,
                        CS_SIZEREDRAW,
                        0)){
     exit(1);
   }
   hand_frame = WinCreateStdWindow(HWND DESKTOP,
                                   WS VISIBLE,
                                   &f1Flags,
                                   (PSZ) Class,
                                   (PSZ) "IOSTREAMS AND Presenta
                                         tion Manager"
                                   WS VISIBLE, 0,1, NULL);
   while(WinGetMsg(hand_ab, &g_mess, OL,0,0))
   {
     WinDispatchMsg(hand_ab,&g_mess);
   }
   WinDestroyWindow(hand_frame);
   WinDestroyMsgQueue(hand_mq);
   WinTerminate(hand_ab);
}
```

The declaration of the **Canvas** object starts most of the magic in the program in Listing 7.8. The constructor for **textspace** takes a pointer to a **streambuf** object as well as a handle to a window. The two arguments to the **textspace** constructor represent elements from the object-oriented stream world, as well as components from the Presentation Manager. The declaration of **Canvas** looks like:

```
textspace Canvas(Area.rdbuf( ),handle);
```

The constructor gets the handle of the presentation space for the window that is accessible by **WinHandle.** The constructor of **textspace** also initializes its **ostream** component with a pointer to an **ostrstream** object. The **ostrstream** object's buffer component becomes the buffer of the textspace Canvas object. These two actions by the constructor set up the presentation space and the **streambuf** component of the **ostream** object. The next important step in extending the **ostream** class is to overload the **<<** insertion operator. This overloaded function makes a call to the Presentation Manager to send the string that was inserted both to the **streambuf** component and to the presentation space that is connected to the **Canvas** object. The constructor, the overloaded **<<** insertor, and the encapsulation of the presentation space handle and the window handle demonstrate the basic steps in extending the IOSTREAM classes to include the page or space metaphor. Of course, these steps are not enough to make a full-blown presentation space object. There are many other considerations that have to be made. However, this object represents an approach to specializing the IOSTREAM family to include Presentation Manager or Windows-style I/O.

The program in Listing 7.8 extracts a list from a disk file. An **ifstream** class object, **In**, is used for this purpose. The file access functions in OS/2 are very similar to the standard nonobject-oriented file I/O functions in the C++ standard library. Therefore, those functions can be totally replaced by the object-oriented **ifstream**, **ofstream**, and **fstream** classes. As the list of numbers is being extracted, the numbers are being converted to strings during their insertion into the **Out ostrstream** object. Once the list is extracted, it is inserted into the **Canvas** using:

```
Canvas << Out.str( );
```

This insertion into the **Canvas textspace** object has the same interface as any other IOSTREAM insertion. This is another example of single interface multiple implementation. In this instance, the insertion operator paints a text string onto a presentation space. We will come back to the **textspace** object in Chapters 8 and 9, where we extend the IOSTREAMS to deal with bitmaps, color, and palettes.

CHAPTER 8

Multimedia Device Access

For there is reason to believe that these technologies might constitute the central phase in a postindustrial rite of passage between organically human and cyberpsychically digital lifeforms.

DAVID THOMAS—*OLD RITUALS FOR A NEW SPACE*

The premiere multimedia device is the graphic display unit. The graphic display unit is a combination of the graphic adapter chip or card and the graphic display technology that comes in the form of high-resolution monitors, multicolor monitors, and so on. To access the graphics display unit, there are two popular graphics APIs available that give the programmer full access to the visual representation power, the Presentation Manager GPI (Graphics Programming Interface), and the Windows GDI (Graphics Device Interface).

Windows Graphics Device Interface (GDI)

The **Windows GDI** offers a number of functions to accomplish device-independent graphics I/O programming. These functions can be categorized as:

- *Device context functions*
- *Drawing tool functions*
- *Color palette functions*
- *Drawing attribute functions*
- *Ellipse and polygon functions*
- *Mapping functions*
- *Coordinate functions*

217

- *Region functions*
- *Clipping functions*
- *Line-output functions*
- *Ellipse and polygon functions*
- *Bitmap functions*
- *Text functions*
- *Font functions*
- *Metafile functions*
- *Printer control functions*
- *Printer escape functions*
- *Environment functions*

Device Context Functions

The device context functions are used to create, delete, and restore the device context. These functions are used to access the output devices. The GDI passes calls to the device driver from the application, then the device driver translates these calls into operations that are executed by the hardware.

The DC (device context) data block contains information that describes the device context. There are a number of functions that affect or use this information from the DC data block. The device context attributes can describe the selected drawing objects, such as a brush, a font, and the font's color. They also describe other important information, such as the way objects are mapped or drawn to the device, and the clipping region. Device contexts can be saved by using the **SaveDC( )** function, and the **RestoreDC( )** function can be used to restore the saved device context. The **DeleteDC( )** function deletes the device context when passed a device context handle.

Compatible Device Contexts

Windows can treat a part of the memory as a virtual device by using the **CreateCompatibleDC( )** function. A device context is given the same attributes as a device with bitblt capabilities. In this case, there is no actual output device connected. The program using the compatible device context creates a bitmap for the device context. The output directed to this device context is drawn on the bitmap. The contents of the bitmap can be copied directly to the actual device once connected. The contents of the device can be copied to the bitmap. The bitmap can also be sent to memory before it is sent to a device.

Information Contexts

The **CreateIC( )** function is used to create an information context for a device. It is a device context that cannot write to a device. The information context can be used to gather information about a device. If an information context is created, the **Get-DeviceCaps( )** function can be used to extract the device technology, the color palette, the raster capabilities, and the physical size, along with other information about a device. The device handle and the capability request are parameters for this function.

Drawing Tools

The drawing tool functions can create and delete the tools the GDI uses when creating output for a device. A program can use a bitmap, a brush, or a pen when creating output. The brush and pen can be used together. The pen is used to outline an object, and the brush used to fill the object. The pen uses solid colors, and the brush or bitmap can use solid or a combination of colors. The combination of colors will depend on the capabilities of the output device. The GDI has seven predefined brushes, three predefined pens, and six predefined hatch patterns. The hatches can be used as a brush pattern. A hatch can be selected by using the **CreateHatchBrush( )** function. The **GetStockObject( )** function is used to select one of the predefined brushes or pens.

Drawing Attribute Functions

The drawing attribute functions affect the appearance and color of Windows output. The functions can set or return background color or mode, drawing color, text color, polygon filling mode, and the stretching mode.

The line output can be solid or broken. If the line output is broken, the space between the lines can be filled with a background mode and color. The brush output can be solid, hatched, or patterned. The space between the hatching can be filled similarly to the spaces between broken lines. When a brush is created, the color on the surface and the brush color are combined to create a new color. This is the default operation, but a different operation can be utilized by using the **SetROP2( )** function.

When a bitmap is copied to a device, it may be necessary to expand or shrink the bitmap before drawing to the device. The **SetStretchBltMode( )** function sets the stretch mode that will be used for the device. The **SetBkColor( )** function is used to set the color of the text background. Each text character is placed in a rectangular region called the *character cell*. The unused portion of the character cell has a color that is set by the **SetBkColor( )** function. The **SetTextColor( )** function sets the color of the actual character.

Mapping Functions

The mapping functions can alter or return information about the mapping modes. A logical output space is created and mapped to a display. Mapping modes determine the relationship between the units in logical space and the pixels on the device. There are eight mapping modes that define the logical units as physical units. These modes include MM_HIENGLISH mode, which defines a logical unit as $\frac{1}{1,000}$ of an inch on the device; MM_HIENGLISH, which defines a logical unit as $\frac{1}{100}$ of a millimeter on the device; and MM_TEXT mode, which defines a logical unit as a pixel on the device. These mapping modes are considered constrained because the scaling factor is fixed and the number of logical units mapped to the physical units cannot be altered by the program using them. Six of the eight mapping modes are constrained. MM_ISOTROPIC is a partially constrained mode and MM_ANISOTROPIC is an unconstrained mapping mode. A partially constrained mode means that the program using it has some control over the scaling factor, and an unconstrained mode means the program using it has complete control over the scaling factor.

Once the mapping mode has been set by using the **SetMapMode( )** function, the **SetViewportExt( )** and the **SetWindowExt( )** functions are used to set the *x* and *y* extents of the viewport and window. The *x* and *y* extents determine how much the GDI will stretch or compress the logical coordinate system units to fit the device coordinate system units. The *x* and *y* extents also determine the orientation of both axes in the logical and device coordinate systems. For example, if the *y* extent in the window is positive, and the *y* extent in the viewport is negative, the GDI will map the positive *y* axis of the logical coordinate system to the negative *y* axis on the device coordinate system. The **SetViewportExt( )** and the **SetWindowExt( )** functions have the device context handle and the *x* and *y* extents as parameters.

Coordinate Functions

The coordinate functions convert client coordinates to screen coordinates, screen coordinates to client coordinates, logical points to device points, and device points to logical points. The coordinate functions also determine the location of a point in a window or child window.

Region Functions

These functions can create, alter, or retrieve information about regions. *Regions* are polygonal areas within a window that can be filled with graphics output. They are used along with clipping functions. Creating a region includes creating an elliptical, polygonal, or rounded rectangular region. Altering the region includes combining two regions into a new region, filling a region with a brush pattern, inverting the color of the region, moving a region, or drawing a border around the region. Information retrieved about a region includes the coordinates of a bordering rectangle of a region, determining whether a point is within a region, or determining whether two regions are identical.

Clipping Functions

The clipping functions can create, test, or alter a clipping region. A clipping region is the part of the client area of a window where the GDI creates output. Any output sent outside the clipping region will not be visible. The **SelectClipRgn( )** function selects a clipping region. The **PtVisible( )** function determines whether a point is within a region. The **OffsetClipRgn( )** function moves a clipping region. The **RectVisible( )** function determines whether part of a rectangle is within a region. The **ExcludeClipRect( )** function will exclude a rectangle from a clipping region. The **GetClipBox( )** function copies the dimensions of a bounding rectangle. The **IntersectClipRect( )** function will form the intersection of a rectangle and a clipping region.

Line-Output Functions

The line-output functions create from a simple line to a complex line output using the selected pen. Some of these functions require the starting point and the ending point as coordinates. The line-output function coordinates are in logical units. The GDI maps the line from the logical coordinate system to the physical coordinate system on the device, using the selected mapping mode. The default map maps a logical unit to one pixel in physical space.

Ellipse and Polygon Functions

The ellipse and polygon functions create ellipses and polygons. The perimeter of the objects is drawn using the selected pen, and the interior of the object is filled with the selected brush. These functions also require that the coordinates are in logical units. These logical units are used by GDI to determine the location and size of the object in logical space. The mapping mode is used to map the object to the physical space. The default map maps a logical unit to one pixel in physical space.

Color

The value of a color in the Windows GDI has the form of COLORREF. The COLOR-REF value can determine a color in three ways:

- An explicit RGB value
- An index to logical-palette entry
- As a palette-relative RGB value

An explicitly expressed RGB value for a color is a long integer that contains red, green, and blue. The first low-order byte (8 bits) represents the intensity of red, the second order of bytes represents the intensity of green, and the third order of bytes represents the intensity of blue in the color. The lowest intensity value is 0 and the highest intensity value is 255. The RGB macro accepts the values of the intensities of the three primary colors and then returns an explicit RGB COLORREF value. A GDI can receive this value as a parameter. The function passes the COLORREF value to the device driver that selects the closest color from the physical color table.

The function **GetNearestColor( )** will return the closest logical color of a physical color a device can represent, given a logical color.

If a raster device cannot produce the color, dithering will be used to produce a color closest to it. Dithering is when the pixels of the color available to the device are mixed. If the device is monochrome, depending on the RGB value, the device driver will select black, white, or shades of gray. If the sum of the RGB value is zero, the device driver will select black. If the sum is 765, the driver will select white. If the sum is between zero and 765, the driver will select a shade of gray. The **GetRValue( )**, **GetGValue( )**, and the **GetBValue( )** functions will extract the red, green, and blue values from the RGB COLORREF value.

Palette in the GDI

The palette is an index of colors that are used at a given time. The Windows color palette is a buffer between the program using the colors and the system. The buffer allows the program to use as many colors as needed without it affecting the other Windows programs or its own color display. Windows will select the closest matching color from that palette for the inactive windows.

A program uses the system palette by creating and using one or more of the logical palettes. The program, instead of using the explicit RGB COLORREF value, will refer to the index in the logical palette. When a request is made for a color, Windows references the system palette for a match. This is called *realizing* the palette. The **RealizePalette( )** function is used to realize the palette. If a match is not possible, then an entry is made in the system palette if there is an unused entry available (meaning if there is an entry in the system palette that is not occupied by a color). If there are no available entries, Windows will attempt to match the color from the logical color palette with one of the color entries in the system palette. A match for the color for the foreground window or active window is attempted first. Other color requests from inactive windows are filled according to the window that had the most recent focus.

In order to use a palette, a logical color palette must be created before drawing objects to a display device. The **CreatePalette( )** function is used to create a palette. The **SelectPalette( )** function is called to select the palette for the device context for the output device. The GDI functions that request a color accept the index entry of the logical palette. This entry is a long integer value, where the first bit in the high order of the value is one, and the two low-order bytes are the palette index number. The PALETTEINDEX macro returns the palette entry number in the logical palette if given the COLORREF value.

A palette index can also be determined by using a palette-relative RGB COLORREF value. This value is identical to the explicit RGB COLORREF value, except that the second bit instead of the first bit of the high order is one.

The **GetPaletteEntries( )** function is used to retrieve entries from the logical palette. The **GetSystemPaletteEntries( )** function is used to retrieve a range of palette entries from the system palette. The **GetSystemPaletteUse( )** function is called to determine whether the program has access to the full system palette. To allow the program to use the full system palette, call the **SetSystemPaletteUse( )** function. The **UpdateColors( )** function performs a pixel-by-pixel translation of each pixel's current color to the system palette.

Bitmap Functions

The bitmap functions are used to display, create, load, or alter a bitmap. A *bitmap* is a matrix of memory that contains values representing pixels of color. This bitmap is copied with a given resolution to a corresponding matrix on the surface of any type of graphics device. The **CreateBitmap( )** function creates a bitmap. The program must provide the width, height, number of color planes, number of bits per pixel display, and an array that contains the initial bitmap bit values in the argument list. The **CreateBitmapIndirect( )** function creates a bitmap described in a data structure. The array that contains the initial bitmap bit values must be supplied in the argument list. The **LoadBitmap( )** function loads a bitmap from the resource file. The module's executable file that contains the bitmap and the character string name of the bitmap must be supplied in the argument list. The function **GetPixel( )** returns the RGB value of a pixel. The program must supply the handle to the device contexts and the logical x and y coordinates in the argument list. The **CreateBitmap( )**, **CreateBitmapIndirect( )**, **LoadBitmap( )**, and **GetPixel( )** are four of the 16 bitmap functions supplied by the GDI. The other bitmap functions include functions that copy bitmaps from a resource file, create bitmaps that are compatible with a specified device, fill surface within borders, create bit patterns, and return dimensions of a bitmap and the bits in memory for a specific bitmap.

The GDI provides functions that translate the *DIB* (device-independent bitmap) specification into a device-specific format. The DIB specification is composed of two components: The first component is the **BitmapInfo** data structure that determines the format and the optional table of colors for the bitmap. The second component is an array of bytes that contain the bitmap values. The bitmap values can be the color values or the indexes of the color table. The bitmap translating functions can create a device-specific memory bitmap from a DIB specification by using the **CreateDIBitmap( )** function. The bits in memory for a specific bitmap from a DIB are returned by the **GetDIBits( )** function. The **SetDIBits( )** function set the bits of a bitmap to the values given in a DIB specification. The **SetDIBitsToDevice( )** function sets the bits from a DIB directly on a device surface. The **StretchDIBits( )** function moves a DIB from a rectangle into another rectangle compressing or stretching the bitmap to fit it into the destination rectangle.

Text Functions

The text functions return and compute information about the text, alter the text justification, alter the text alignment, and write the text on a device or some type of display surface. The **GetTabbedTextExtent( )**, **GetTextAlign( )**, **GetTextExtent( )**,

GetTextFace( ), and **GetTextMetrics( )** functions return and compute information about the text. They compute such information as the width and height of text without tab characters, as well as a string of text with the tab characters. The text functions can return the mask of the text alignment flags with the **GetTextAlign( )** function. The font name can be copied to a buffer with the **GetTextFace( )** function. The **GetTextMetrics( )** function fills the buffer with the metrics of the selected font. The **TextOut( )** function writes character strings using the current font. The **SetTextJustification( )** function justifies a line of text.

Font Functions

The font functions can select, remove, create, or return information about the fonts. Fonts are the subset of a typeface. Typeface is a set of characters that share a common design. The typeface and fonts are categorized. The font functions can add a font resource to the system font table or remove a font from the table, create a logical font, and list the fonts that are available on a given device. The font functions can also return the width of individual characters and alter the algorithm the font mapper uses. Each character is contained in a rectangular space called the *character cell*. Each character cell has a specific number of rows and columns and six points of measurement: ascent, baseline, descent, origin, height, and width. The height and width of the font are referring to the height and width of the character cells. The characters can be altered by changing the shape and size. The fonts can be italic, bold, underlined, and strike-out. Strike-out means that a horizontal line is drawn through each character. Leading can be added. Leading is the distance between the baselines of two adjacent rows of text.

Metafile Functions

A metafile is an aggregate of GDI commands that create text or images. A metafile stores the graphics commands used to create text or an image. The metafile functions can create, delete, copy, retrieve, play, and return information about metafiles. These metafiles can be used in programs that repeatedly use a specific text or image. They can also be used repeatedly on a number of different devices. A metafile must be created in a special device context. The **CreateMetaFile( )** function is used to return the device context of a metafile. The functions used in a metafile is a subset of functions the GDI uses to create output. The device context for a metafile uses the default attributes of the output device in use when the metafile is played.

Metafiles can be deleted from memory by using the **DeleteMetaFile( )** function. The metafile is deleted from memory and the device handle is invalidated. Windows can change the way metafiles are played. The **EnumMetaFile( )** function can be used to return information about a specific metafile. The information returned can be used to modify, query, copy, or play a single record in the metafile. The **PlayMetaFile-Record( )** function can be used to play the single record.

Printer Control Functions

The printer control functions are used to return information about a printer and modify the initialization state. The printer driver provides the information. The **DeviceCapabilities( )** function returns the capabilities of a printer device driver. The **DeviceMode( )** function sets the printing modes for a device. The **ExtDevice-Mode( )** function returns or changes the device initialization information for a specific printer driver.

Printer Escape Function

The Escape function allows a program to access the facilities of a specific device that is not available through the GDI. The program calls the Escape for the printer device context, and the function regulates the flow of printer output from the Window program. It returns the information about the printer, then changes the settings of the printer.

Environment Functions

These functions can alter and return information about the environment that is associated with an output device. The **GetEnvironment( )** function copies environment information into a buffer. The **SetEnvironment( )** function copies the data to the environment associated with the attached device.

OS/2 Graphics Programming Interface (GPI)

The OS/2 Presentation Manager Graphics Programming Interface (GPI), like the Windows GDI, offers the programmer more than 200 functions to accomplish device-independent graphics programming. The Presentation Manager provides an extra layer of abstraction called the *presentation space* that is connected to an associated device context. The device context translates the presentation space device-independent information to device-dependent information that is sent to the device drivers for the displaying and printing of graphics primitives. The presentation space makes calls to the number of GPI functions that can be divided into these categories:

- Presentation spaces and device context
- Graphics primitives
- Line and arc primitives
- Area primitives and polygons
- Character string primitives and fonts
- Marker primitives
- Color and mix attributes

- Bitmaps and metafiles
- Paths and regions
- Retained and nonretained graphics
- Correlation
- Clipping and boundary determination
- Coordinate spaces and transformation operations and functions
- Print job submission and manipulation

Presentation Space and Device Context Functions

A presentation space is a data structure in which information about the graphics output is stored. A presentation space is needed for each output device as well as for each window on the display screen. There are three different types of presentation spaces: *standard micropresentation space, cached micropresentation space,* and a *normal presentation space.* There are functions that are used for each type of presentation space.

The standard micropresentation space is created for drawing on any type of output device, as long as the space is not in retain mode or retain and draw mode. The **GpiCreatePS( )** function is used to create a standard micropresentation space. This function accepts an anchor handle, a device context handle, and the size of the presentation space. The **GpiDestroyPS( )** function is used to close the space. The **WinGetScreenPS( )** function is used when the presentation space will represent the entire display screen. The **WinReleasePS( )** function is used to close the space.

The cached micropresentation space is created when an application uses a large number of windows, and each window needs a temporary space and device context for a short sequence of operations. These spaces will belong to the system instead of the program, and are allocated on a temporary basis. These spaces are for output only to a window on a display device. The **WinBeginPaint( )** function is used in response to a WM_PAINT message. The space is created and automatically associated with a window device context. The **WinEndPaint( )** function can close any type of presentation space. The **WinGetScreenPS( )** and the **WinReleasePS( )** function can also be used with this type of space. The **WinGetPS( )** function is used when the space represents the entire desktop or any other window. The **WinReleasePS( )** function can also be used to close the space.

The normal presentation space is created when the program requires the same presentation space to send output to multiple devices. The **GpiCreatePS( )** function can be used to create this type of space, and the **GpiDestroyPS( )** function is used to close the space.

The presentation space has to be connected to a device context in order for graphics to be displayed or printed. When they are linked, any graphics directed to the space will automatically be sent to the device context and displayed on the output device. There are three types of device contexts associated with the three types of presentation spaces: *cached, window,* and *normal* device contexts.

The device context can be obtained or created, associated with a space, and closed. The **DevOpenDC( )** function creates a nondisplay device context. The **Dev-CloseDC( )** function is used to close the device context. If a device context was created by the **WinOpenWindowDC( )** function, this type of device context will automatically be deleted when the space for that context is deleted.

The device context can retrieve information about the capabilities of the device. The **DevQueryCaps( )** function can retrieve the device technology of an output device, or determine whether the device is raster or vector. It can retrieve the maximum window dimensions of a video display device, the page dimensions, the character-box dimensions, and the dimensions of a marker-box. The pel resolution, color capabilities, and the mix-mode capabilities can also be retrieved by this function.

Graphic Primitives

There are four different types of graphics primitives: *lines and arcs, areas, text,* and *marker symbols.* The line and arc primitives are for drawing simple objects. They are governed by the attributes found in the LINEBUNDLE data structure. These attributes are: line width, geometric width, line type, line end, line join, line color, and line mix. All of these attributes, except line end and line join, have default settings but can be redefined. The **GpiLineWidth( )** and **GpiLineWidthGeom( )** functions are used to redefine the line width and geometric width. The **GpiSetLineType( )** can set the line type. The **GpiSetAttrs( )** functions that have an LBB_COLOR as a parameter sets the color. The same function name with an LBB_MIX_MODE parameter sets the line-mix attribute.

In addition to the attributes that an arc primitive shares with a line, the arc primitive also has other attributes: circles and ellipses. Multiple arcs contain a *fillet*, which is a curve that is tangential to the two lines defined by three control points. *Splines* are curves that are tangential to the first and last of three intersecting lines. A unit circle at the point of origin is used to define a full arc, partial arc, or three-point arc. The **GpiFullArc( )** function is used to create a full arc. The **GpiPartialArc( )** function is used to create a partial arc, and the **GpiPointArc( )** function is used to create a three-point arc. The **GpiSetArcParams( )** function is used to set the shape, orientation, size, and drawing direction of the arc.

An area primitive can be created, outlined, and filled with custom-filled patterns from a bitmap or a font symbol. The attributes of an area primitive are defined by the data structure AREABUNDLE that contains pattern symbol, pattern reference point, pattern set, foreground color, background color, foreground mix attribute, and background mix mode. All of these attributes have a default setting but can be redefined. The **GpiSetPattern( )** function can set the pattern symbol. The **GpiSetPatternRefPoint( )** function can set the pattern reference point. The **GpiSetPatternSet( )** can set the pattern set. The **GpiSetAttrs( )** function with an ABB_COLOR parameter can define the foreground color. The same function name with an ABB_BACK_COLOR parameter can set the background color. The same function name with an ABB_MIX_MODE parameter can define the foreground mix, and the **GpiSetAttrs( )** function with the ABB_BACK_MIX_MODE parameter can define the background color mix.

The text or character primitives are printed or displayed, and are limited to a length of 256 characters. The text appearance is determined by the font settings chosen. Other attributes concerning the fonts can be set in the CHARBUNDLE data structure. The attributes this structure contains are character set, character mode, character cell, character angle, character shear, character direction, character text alignment, character extra, character break extra, foreground color, background color, foreground color mix, and background color mix. The character mode defines the extent to which a font can be affected by the attributes in the CHARBUNDLE data structure.

All the attributes in the CHARBUNDLE data structure have default values that can be reset by calls to their corresponding functions. The **GpiSetCharSet( )** function can redefine the character set attribute. The **GpiSetCharMode( )** function sets the character mode. The **GpiSetCharBox( )** function sets the dimensions of a character cell. The **GpiSetCharAngle( )** function defines the angle of the character. The angle is defined by the x axis and a vector drawn through the point of origin to a specified point. The **GpiSetCharShear( )** function sets the angle formed by the vertical lines of the character cell. The character shear can affect the positioning and the shape of the characters in a string. The **GpiSetCharDirection( )** function defines the direction of the character string in relation to the baseline. This direction can be from left to right (default direction), right to left, top to bottom, or bottom to top. The **GpiSetText-Alignment( )** function defines the alignment of the characters, with respect to the boundary of the output. The **GpiSetCharExtra( )** and the **GpiSetCharBreakExtra( )** functions specify the space between the character cells. The space between words can be increased by increasing the size of the break character. The colors of the background, foreground, and color mixes are set by the **GpiSetAttrs( )** function accepting a CBB_COLOR parameter to set the foreground color; CBB_BACK_COLOR parameter to set the background color; CBB_MIX_MODE parameter to set the mix of the foreground; and the CBB_BACK_MIX_MODE parameter to set the background color mix.

Marker primitives are small objects the same size as a system font and are used to indicate plotted points on a line graph. The **GpiMarker( )** function draws a marker at the center of a point specified by its argument. That point becomes the new current position when a marker is drawn. The **GpiPolyMarker( )** function draws multiple markers in a presentation space. The attributes of the marker primitives are contained in the data structure MARKERBUNDLE. The attributes in this structure are: marker symbol, marker box, marker set, foreground and background color, and the foreground and background color mix.

All the marker attributes have corresponding functions that redefine their values from the default values. The **GpiSetMarker( )** function sets the type of marker symbol. The default symbol is a cross. There are 11 different marker symbols including an eight-point star, a solid diamond, a small circle, and a square. The **GpiSetMarker-Box( )** function sets the size of the marker. The default size is the size of one character. The **GpiSetMarkerSet( )** function sets which marker sets will be used. The **GpiSetAtrrs( )** function also sets the foreground and background color and color mix used.

Colors and Mix Attributes

Mix attributes control how primitives are combined with already existing drawings. They also affect the way colors result when primitives of different colors overlap. Foreground and background attributes also have mix attributes.

Color is implemented in Presentation Manager in much the same way as already explained. The RGB components of a color are stored in either an RGB or RGB2 data structure or in a long integer 32-bit value. The color fields in this integer value and RGB2 work in the same way. The first byte in the RGB value, stored as a long integer, is a flag value set to 0. The remaining 24 bits are for the color intensities.

A logical color table is assigned to a presentation space. These colors are the colors that will be specifically used for that space. When a program uses color from the logical color table, the Presentation Manager maps the index from the logical color table to the closest match in the physical color table. The table contains a number of entries, each of which will represent a different RGB color. The Presentation Manager has a default color table (Table 8.1). The first three entries in the table, CLR_DEFAULT, CLR_BACKGROUND, and CLR_NEUTRAL, are used in a program for the purpose they serve, not for the colors they represent. The purpose does not change from device to device even though the color that fulfills that purpose may be different. The CLR_BACKGROUND color for a device will be the natural background color for that device. For example, for a printer, the natural background color is white, which is also the natural background color for a window. CLR_NEUTRAL and CLR_DEFAULT are the natural foreground colors or contrasting colors. For a printer or a window, this would be black.

A logical color table can be redefined in three ways: The default color table can be entirely replaced or partly replaced; color definitions can be added to the default color table; or the logical color table can be reset to the default color table. The **GpiCreateLogColorTable( )** function can be used to do this. In order to add to the table or replace some of the colors, an array of color indexes and their associated colors is supplied to this function. To replace or add to the table, the program would call the **GpiCreateLogColorTable( )** function with an LCOLF_INDRGB argument. The program passes an array of indexes and the associated colors. The indexes do not have to be consecutive. If the program wants to replace a section of the table, the **GpiCreateLogColorTable( )** function is called with the LCOLF_CONSECRGB argument. The program passes an array of the RGB values and the starting index position. The values will be placed in the table, starting with the index and consecutively replacing the color values. When referring to color by the index, the logical color table would have to be in the INDEX MODE. When passing a color to GPI functions, the index of the color is used. If the actual values of the colors are to be used, the logical color table will have to be in the RGM MODE.

Table 8.1 Default Color Table for Presentation Manager's GPI

Color Index	Index Number	Effect
CLR_FALSE	–5	All bits are set to 0.
CLR_TRUE	–4	All bits are set to 1.
CLR_DEFAULT	–3	Default value
CLR_WHITE	–2	White
CLR_BLACK	–1	Black
CLR_BACKGROUND	0	Natural background color for the device
CLR_BLUE	1	Blue
CLR_RED	2	Red
CLR_PINK	3	Pink
CLR_GREEN	4	Green
CLR_CYAN	5	Cyan
CLR_YELLOW	6	Yellow
CLR_NEUTRAL	7	Neutral—The contrasting color to CLR_BACKGROUND
CLR_DARKGRAY	8	Dark gray
CLR_DARKBLUE	9	Dark blue
CLR_DARKRED	10	Dark red
CLR_DARKPINK	11	Dark pink
CLR_DARKGREEN	12	Dark green
CLR_DARKCYAN	13	Dark cyan
CLR_BROWN	14	Brown
CLR_PALEGRAY	15	Pale gray

The foreground color can be set by using the **GpiSetColor( )** function. The function call requires either the index from the logical color table or the RGB value for the color. This will depend on the mode the logical color table is in. A color from the system color table can also be specified. A foreground color for a specific primitive type can be set by using the **GpiSetAttrs( )** function. The background color is set by using the **GpiSetBackColor( )** function. The **GpiQueryBackColor( )** function can be used to determine the background color of a character, and **GpiQueryColor( )** function can be used to determine the foreground color of a character. These functions should be used to ensure the primitive color is different from the background color. To determine the background or foreground colors of a certain type of primitive, the **GpiQueryAttrs( )** function is used.

There are a number of functions that retrieve information about the color tables. The **GpiQueryColorData( )** function can be used to get information about the logical and physical color tables. This function can return the format of the current logical color table, and the smallest and largest indexes in the logical color table. The smallest number is 0, and the largest number is never less than 15. The **GpiQueryRealColors( )** function returns the RGB value of each of the colors in the physical color table. The **GpiQueryNearestColor( )** function, with an RGB value as the parameter, will return the RGB value of the physical color table closest to that color. To determine which colors are in the physical color table, call the **GpiQueryRealColor( )** function. The **GpiQueryRGBColor( )** function will return the RGB value of an index in the logical color table. The value returned will be the RGB value from the physical color table that the index would reference.

To change the physical color table, the program calls the **GpiCreatePalette( )** function. This function can also prevent dithering by setting the LCOL_PURECOLOR in the flag. For all 256 colors, the flag can be set to LCOL_OVERRIDE_DEFAULT_COLORS. The values in the palette can be changed by using the **GpiSetPaletteEntries( )** function. To delete the palette, pass the palette handle to the **GpiDeletePalette( )** function. If complete information about the palette is needed, the **GpiQueryPaletteInfo( )** function is called.

Foreground and background colors can be mixed. The mix attribute is a bitwise operation on the color indexes in the device's logical color table. The bits are ORed (OR), exclusive ORed (XOR), and AND together to produce a color mix. There are 17 foreground mix attributes, and four background mix attributes. The overpaint mix attribute will replace color instead of mixing the colors. This is the default mix attribute.

Bitmaps and Metafiles Functions

To display a bitmap image, the display device must be of a type *raster device*. A raster device displays images that are composed of pixels. It is different from a *vector device* that displays images composed of lines. The Presentation Manager has functions that work with both raster and vector images.

Bitmaps can be created by an application, or by using the PM Icon Editor. To create a bitmap in a program, the **DevOpenDC( )** function is called to create a memory device context. A graphics presentation space is then associated with the memory device context. The **GpiCreateBitmap( )** function is used to define the bitmap, and the **GpiSetBitmap( )** function is used to designate the bitmap as the current selected memory device context. Then, the drawing functions are used to draw objects to the presentation space of the bitmap. The **GpiBitBlt( )** function copies the bitmap from the presentation space to the device contexts associated with a screen. The image appears on the video display.

Bitmaps can be drawn on a raster display screen or printer by using the **GpiImage( )** and **WinDrawBitmap( )** functions. **WinDrawBitmap( )** will draw a bitmap image by copying the image into a window that is linked to a target presentation space. The **GpiImage( )** function draws a nonstandard, monochrome bitmap. The bitmaps are stored in the opposite order from the standard bitmap. In this case, the first pel is the upper left corner of the bitmap image. Bitmaps are transferred using the **GpiDrawBits( )**, **GpiBitBlt( )**, and **GpiWCBitBlt( )** functions. The **GpiDraw-Bits( )** function copies a bitmap image data from storage into a bitmap that has been selected into a device context associated with a space or to a device. The **GpiBit-Blt( )** function directs a bitmap to devices other than the screen. It can take part of a bitmap and change the size and the appearance in the process of copying it to another device context. The **GpiBitBlt( )** function can copy a bitmap from a memory to another memory device context. It can copy a bitmap from a memory to the device context of an output device, and vice versa. It can also copy a bitmap from one device context of a device to another device context of a device. The **Gpi-WCBitBlt( )** function retains the bitmap data in the segment store of the target presentation space.

Metafiles contain the instructions that contribute to the final version of a picture. When a graphics program executes an image, the image is lost. Metafiles retain a picture after the program has executed the image. They are in three forms: a *memory metafile*, a *disk metafile*, and an *editable metafile*. The memory metafile exists in memory and is managed by the Presentation Manager. A disk metafile exists on a disk as a file with an .MET extension. A editable metafile is loaded into the program's memory and is editable by the program.

The metafile saves the resources that are associated with the image. A program that is not retaining segments can use a metafile. Metafiles are available while the program is running, regardless of how many presentation spaces are being used. If the metafile is given the exact same starting conditions as the presentation space, an identical picture will be retained and executed. Different processes and threads within a program can display an image stored in a metafile without having to own the metafile. Images that are used often in a program could be stored in a metafile.

Metafiles, unlike bitmaps, which store information on a pixel-by-pixel basis, store image information graphics commands called *graphics orders* that the operating system uses to construct the picture. Graphics orders are graphics functions, including attribute setting instructions that create the picture. The metafile's contents are similar to the contents in a presentation space. It can contain data generated from a GPI function. Any information that is not of a graphic nature is ignored by the metafile. The images stored in the metafile can be redrawn by executing the contents of the metafile, a process called *playing the metafile*. The **GPIPlayMetafile( )** function is used to play the metafile. This function requires the metafile handle, a byte count of a descriptive record, and a descriptive record as parameters. The descriptive record is a natural-language description of the picture's contents. The array specifies how the operating system alters your application's presentation space before playing the metafile.

Path and Region Functions

A path is a collection of graphics primitives that are stored in GPI memory. The path attributes are not stored in a separate data structure, such as line or area. The path attributes are stored in both the LINEBUNDLE and the AREABUNDLE data structures. The purpose of the path determines the attributes that are in effect. Type, color, and mix mode take effect only when a path is outlined using the **GpiOutlinePath( )** function. The end, geometric width, and join take effect only when a path is converted to a geometric wide line, using the **GpiStrokePath( )** or **GpiModifyPath( )** function.

The operations performed on a path define the applicable path attributes. The operations require separate function calls instead of specifying the options with the **GpiBeginPath( )** function. These operations can be performed on a path: outline, fill, modify, stroke, convert to clip path, and convert to region. These operations are performed by the **GpiOutlinePath( )**, **GpiFillPath( )**, **GpiModifyPath( )**, **GpiStrokePath( )**, **GpiSetClipPath( )**, and the **GpiPathToRegion( )** functions, respectively. Once these functions are performed, the paths are deleted.

Regions are composed of one or more rectangles used to define clipping boundaries in device coordinates for multiple intersecting rectangles. The sides of the rectangle are parallel to the x and y axes of the coordinate space. Regions are device-dependent and defined in device coordinates. The regions are created for the device currently associated with the presentation space.

The regions, like paths, do not have a separate data structure containing their attributes. Regions provide a definition of an operation. They can be identified as visible entities by using the **GpiPaintRegion( )** or **GpiFrameRegion( )** function. The **GpiPaintRegion( )** function paints the region in the presentation space. The functions have a region handle as a parameter. The **GpiFrameRegion( )** function draws a frame around a region by tracing the inner perimeter with a rectangle. The function accepts a handle to a region, and the frame thickness. The attributes of the region are stored in the AREABUNDLE data structure.

The region has operations that can be performed on it. The operations are: creating regions; drawing regions; moving regions; determining region characteristics; converting a path to a region; converting a region to a clip region; and deleting regions. The **GpiCreateRegion( )** function defines the region. The function has a total number of rectangles and the coordinates of each rectangle that contributes to the region. The **GpiCreateRegion( )** function returns a handle to the region created. To delete a region, the **GpiDestroyRegion( )** function is used. The **GpiDestroyRegion( )** function has the region handle as the parameter. A region can be moved by using the **GpiOffsetRegion( )** function. The function has a region handle and an offset value that is added to every coordinate point of the region. There are a number of functions that are used to determine the characteristics of the region.

Retained and Nonretained Graphics

Retained and nonretained graphics are the two types of graphics output. In retained graphics, the entire graphics picture is stored for additional displays and editing in a presentation space model. Retained graphics are stored in segments. Therefore, the images can be altered and part of the image erased without having to re-create the whole image. The image can be created with a single function call. The call accesses the storage area of the image that contains all the GPI functions used to create the image. The image can be redrawn in any number of segments for any number of device contexts. These segments can be scaled, moved, or rotated, and recorded in a metafile.

To create retained graphics, the drawing mode should be in either the retain mode, or the draw-and-retain mode. In the retain mode, graphics are drawn and retained in a segment. They are not sent to a device context for immediate display on an output device. In the draw-and-retain mode, the graphics are drawn on the output device and stored in a segment. The **GpiOpenSegment( )** function is used to signal the start of a graphics segment. Once the segment is opened, the subsequent function calls become a part of the retained graphics. A presentation space can have a number of segments. Each segment will have its own segment attribute values. New elements can be added to the graphics segments, or they can be altered.

Nonretained graphics are immediately sent to the output device. For these graphics, if part of the picture is erased or needs to be repeated, the program must re-create the entire picture with the GPI function calls. When using the nonretained graphics, all the attribute segments are set to OFF. They can also be recorded in a metafile. They can be drawn in a draw mode, or a draw-and-retain mode. While the primitives are being drawn, they are considered to be in a retain mode. Once drawn, they are considered retained. Nonretained graphics can be easily converted to retained graphics.

Correlation

Correlation is the process of determining which primitives in a picture are at a specified position on the display. The process will be different if the primitive is a retained or nonretained graphic. Before the primitive is drawn, the presentation space must be in a state that supports correlation if dealing with nonretained graphics. The correlation would have to be performed while the graphics are being drawn. When dealing with retained graphics, segments can be replayed. The correlation can be performed after the primitives are drawn.

When performing correlation on nonretained graphics, the **GpiSetDrawControl( )** function is called in order to switch on the correlation flag. Then, the **GpiAperture-Size( )** function is called to change the size of the aperture if necessary. The **GpiSet-AperturePosition( )** function is called to position the aperture. The *pick aperture* is the area of interest. It is a small rectangle around a coordinate position sent to the program by the operating system. The correlation determines what object is in the area of interest. The coordinate position is the argument for the **GpiSetAperturePosition( )** function.

Since the retained graphics can be redrawn, a correlation state for the presentation space is not necessary. Correlations for retained graphics are processed through the segment IDs and tags throughout the segment. To correlate for retained graphics, the **GpiOpenSegment( )** function is called. Then, the **GpiSetSegmentAttrs( )** function is called to set the attributes of the segment. Finally, the **GpiSetTag( )** function is called at the appropriate locations within the segment. This function inserts a tag, a long integer value, at the current element pointer position. The tag is an identifier for the primitives. It becomes a part of the segment.

Clipping Boundary Determination

There are different types of clip areas. The *clip path* is for world coordinates. The clipping area can have curved edges. The clipping area can be rotated. The *viewing limit* is for model space. The clipping boundary is always rectangular. They can also be rotated. The *graphics field* is for page space, and the *clip region* is for device space. Each type of clipping area has functions associated with it.

The **GpiBeginPath( )**, **GpiModifyPath( )**, and **GpiSetClipPath( )** functions, along with line and arc functions, are used by the clip path clipping areas. The **GpiBegin-Path( )** function is used to begin the path definition. The **GpiEndPath( )** function is used to end the path definition. The **GpiModifyPath( )** function is used before the path is converted to a clip path. When modified, the line is converted to a geometric line by using the current geometric width, line-join, and line-end attributes. Then the shape is used for the clip path.

The viewing limit window is defined with the **GpiSetViewingLimits( )** function. When a line intersects the viewing window, the part of the line outside the window is clipped. The points on the boundary window are not clipped, as they are considered part of the window. The viewing window does not clip by default. All graphic objects are transformed to the model space.

The graphics field is defined by the **GpiSetGraphicsField( )** function. This type of clipping area has to be defined before any drawing takes place. Only the graphics in this clipping area will be visible on the output device. Intersecting lines to this clipping area will be clipped if outside the area. If on the boundary, they are considered part of the area.

Coordinate Space and Transformation Functions

Most GPI draws the output in a conceptual area called a *world coordinate space*. The world coordinate space is a Cartesian coordinate grid mapped on the presentation space for scaling the object being drawn. Each component of the image is called a *subpicture*. The subpicture is scaled to the world coordinate space in a way that is convenient for that subpicture. Each subpicture can be scaled separately, starting at the point of origin (0,0). Thus, a separate world coordinate space exists for each subpicture. The subpicture is transformed in order to be displayed on the output device. Transformations are operations performed on an object, which change the object in four ways: translation, rotation, scaling, and shearing. The transformation allows the program to control the location, size, orientation, and shape of the object on the output device. There are five coordinate spaces and transformations that can transform an object from one space to another.

Most drawing coordinates occupy the world coordinate space. The world coordinate space is specified when the presentation space is crated. There are two types of world coordinate spaces: short and long. The short world coordinate space has a maximum coordinate of (32767,32767) and a minimum coordinate of (–32768, –32768). The long world coordinate space has a maximum coordinate of (134217727, 134217727) and a minimum coordinate of (–134217728,–134217728). The world coordinates do not have to be within the range of the presentation space. Transformations are performed to scale the image.

Model space is where the separate components of a picture are brought together conceptually. To place an object from world coordinate space to model coordinate space, the appropriate transformation is used. Even if the object has components that have separate world coordinate spaces, they can be transformed. If a program has more than one model space, the components are placed in page space. Page space is where a complete picture is placed for viewing on display output devices. The page coordinate units can be pixels, inches, meters, or some other physical measurement.

Device space is the coordinate space where a picture is drawn before it appears in a display screen window or a printer. The units are device-specific units. The units can also be physical measurements as well as pixels, depending on the page units.

Media space is used for a window only. When a program draws an image in a window, at a certain location, it is not drawn in the device space. Shifting transformations are used to draw an object in a window. This moves the object from the given unitless position to a location in the window.

Print and Job Submission and Manipulation

OS/2 operating system print subsystems are composed of the following software components of the operating system: spooler, print subsystem user interface, queue drivers, printer drivers, file system, and the kernel device drivers. The *spooler* is the central coordinating process for the print subsystem. It can print output from two separately executing programs. The spooler can print in the background while the user continues to use the program. It can send jobs from the Presentation Manager across a network to a remote server. It can support a number of printers simultaneously.

The *print subsystems user interface* is composed of printer objects. The spooler will implement each object by using a queue. The queue is connected to a logical device that has the configuration data for the device.

The *queue driver* is used to take print jobs from a queue and print the data using the printer driver. The printer driver knows all the specifications of the printer it supports. Each printer driver is unique for each printer supported by the operating system. The file system is involved in both the spooling process and the printing process. The file system intercepts the data when a non-Presentation Manager program creates print data and places it in the queue. The file system sends the data to the appropriate file or device after a printer driver has processed the print job. The *kernel device drivers* are the device drivers for physical devices: the parallel port driver and the serial port driver.

Logical Characteristics of the Graphics Adapter Card

The graphics adapter is the hardware circuitry that gives a computer the capability of displaying graphic images along with text. Regardless of the type of graphic display—gas plasma, liquid crystal, or active or passive matrix—they will all have some fundamental logical concepts. Some of those logical concepts are *pixels, resolution, color model, foreground and background color,* and *palettes.*

Pixels and Resolution

The graphic images and text are placed on a grid of vertical and horizontal lines. The horizontal lines are composed of dots or picture elements called *pixels.* The number of horizontal lines and the number of pixels per line determine the *resolution.* The higher the number of pixels per horizontal line, and the higher the number of horizontal lines, the greater the resolution. A high resolution means that a graphic image can display more detail.

The graphic images and text are placed on a grid of vertical and horizontal lines. Each pixel is represented by a coordinate pair. The pair are two numbers describing the location of the pixel on the display grid or *coordinate system.* The first number in the pair represents the location on the x axis of the coordinate system. The x axis runs horizontally on the display unit. The second number in the pair represents the location on the y axis. The y axis runs vertically on the display unit. The point of origin (0,0) will be either at the top left corner or the lower left corner of the display unit. The resolution of a graphics adapter can be determined by the maximum x value and the maximum y value.

Colors

Graphics adapters have different ways of storing color in memory. The type of graphics adapter or chip will determine the type of memory organization the adapter uses for color. Some adapters are based on *multiplane-per-pixel* display memory. For these types of adapters, four separate graphic images are stored in memory. Each image is called a *bit plane.* Each bit plane stores an image in one of the primary colors, and some adapters have an intensity level plane. The standard VGA adapter is an adapter that uses this technology. Most super VGA graphics adapters are based on the *multibit-per-pixel* display memory. There is only one bit plane. A number of bits represent each of the primary colors. The primary color values adjacent to each other will represent a color.

Colors are defined as *bit patterns.* These bit patterns represent the percentage of the primary color required to produce a color. These percentages, or *intensities,* of colors can range from 0 to 100 percent. For example, if the display hardware uses 24 bits to determine a color, 8 bits would be used to represent the intensity of each of the three primary colors. The values would start from 00000000, which means the absence (0 percent) of that primary color, to 11111111, which means the full intensity (100 percent) of that primary color. This range of values is 0 to 255. If 16 bits were used to determine a color, 5 bits would represent the intensity of each of the three primary colors. The values would start from 00000 to 1111. This range of values is 1 to 15.

The bit pattern for a pixel determines the color, and helps in determining the number of possible colors that can be displayed by the graphics adapter device. For adapters that use the *multibit-per-pixel*, display memory can raise 2 to the power of the number of bits per pixel. For example, adapters that use a 24-bit pattern to determine a color could use this formula:

$2^{24} = 16,777,216$ possible colors

The three primary colors can be from different color systems. The color systems for defining the primary colors are called *color models*. The color models can be RGB, CMY, HSI, or HSB. The RGB color model means that red, green, and blue are the primary colors. The CMY color model means that cyan, magenta, and yellow are the primary colors. The HSI color model represents color as hue, saturation, and intensity. The HSB color model represents color as hue, saturation, and blackness. The RGB color model uses an *additive primary system* to generate color, and CMY uses a *subtractive primary system* to generate color. The additive primary system means that color is generated by combining the three primary colors in various amounts. The subtractive primary system means that color is generated by removing parts of the white light spectrum. Table 8.2 shows the important color models and their descriptions.

From the possible colors, a selection of colors is made that will be used by a program. The number of the selection is determined by the number of colors the device is capable of displaying simultaneously. The color selection is called the *palette*. Some graphics adapters that have a large number of colors shown simultaneously do not use palettes. The different types of graphics adapters each has its own resolution, color, and palette capabilities. Table 8.3 shows the different types of graphics adapters and their display capabilities.

Table 8.2 Important Color Models and Their Descriptions

Model	Description
RGB	Red, green, and blue primaries. An additive primary system.
CMY(K)	Cyan, magenta, and yellow (and black). A subtractive primary system.
YCbCR	Luminance (Y) and two chrominance components (Cb and Cr; used in television broadcasting.)
HSB	Hue, saturation, and brightness. A model based on human perception of color.
HLS	Hue, lightness, and saturation; similar to HSB.

Table 8.3   **Different Graphics Adapters, the Number of Possible Colors, and the Type of Display Memory**

Resolution	Number of Colors	Graphics Adapters
320×200	256	VGA, MCGA
320×200	16	VGA, EGA
640×200	2	VGA
640×200	16	VGA, EGA
640×350	4	VGA
640×350	2	VGA, EGA
640×350	16	VGA, EGA
640×400	256	SVGA
640×480	2	VGA, MCGA
640×480	16	VGA, XGA, XGA-2
640×480	256	8514/A, XGA, XGA-2
640×480	65,536	XGA-2
800×600	2	SVGA
800×600	16	SVGA
800×600	256	SVGA
1024×768	2	SVGA
1024×768	4	SVGA
1024×768	16	SVGA, XGA, XGA-2
1024×768	256	8514/A, SVGA, XGA, XGA-2
1280×1024	16	XGA-2

Palette (Logical Color Tables)

There are two types of color tables: a *physical color table* and a *logical color table*. A physical color table consists of the possible colors that can be generated by a graphics display adapter or chip. For adapters that can display a large number of colors simultaneously, the physical table is a subset of all the possible colors. The logical color table contains the color that will be used by the program. The logical color table for a program can also be considered the palette. It is a subset of the physical color table. Like the palette of an artist, from all the possible colors, a collection of colors is selected to be used on the canvas. For some devices, there is no palette and the colors used are directly from the physical color table. The background and foreground colors are selected from the logical color table. The foreground color can be the text color or the drawing color.

The entries of the logical color table represent the colors that will be used at a given time. Each color is inserted in a given entry. Therefore, when using a color in a program, instead of referring to the specific color value, the entry from the color table can be used. The colors of the table can be changed by storing a different color value at that entry. If a color is removed from that entry and replaced with another color, then the former color on the display will be replaced with the new color. Each entry or the whole table can be replaced. When a program makes a color request, the operating system, using logical color table entry, searches for a match as close as possible in the physical color table and uses that color.

Encapsulation of the Graphics Adapter

These logical concepts, palette, number of possible colors, number of colors displayed simultaneously, background and foreground colors, and resolution can be encapsulated into an object. This object represents the state of the graphics adapter and display unit. A simple graphics adapter object in the Windows environment will be created by using the sum of the functions and information from the GDI. The simple graphics adapter object will inherit an **ioscontext** object, which is derived from the C++ **ios** class. As explained in Chapter 3, the **ios** class is the state class. The **ios** class represents a format state, open mode state, and buffer state of an object. The format state is very useful when sending characters to the display unit. The **ioscontext** object would represent the state of the graphics adapter object. This would include the color state, and the background and text colors. Using multiple inheritance, the **ioscontext** class is also derived from a **logicalpalette** and a **devicecontext** object. The **logicalpalette** object is the logical palette. The **devicecontext** object is the device context and window handle of the display unit. The **logicalpalette** object is derived from a **colors** object. The **colors** object is the color that is placed in the logical palette.

The **devicecontext** object is the window and device handle for an object.

```
// The devicecontext object contains the device context and
// window handle. The device context and window handles are
// passed to the object when instantiated to the constructor.

class devicecontext{
   HDC Dc;
   HWND WinHandle;
public:
   devicecontext(HDC i, HWND j);
}

devicecontext:: devicecontext(HDC i, HWND j);
{
  Dc = i;
  WinHandle = j;

}
```

The **devicecontext** object contains a device context handle and a window handle. They are passed to the object when instantiated to the constructor. The constructor assigns the device handle and the window handle to the data members **Dc** and **Win-Handle.** The device context handle is needed by the other objects when calling GDI functions.

The **devicecontext** object is inherited by the **colors** object. Figure 8.1 shows the class relationship diagram for the **colors** object. The **colors** object is the color that will be placed in the logical color table.

```
// The colors object contains the color that will be placed in the
   logical
// color palette. It is derived from the devicecontext object. It is
   passed the RGB
// values when instantiated to the constructor.

class colors: public devicecontext{
    BYTE logRed;
    BYTE logGreen;
    BYTE logBlue;
    COLORREF Color;

public:
    colors( HDC x, HWND y);
    colors(BYTE red, BYTE green, BYTE blue, HDC x, HWND y);
    BYTE Red(void);
    BYTE Green(void);
    BYTE Blue(void);
    void Red(BYTE Color);
```

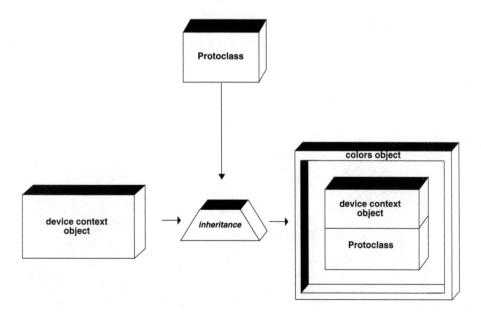

Figure 8.1 *Class relationship diagram of the **color** object.*

```
    void Green(BYTE Color);
    void Blue(BYTE Color);
    COLORREF Color(void);
}
colors:: colors(BYTE red, BYTE green, BYTE blue, HDC x, HWND y)
              :devicecontext(x, y)
{
    logRed = red;
    logGreen = green;
    logBlue = blue;
    Color = PALETTERGB(logRed, logGreen, logBlue);
}
colors:: colors(HDC x, HWND y):devicecontext(x, y)
{
    logRed = 0;
    logGreen = 0;
    logBlue = 0;

}

BYTE colors:: Red(void)
 {
    return(logRed);
 }
BYTE colors:: Green(void)
 {
    return(logGreen);
 }

BYTE colors:: Blue(void)
 {
    return(logBlue);
 }

void colors:: Red(BYTE Color)
 {
    logRed = Color;
 }

void colors:: Green(BYTE Color)
 {
    logGreen = Color;
 }

void colors:: Blue(BYTE Color)
 {
    logBlue = Color;
 }
COLORREF colors:: Color(void)
 {
    return(Color);
 }
```

The **colors** object's protoclass will return a color value. The **colors** object has the three primary colors of the RGB color model, and the colors of type COLORREF as data members. This object has two constructors. Both constructors accept the device context and window handles. One of the constructors initializes the data members **logRed**, **logGreen**, **logBlue**, and **Color** to zero. The other constructor has three primary color parameters. They are assigned to the data members, and the color is determined by a call to the PALETTERGB GDI function. This function accepts three parameters, the primary colors as BYTES, and returns a 32-bit color value of type COLORREF. This is assigned to the **Color** data member. The primary colors can also be assigned individually by the function that bears their name. The functions with the same names and a return type of BYTE returns the primary colors. The **Color** function returns the COLORREF color value.

The **logicalpalette** object is the logical color table. The following is the declaration and implementation of the **logicalpalette** object.

```
// The logicalpalette object creates a logical palette. It is derived
// from colors and device context objects. It fills an array of colors
// objects and assigns the colors to the logical palette. It is passed
// the number of entries, the device context, and window handle when
// instantiated to the constructor.

class logicalpalette: public colors, public devicecontext {
    colors logicalcolors[MAX];
    int NumEntries;
    int NumSysCol;
    int NumSysResCol = 0;
    int NumSysFreCol= 0;
    static HPALETTE PalHan;
    LOGPALETTE logicalpalette;
    LOCALHANDLE LocHan;

public:
    logicalpalette(HDC x, HWND y);
    logicalpalette(int Num,HDC x, HWND y);
    ~logicalpalette(void);
}

logicalpalette::logicalpalette(HDC x, HWND y)
                                :devicecontext(x, y),
                                 colors(x, y)
{
    logicalpalette[0] = 0;
}

logicalpalette::logicalpalette(int Num, HDC x, HWND y)
                                :devicecontext(x, y),
                                 colors(x, y)
{

    NumEntries = Num;
    for (int i = 0; i < NumEntries; i++){
        logicalcolors[i].logRed = (i * 4)%256;
        logicalcolors[i].logGreen = (i * 8)%256;
        logicalcolors[i].logBlue = (i * 16)%256;
    }
}
```

```
        NumSysCol = GetDeviceCaps(HDC, SIZEPALETTE);
        NumSysResCol = GetDeviceCaps(HDC, NUMRESERVED);
        NumSysFreCol = NumSysCol - NumSysResCol;
        if (NumEntries <= NumSysFreCol)
            Entries = NumEntries;
        else
            Entries = NumSysFreCol;
        LocHan = LocalAlloc(LMEM_MOVEABLE, sizeof(LOGPALETTE)*
                            Entries * sizeof (PALETTEENTRY));
        logicalpalette = (LOGPALETTE) LocalLock(LocHan);
        for (int i = 0; i < Entries; i++){
            logicalpalette->palPalEntry[i].peRed = logicalcolors[i].logRed;
            logicalpalette->palPalEntry[i].peGreen = logicalcolors[i].logGreen;
            logicalpalette->palPalEntry[i].peBlue = logicalcolors[i].logBlue;
            logicalpalette->palPalEntry[i].peFlags = PC_RESERVED;
        }
        PalHan = CreatePalette(logicalpalette);
        SelectPalette(HDC, PalHan, FALSE);
        RealizePalette(HDC);
    }

    void logicalpalette::~palette(void)
    }
        DeleteObject(PalHan);
    }
```

The **logicalpalette** object is derived from the **colors** and **devicecontext** objects. Figure 8.2 shows the class relationship diagram for the **logicalpalette** object. The **logicalpalette** protoclass will fill an array of colors objects and will fill, create, select, and realize a logical palette. The data member **logicalcolors** is an array of colors objects. The object is passed the number of entries, **Num**, that it will create in the logical color table in one of its constructors. In this constructor, **Num** is assigned to the **NumEntries** data member and the **logicalcolor** array is filled. Then the logical palette, **LogicalPalette** is assigned these colors. In the constructor, the **GetDeviceCaps( )** function returns the size of the system palette that is assigned to the **NumSysCol** data member. Then the **GetDeviceCaps( )** function is used to retrieve the number of reserved entries in the system palette. The remaining entries are free to be filled by the program. This value is stored in the **NumFreSysCol** data member. Memory is allocated to store the size of the logical palette by using the **LocalAlloc( )** function, and a handle to this allocated memory is returned. The handle to this location is stored in the **LocHan** data member. The LOGPALETTE data structure has a PALETTEENTRY structure that stores the RGB values of the color. The **LocalLock( )** function retrieves a pointer to the memory object. It is typecast as a pointer to a LOGPALETTE. The FOR loop assigns the RGB values from the colors array to the RGB variables in the **logicalpalette**. Once the **logicalpalette** structure is filled, the **CreatePalette( )** function is called. The **CreatePalette( )** function creates the palette and returns a handle to the logical color table. The **SelectPalette( )** function associates the created palette with the device context. The palette then has to be *realized* by using the **RealizePalette( )** function.

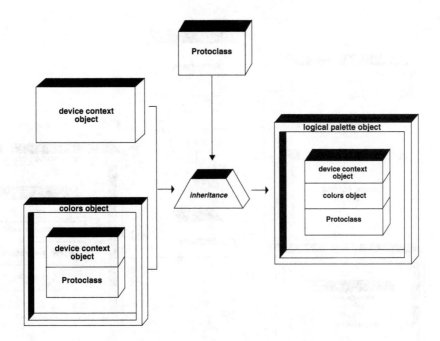

Figure 8.2 *Class relationship diagram of the **logicalpalette** object.*

The **ioscontext** object is derived from the **logicalpalette** and **devicecontext** objects. It is also derived from the **ios** class. The **ioscontext** object is an example of combining IOSTREAM classes with user-defined objects. Figure 8.3 shows the class relationship diagram of the **ioscontext** object. The **ioscontext** protoclass will set background and text colors.

```
// The ioscontext object contains the text and background color of the
// display unit. This object is the state of the simplegraphicadapter
// object. It is derived from logicalpalette, devicecontext, and ios
// class. It is passed the text color, background color, the device
// context, and window handle when instantiated to the constructor.

class ioscontext: public logicalpalette, public devicecontext,
                  public ios{
    long BkgrdColor;
    long TxtColor;

public:
    ioscontext(HDC x, HWND y, streambuf *Buffer);
    ioscontext(long BColor, HDC x, HWND y, streambuf *Buffer);
    ioscontext(long TColor, HDC x, HWND y, streambuf *Buffer);
    ioscontext(long BColor, long TColor, HDC x, HWND y, streambuf
```

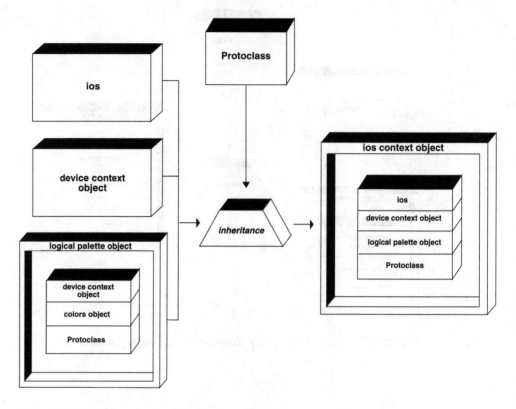

Figure 8.3   *Class relationship diagram of the **ioscontext** object.*

```
*Buffer);
   long BkgrdColor(void);
   long TxtColor(void);
}

ioscontext:: ioscontext(HDC x, HWND y) :devicecontext(x, y), logical
                        palette(x,y), ios(Buffer)

{
   BkgrdColor = 0;
   TxtColor = 0;
   PnColor = 0;

}

ioscontext:: ioscontext(int BColor,HDC x, HWND y)
                        :devicecontext(x, y),
                        logicalpalette(x,y),
                        ios(Buffer)

{
```

```
    BkgrdColor = BColor;
    SetBkColor(Dc, PALETTEINDEX(BkgrdColor));
}

ioscontext:: ioscontext(int TColor, HDC x, HWND y)
                        :devicecontext(x, y),
                        logicalpalette(x,y),
                        ios(Buffer)
{

    TxtColor = TColor;
    SetTextColor(Dc, PALETTEINDEX(TxtColor));
}

ioscontext:: ioscontext(int BColor, int TColor, HDC x, HWND y)
                        :devicecontext(x, y),
                        logicalpalette(x,y),
                        ios(Buffer){

    BkgrdColor = BColor;
    TxtColor = TColor;
    SetBkColor(Dc, PALETTEINDEX(BkgrdColor));
    SetTextColor(Dc, PALETTEINDEX(TxtColor));
}

long ioscontext:: BkgrdColor(void)
{
    return(BkgrdColor);
}

long ioscontext:: TxtColor(void)
{
    return(TxtColor);
}
```

The background color, **BkgrdColor**, and the text color, **TxtColor**, are passed and assigned to the object data members at the same time, or separately through the constructors at the time of instantiation. The constructors also set the text and background colors.

The **simplegraphicadapter** object is derived from the **ioscontext** and **devicecontext** objects. Figure 8.4 shows the class relationship diagram for the *simplegraphicadapter* object. The protoclass will determine the horizontal and vertical resolution, the possible colors, and the colors that can be displayed at one time for a graphics adapter.

```
// The simple graphic adapter object contains the resolution, possible
// colors, number of colors in the device table, the number of planes,
// and the number of bits per pixel. It is derived from ioscontext and
// devicecontext objects. It is passed the device context and window
// handle when instantiated to the constructor.

class simplegraphicadapter:: public ioscontext, public devicecontext{
    int HorizonRes;
    int VertRes;
```

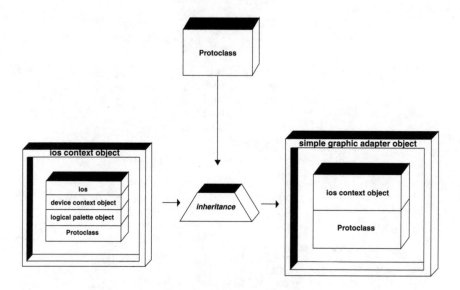

Figure 8.4   *Class relationship diagram of the **simplegraphicsadapter** object.*

```
    int PossColors;
    int DispColors;
    int ColorPlanes;
    int BitsPerPix;
public:
    simplegraphicadapter(HDC x, HWND y)
    int HorizontalRes(void);
    int VerticalRes(void);
    int PossibleColors(void);
    int DisplayColors(void);
    int ColorPlanes(void);
    int BitsPerPixel(void);
}

simplegraphicadapter:: simplegraphicadapter(HDC x, HWND y)
                                    :devicecontext(x, y),
                                    ioscontext(x, y)
{
    HorizonRes = 0;
    VertRes = 0;
    PossColors = 0;
    DispColors = 0;
    ColorPlanes = 0;
    BitsPerPix = 0;

}
```

```
void simplegraphicadapter:: HorizontalRes(void)
{
    HorizonRes = GetDeviceCaps(Dc, HORZRES);
    return(HorizonRes);

}

void simplegraphicadapter:: VerticalRes(void)
{
    VerticalRes = GetDeviceCaps(Dc, VERTRES);
    return(HorizonRes);

}

int simplegraphicadapter:: Possiblecolors(void)
{
    ColorPlanes = GetDeviceCaps(Dc, PLANES);
    BitsPerPix = GetDeviceCaps(Dc, BITSPIXEL);
    if(ColorPlanes = 1)
        Posscolors = pow(2, BitsPerPixel);
    else
        Posscolors = 0;
    return(Posscolors);

}
int simplegraphicadapter:: DisplayColors(void)
{
    DispColors = GetDeviceCaps(Dc, NUMCOLORS);
    return(DispColors);
}

int simplegraphicadapter:: ColorPlanes(void)
{
    ColorPlanes = GetDeviceCaps(Dc, PLANES);
    return(ColorPlanes);
}

int simplegraphicadapter:: BitsPerPixel(void)
{
    BitsPerPix = GetDeviceCaps(Dc, BITSPIXEL);
    return(BitsPerPix);
}
```

The device context and window handle are passed to the object at the time the object is instantiated. The member function **HorizontalRes( )** will return the horizontal resolution by using the **GetDeviceCaps( )** function. The value is stored in the **HorizonRes** data member. The vertical resolution is returned by the **VerticalRes( )** member function. The **GetDeviceCaps( )** function is called and returns the value. This value is assigned to the **VertRes** data member. The **PossibleColors( )** member function calculates the number of possible colors for an adapter with one bit plane. If the adapter has more than one bit plane, then a zero value will be returned. The number of possible colors is stored in the **PossColors** data member. The **Display-Colors( )** member function will return the number of colors that can be displayed at one time. The **GetDeviceCaps( )** function is called with the NUMCOLORS capability argument. The NUMCOLORS is the number of colors in the device color table. This is the number of pure colors that are produced by the device at one time. This value is stored in the **DispColors** data member and returned by the **Display-Colors( )** member function. The **ColorPlanes( )** and **BitsPerPixel( )** member functions return the number of color planes and the number of bit per pixel, respectively. The number of color planes is stored in the **ColorPlanes** data member, and the number of bits per pixel is stored in the data member **BitsPerPix**.

An ios Extension

The **ioscontext** object is derived from the **ios** class. The **ios** class contains the format state, the buffer state, and the open mode state of the IOSTREAM classes. The **ioscontext** object's member functions and data members describe the state of the display unit. This extends the **ios** class to a descendant that reveals the state of a palette, and the state of the text and background colors. The **ios** class will contain the format state of characters that are sent to the display unit.

By inheriting **ios** class, the **ioscontext** object can set the format state of data sent to a display unit. The format states of **ios** can be: scientific, fixed, showpoint, and so on. For example, if the format state of **ioscontext** is fixed, after the object is instantiated, a message to the object would look like this:

```
ioscontext Context;
Context.setf(ios::fixed);
```

The protoclass of **ioscontext** will set the text and background colors.

Multimedia Devices

The combination of graphics with text in one medium represented the start of the multimedia generation of computing. Since the arrival of the graphics card and other high-resolution graphics technology on the scene, sound cards, sound chips, midi, video capture cards, and various full-motion video technologies have appeared as regulars in desktop computing. These technologies are often referred to under the catch phrase *multimedia devices*. The PC is now called the MPC (Multimedia PC). Multimedia devices are virtually standard components in desktop computers. The sound cards, video boards, and midi devices are no longer just add-in peripherals for gamesters. The multimedia devices are finding their way into education, business, industrial, and scientific applications. Two important developments have occurred to accent the fact that multimedia devices have earned their place among standard peripherals:

- *The new operating systems have built-in support for multimedia devices.*
- *New standardized multimedia file formats exist that are also supported by the new operating systems.*

The addition of multimedia devices to the ranks of other standard computer peripherals has increased the need for multimedia operating systems and multimedia I/O programing skills. OS/2's Multimedia Presentation Manager and Windows NT have layers of built-in support for multimedia devices. Windows has the Waveform Audio API, which allows applications to record and play back digitized sound. OS/2 has the Waveform Audio Media Control Driver that works with the Sync/Stream Manager. The Sync/Stream Manager also allows applications to access audio technology. Both Windows and OS/2 support the MMIO(Multimedia Input/Output) file functions. The MMIO functions give applications comprehensive access to files containing multimedia data. We discuss MMIO in Chapter 9. Both Windows and OS/2 support the MCI(Media Control Interface). Through this interface, the programmer can access the multimedia peripherals connected to the desktop computer. The multimedia APIs are well documented in the MDKs (Multimedia Development Kit) that are available from IBM and Microsoft. We will look briefly at the most general multimedia API, and we will discuss how it can be combined with the IOSTREAM classes to achieve a *multimedia stream*.

Media Control Interface for Multimedia Devices

The Media Control Interface (MCI) is an API for accessing I/O devices in a multimedia-based environment. The MCI can control audio, video, midi, timer, joystick, and CD-ROM type devices. The MCI provides the programmer with a device-independent method to access multimedia type hardware connected to a computer. Without something like the MCI API, the programmer would have to be aware of hardware-dependent memory requirements, port addresses, sequencing, and timing values. These specifics would be different for every kind of multimedia device connected to the computer. Fortunately, the MCI is available to programmers using the MMPM/2 for OS/2 or the Windows environment.

To access the MCI in the Windows programming environment, the programmer must have access to **mmsystem.h**, **mmsystem.lib**, and **mmsystem.dll** To use the MCI interface in the MMPM/2 environment, the programmer must:

```
define INCL_MCIOS2
#include os2me.h
```

This will include the appropriate header files for MCI access in the MMPM/2 (Multimedia Presentation Manager) environment. The MDK available from IBM contains a host of tools that allow powerful multimedia development. The examples of MCI in this book were developed and tested in the MMPM/2 environment using the IBM MDK and the CSet++ compiler. The MCI in the Windows environment supports the same basic concepts. With the exception of some minor naming differences, the core MCI access under OS/2 and Windows works the same.

Besides controlling multimedia type devices, the MCI API can be used to share devices with other applications and group devices for purposes of synchronization, acquisition, and collective use. The services provided by the MCI under MMPM/2 are accessible using functions from two categories.

High-level macro service functions

Media control interface application functions

The MCI High-Level Macro Service Functions

The high-level macro service functions offer very easy access to multimedia devices connected to the desktop. There are three functions in this category:

```
mciPlayFile()
mciPlayResource()
mciRecordAudioFile()
```

These functions can access audio devices, video devices, midi devices, and so on. The complexity of the underlying device is hidden from the application programmer. Ordinarily, the programmer is responsible for loading in the multimedia file, decoding the file, initializing the appropriate hardware device (with device-specific idiosyncrasies in mind), sending the decoded data to the device, ensuring that there are no device locks or timing snafus, and, when all is said and done, closing the device. The MCI functions, especially the high-level macro service functions, remove this responsibility from the programmer. With one function call, the application can play a movie, wave file, or midi file. The trade-offs for this simplicity are speed and efficiency. However, for simple multimedia I/O needs, the high-level macro service functions offer an easy, straightforward entry into multimedia I/O programming. For example the:

```
mciPlayFile (hwnd, "solar.wav",0,0,0);
```

opens the **solar.wav** file, initializes the connected audio device, plays the wave file, and then closes the device. Table 8.4 shows the high-level macro service functions and their descriptions.

Table 8.4   High Level Macro Service Functions and Their Descriptions

Function Names	Description
mciPlayResource	Plays a multimedia resource that has been bound into an application.
mciRecordAudioFile	Records digital audio into a file specified by the caller. Records only the digital audio.
mciPlayFile	Plays a multimedia file or audio elements of a compound file.

The Media Control Interface Application Functions

The media control interface application functions offer more specific control than the high-level macro functions. Also, the media control interface application functions are more efficient than the high-level macros. There are six functions in this category:

```
mciSendString()
mciSendCommand()
mciSetSysValue()
mciGetDeviceID()
mciQuerySysValue()
mciGetErrorString()
```

Table 8.5 shows the descriptions of these functions. The first two functions control the I/O to the multimedia devices. The **mciSendString( )** function sends a command to a media device driver in the form of a string. This string is parsed, translated, and then sent to the media device driver. The **mciSendString( )** function provides the programmer with very high-level access to multimedia devices and the MCI. For example, the sequence of **mciSendString( )** commands in Listing 8.1 opens a wave file, plays the wave file, and then closes the file. Ordinarily, this would require considerably more effort on the part of the application programmer.

Listing 8.1

```
mciSendString ("open ding.wav alias wave1 wait" NULL,0,0,0);
mciSendString ("play wave1 wait",NULL,0,0,0);
mciSendString ("close wave1 wait",0,0,0);
```

Table 8.5 Media Control Interface Application Functions and Their Descriptions

Function Names	Description
mciSendString	Sends a command to a media device driver using string buffers.
mciSendCommand	Sends a command to a media control driver using flags and structures.
mciSetSysValue	Sets or alters systemwide values such as the closed captioning flag or working path for temporary files.
mciGetDeviceID	Retrieves the device ID corresponding to the alias of a device.
mciQuerySysValue	Queries multimedia Presentation Manager/2 system values.
mciGetErrorString	Fills the caller's buffer with the error code string.

Whereas the **mciSendString( )** function sends the string to a parser and then to the media control device, the **mciSendCommand( )** function sends the command directly to the media control device. Actually, the **mciSendString( )** function calls a string parser. The string parser parses the string into commands that are eventually sent to the **mciSendCommand( )** function. This means that calls directly to the **mciSendCommand( )** function are faster than calls to **mciSendString( )**.

Although the MCI is not object-oriented, the center of focus in MCI programming is a generic multimedia object. This object represents some I/O device or set of devices that have a basic set of multimedia attributes. The MCI controls connected devices through three levels of commands:

- System commands
- Required commands
- Basic commands

The *system commands* are sent directly to the media control manager. These commands can be used to acquire the resources for a device, or group multiple devices together to be treated simultaneously. The system commands can also be used to get information on the devices that are installed in the system or to make global changes; for example, setting volume for all the devices in a system.

The *required commands* are a core set of commands that are recognized by every multimedia device connected to the system. The core commands are:

```
open
close
status
info
capability
```

An MCI system command can be used to determine whether a certain device is connected to the system, and if it is, that device will respond to one of the required commands. In this sense, the device is like an object that can respond to at least the five basic messages or commands. For example, if a CD player is connected to the system, the **mciSendString( )** function can be used to send the **open** command to the CD player:

```
mciSendString ("open cdaudio alias mycd wait" NULL,0,0,0);
```

The **close** command could be sent by the **mciSendString( )** function to close the CD device:

```
mciSendString ("close mycd wait",0,0,0);
```

To obtain more characteristics of the device, the **mciSendString( )** can send the **capability** command to the device. The **capability** command returns true or false to a query. The basic queries are:

```
can record        has audio         preroll type
can eject         has video         preroll time
can play          compound device   device type
can save          uses files        message command
can setvolume     can lockeject
```

The queries can be used to understand what functionality is supported by the multimedia devices connected to the system. For instance, the **mciSendString( )** function:

```
mciSendString ("capability mycd can eject" ReturnString,0,0,0);
```

can be called to determine if the device named ***mycd*** can eject. The result to this query would be placed in the **ReturnString** parameter. The *required commands* are used to determine the baseline functionality of the connected device.

The last category of commands that the MCI uses to control multimedia devices are the *basic commands*. The basic commands are specific to a class of devices. For example, all wave audio devices should recognize the **play** command or **record** command, or all CD type devices would recognize the **seek** command. The basic commands that the devices recognize can control the majority of the input, or output of the connected multimedia device. The basic commands in the MMPM/2 are:

```
load      seek
pause     set
play      setcuepoint
record    setpositionadvise
stop      status
save
```

These commands can be used to program sound cards to play midi and wave files. These commands can be used to control CD players, or record digitized sound. Some of these commands are recognized by video devices connected to the computer.

The MCI API gives the programmer complete access to the connected multimedia devices. However, the MCI is large, containing more than 100 functions. It is advantageous to use *object orientation* when programming multimedia devices through the MCI. The object-oriented I/O paradigm is compatible with the MCI. The easiest approach to using object-oriented I/O techniques with the MCI using C++ is to model user-defined classes to encapsulate the required commands, basic commands, and the basic attributes. In this way, the programmer can have a C++ object for every multimedia device connected to the computer. Because of the size of the MCI, the largest advantages of using C++ objects are organization and access. The C++ object serves to package the function calls and return values into a comprehensible unit.

Multimedia Object-Oriented Streams

In Chapter 7, we demonstrated how a *space stream* could be constructed in an MMPM/2 or Windows environment. The space stream extends the **ostream** class. The space stream encapsulates the idea of painting a stream of text to a canvas. The multimedia stream would encapsulate I/O going to and from audio, video, joystick, timer, and midi devices. This stream is different from the multimedia streams that are processed by the Sync/Stream Manager in OS/2. The *multimedia stream* will be an extension to IOSTREAM components. The multimedia stream can organize I/O to and from the differing multimedia devices into one coherent stream interface, using the **<<** inserters and **>>** extractors, or using the **sputn( )**, **sgetn( )**, **read( )**, and **write( )** interfaces. In this way, the programmer can keep a consistent interface regardless of whether the I/O is to or from printers, files, joysticks, communication ports, sound cards, graphics adapters, and so on.

One of the key goals in object-oriented programming is to maintain common interfaces for similar operations. Sending output to a sound card, or video capture card, should look the same as sending output to a file or printer. Through polymorphism and operator overloading, the C++ programmer can achieve the common interface advantage, which is especially important in the face of the mammoth APIs that are found in the new breed of operating systems.

Listing 8.2

```
// This program demonstrates how to build and use a multimedia
// stream using the MCI.

#define INCL WIN
#define INCL GPI

#include <os2.h>
#include <stdlib.h>
#include <stdio.h>
#include <string.h>
#include <fstream.h>
#include <strstrea.h>
#include <iomanio.h>
#define INCL MMOS2
#define INCL MCIOS2
#define INCL 32
#include "os2me.h"

class textspace : public ostream{
protected:
    HPS PSpace;
    HWND WinHandle;
    POINTL Coord;
    long int Tab;
public:
    textspace(streambuf *Buffer, HWND Handle);
```

```
      ~textspace(void);
      HPS space(void);
      void setxy(long X, long Y);
      long int tab(void);
      void tab(long X);
      long getx(void);
      long gety(void);
      friend textspace &operator<<(textspace &Out, char *Text);
};

HPS textspace::space(void)
{
  return(PSpace);
}

textspace::textspace(streambuf *Buffer,HWND Handle) : ostream(Buffer)
{
  Coord.x = 10;
  Coord.y = 10;
  Tab = 5;
  PSpace = WinGetPS(Handle);
  WinHandle = Handle;
}

void textspace::setxy(long X, long Y)
{
  Coord.x = X;
  Coord.y = Y;
}

textspace::~textspace(void)
{
  WinReleasePS(PSpace);
}

long int textspace::tab(void)
{
  return(Tab);
}

void textspace::tab(long X)
{
  Tab = X;
}

long textspace::getx(void)
{
  return(Coord.x);
}

long textspace::gety(void)
{
  return(Coord.y);
}

textspace &operator<<(textspace &Out,char *Text)
{
```

```
      Out.rdbuf( )->sputn(Text,strlen(Text));
      GpiCharStringAt(Out,PSpace,&Out.Coord,strlen(Text),(PCH)Text);
      return(Out);
}

textspace &tab(textspace &Mstream)
{
  Mstream.setxy(Mstream.getx( ), (Mstream,gety( ) + Mstream.tab( )));
  return(Mstream);
}

class mcios : public ios{
protected:
   char MciErrorDesc[50];
   unsigned long MciErrorCode;
   void mciError(char *Error);
public:
   mcios(streambuf *Buffer);
};

class mcistream : public mcios{
protected:
   HWND WindowHandle;
   char MessageBack[50];
   unsigned long ReturnValue;
public:
   mcistream(HWND Handle,streambuf *Buffer);
   friend mcistream &operator<<(mcistream &Out,char *Expression);
};

mcios::mcios(streambuf *Buffer) : ios(Buffer)
{
  MciErrorCode = 0;
  strcpy(MciErrorDesc,"");
}

void mcios::mciError(char *Error)
{
  strcpy(MciErrorDesc,Error):
}

mcistream::mcistream(HWND Handle,streambuf *Buffer):mcios(Buffer)
{
  ReturnValue = 0;
  WindowHandle = Handle;
}

mcistream &operator<<(mcistream &Out,char *Expression)
{
  Out.bp->sputn(Expression,strlen(Expression)):
  Out.ReturnValue = mciSendString((PSZ)Expression,
                                  (PSZ)Out.MessageBack,
                                   strlen(Out.MessageBack),
                                   Out.WindowHandle,0);
    mciGetErrorString(Out.MciErrorCode,(PSZ)Out.MciErrorDesc,
                  strlen(Out.MciErrorDesc));
```

```
      return(Out);
}

MRESULT EXPENTRY window func(HWND,ULONG,MPARAM,MPARAM);
MRESULT EXPENTRY window func(HWND handle, ULONG mess, MPARAM
                                  parm1, MPARAM parm2)
{
   HPS PSpace;
   POINTL Coord;
   CHAR ch;
   SHORT i;
   static char List[400] = "";
   char Number[25] = "";
   char Other[80] = "";

   ostrstream DeviceCommand(Other,79);
   mcistream WaveDevice(handle,DeviceCommand.rdbuf( ));

   switch(mess)
   {
      case WM COMMAND :
        switch(SHORT1FROMMP(parmi))
        {
          case 101 :
            ifstream In("file1.txt");
            double Value;
            int N = 0;

            ostrstream Area(List,399);
            textspace Canvas(Area.rdbuf( ),handle);
            Canvas.setxy(10,300);
            Coord.y = 400;
            WaveDevice << "open whoops.wav alias wave1 wait"
                       << "play wave1 wait"
                       << "close wave1 wait";
            GpiSetColor(Canvas.space( ),CLR_DARKCYAN);
            while(!In.eof( ) && !In.fail( ) && N < 10)
            {
               {
                 ostrstream Out(Number,24,ios::trunc);
                 In >> Value:
                 if(!In.eof( )){
                   Out << Value;
                   }
                 Coord.y -= 15;
                 Canvas.setxy(10.Coord.y);
                 Canvas << Out.str( ) << tab;
               }
            }
            In.close( );
            WaveDevice << "open boing.wav alias wave1 wait"
                       << "play wave1 wait"
                       << "close wave1 wait":
            break;
        }
```

```
        case WM ERASEBACKGROUND:
          return(MRESULT) TRUE;
        default:
          return WinDefWindowProc(handle,mess,parml,parm2);
      }
    return(MRESULT) FALSE;
}

void main(void)

{

    HAB hand_ab;
    HMQ hand_mg;
    HWND hand_frame;
    QMSG q_mess;
    ULONG flFlags;
    unsigned char Class[] = "MYCLASS";
    flFlags = FCF MENU |
              FCF TITLEBAR |
              FCF SIZEBORDER |
              FCF MINMAX |
              FCF SYSMENU |
              FCF VERTSCROLL |
              FCF HORZSCROLL |
              FCF SHELLPOSITION;
    hand_ab = WinInitialize(0);
    hand_mq = WinCreateMsoQueue(hand_ab.0);
    if(!WinRegisterClass(hand ab,
                        (PSZ) Class,
                        (PFNWP) window_func,
                        CS_SIZEREDRAW,
                        0)){
      exit(1);
    }
    hand frame = WinCreateStdWindow(HWND DESKTOP,
                                    WS VISIBLE,
                                    &flFlags,
                                    (PSZ) Class,
                                    (PSZ) "IOSTREAMS AND Presenta
                                          tion Manager",
                                    WS_VISIBLE,0, 1, NULL);
    while(WinGetMsg(hand_ab, &q_mess, OL, 0,0))
    {
      WinDispatchMsg(hand_ab, &q_mess);
    }
    WinDestroyWindow(hand_frame);
    WinDestroyMsgQueue(hand_mq);
    WinTerminate(hand_ab);
}
```

The program in Listing 8.2 demonstrates a simple example of a *multimedia stream*. We used the MCI as the basis for this stream. Through encapsulating the

MCI, the multimedia stream has I/O access to any multimedia device connected to the system. The program in Listing 8.2 extends the IOSTREAM functionality by adding two classes:

- **mcios** class
- **mcistream** class

The **mcios** class extends the **ios** class to represent the error state of a multimedia device. The **mcistream** class is a translator that translates command strings to multimedia I/O using the **mciSendString( )** function. The **mcistream** and **mcios** classes are skeletons that can be fully developed to encapsulate the entire MCI functionality under MMPM/2 or Windows. Here, we present a frame of reference for the C++ programmer who wants to know how to integrate the IOSTREAM classes with the multimedia APIs. This approach in extending and integrating the IOSTREAMS is incremental. It does not force the programmer to adapt a foreign methodology or an entire design philosophy. Using inheritance and operator overloading, the programmer can have complete control of how much of the I/O programming is object-oriented. By extending the IOSTREAMS incrementally, the programmer can mix Windows or OS/2 programming with the IOSTREAMS without compromising.

The program in Listing 8.2 overloads the << insertion operator to accept strings that will be sent to the MCI through the **mciSendString( )** function. The statement:

```
WaveDevice << "open whoops.wav alias wave1"
           << "play wave1 wait"
           << "close wave1 wait";
```

causes the wave file **whoops.wav** to be played. Notice the common interface that the **WaveDevice** now has with all the other IOSTREAM classes. Once the consumer of a C++ IOSTREAM object knows how to insert one object into a stream, the rest comes easily. This common interface should not be taken for granted. It can decrease the learning curve for complex I/O programming. Also, notice that the commands that are inserted into the **WaveDevice** are strung together in one statement. This is another advantage of encapsulating the MCI. It improves source code readability and relieves the programmer from the drudgery of remembering function arguments. The << inserter also calls the **mciGetErrorString( )** function. Ordinarily, we would have made this call in the **osfx( )** function. However, for exposition purposes, we put it directly in the << inserter function. This call sets the **MciErrorCode** value and the **MciErrorDesc** value of **mcios** object. The << inserter also places the command string in the **mcios** buffer through a call to the **sputn( )** member function. This processing is analogous to the processing done in the built-in inserters. It is important that the general semantics of the IOSTREAMS remain intact when they are being extended.

The **WaveDevice** object is constructed with a handle to the main window, and a **streambuf.** These are the fundamental components that the **WaveDevice** needs to communicate with both the IOSTREAMS and the MMPM/2 environment. The program in Listing 8.2 also utilizes the **textspace Canvas** object created in Chapter 7. We included this object to demonstrate how a common interface across device and object types looks. The **window_func( )** in Listing 8.2 contains a potpourri of IOSTREAM objects. This function contains an **ifstream** object named **In**, an **ostrstream** object named **DeviceCommand**, a **mcistream** object named **WaveDevice**, an **ostrstream** object named **Area**, and a **textspace** object named **Canvas**. These are all members of the IOSTREAM classes.

The **In** object is connected to a text file containing numbers. The **DeviceCommand** and **Area** objects are memory objects. The **WaveDevice** object is connected to a generic device representing any multimedia device connected to the system, and the **Canvas** object is connected to a display unit in graphics mode. Although these IOSTREAM objects are all tied to different types of devices, they are used in the same way and have the same interface. This makes the entire function more comprehensible. If we were to replace these objects with their nonobject-oriented counterparts, the source code would be longer and more difficult to read, manage, and modify.

In this chapter, we discussed the multimedia devices, some of their characteristics, and how they can be accessed through the operating environment APIs. We also demonstrated how these devices can be encapsulated in the C++ environment. Finally, we demonstrated how these devices can be accessed using the object-oriented stream interface. We constructed **color** objects, **palette** objects, **ioscontexts**, **mcios** objects, and **mcistreams**, and demonstrated one approach to implementing the multimedia stream. In the next chapter, we shall discuss the file formats that are used in the multimedia environment, and how object orientation can be used to simplify and organize the multimedia files otherwise known as *blobs*.

CHAPTER 9

Blob Streams

> *In possessing a threshold of this kind, hearing is exactly in line with all the other senses; with each our brains are conscious of nothing at all until the stimulus reaches a certain "threshold" degree of intensity. The threshold of seeing, for instance, is of special importance. . . .*
>
> SIR JAMES JEANS—*MATHEMATICS OF MUSIC*

Blobs—Two Definitions

There can be two definitions of Blobs.

Blobs—An Informal Definition

Blob stands for binary large object. Blobs have become ubiquitous. Blobs can be found in word processing documents, spreadsheets, and databases. Blobs can be found zipping up and down the Internet at millions of bits per second. Blobs can be both seen and heard. Blobs are the substance of multimedia applications. Blobs can be sent to and received from faxes and modems. Blobs can contain other blobs. Blobs embody the state of the art in information representation and organization for desktop computers. Blobs are containers for information.

Blobs—A Formal Definition

A blob is a *data structure*. Data structures are organizations, or representations, of computer-based information. Data structures cannot be discussed without discussing the *algorithms* used to access the data structures. An algorithm is a well-defined set of steps that are used to describe a process. In connection to data structures, algorithms are used to process, store, retrieve, and manipulate the data components of the data structure. The two key characteristics of algorithms are:

1. Each step must be stated in a nonambiguous manner.
2. The steps must implement a finite process.

The process that an algorithm implements is usually used to solve a problem or execute a task. Algorithms are *politically correct* procedures. Data structures are incomplete without algorithms. Without algorithms to access and manipulate blobs, the blobs are also incomplete. Data structures can reside in the internal memory of the computer, or as files in external memory of the computer. When a blob exists in internal memory, it is referred to as a data object. When a blob resides on an external medium, it is referred to as either a file, resource, or persistent object.

The blob data structure will usually contain data that has been stored in a nontrivial way. The data must be inserted into or extracted from the structure, using a sequence of well-defined steps. The sequence of well-defined steps is the blob's algorithm. The stored data is sometimes compressed, or encrypted. This requires that the blob's algorithm perform compression, decompression, encryption, or decryption. The stored data is sometimes coded. This also requires that the blob's algorithm perform coding and decoding. Many blobs' data structures represent data that has been recursively stored. When this is the case, the blob's algorithm must be capable of recursively processing the data components of the blob.

Data structures and algorithms are of central importance and significance in all but the most trivial computer programming. As blobs conquer the world, a thorough understanding of data structures, algorithms, and the objects that encapsulate them will be necessary. In this chapter, we will discuss the fundamental types of blobs that the C++ programmer is likely to encounter. We will discuss some of the support available for blobs in the Microsoft Windows environment and in the OS/2 environment, and, finally, we will give some examples of how the IOSTREAMS can be used to encapsulate a blob stream.

A Short History of the Blobs

In computer programming, the concept of a file originally referred to a collection of characters, text, or numbers electronically or magnetically recorded into a single unit. The single unit of information would reside on some computer-based storage medium (i.e., on floppy disks, micro fiche, or magnetic tape). This unit would be stored in either in ASCII, EBCDIC, or binary format. The concept of the electronic file was born in the era when computers were used as either giant number crunchers or word processors. In this era, file processing involved the storage and retrieval of textual information, numerical information, or some combination thereof.

Today, a file on a desktop computer could contain animation sequences, graphics, digitized sound, voice, full motion video, and music, as well as textual and numerical information. Notice that we did not mention holographic images! The concept of the traditional file falls short of the type of entities that are storable and retrievable using current technologies. The blob has become a catchall term referring to files that contain more than textual or numerical information. Formally, a file is a data structure and usually exists on an external medium accessible by a computer. The file can be read into memory, at which point it becomes a data or memory object.

Blobs originated as graphics files. These graphics files were the result of graphics and paint editors, such as MacPaint, DP Paint, and PC Paintbrush. The images that were created with graphics editors or paint editors could be stored as binary files containing bitmaps or sequences of commands (records). If the binary file consisted of bitmaps, the file represented a *raster* image. If the file consisted of a sequence of commands or records, the file represented a *vector* image. Originally, every graphics editor had its own unique format for storing graphics information. Sometimes, the graphics file was created within application programs using graphic primitives, and saved to disk for later use. The storing of information that represented graphics into binary files ushered in the first generation of blobs. Around the same time, binary files representing sound were introduced by such companies as Creative Labs, the company that produces the Sound Blaster adapter card. These files representing sound could be stored on a disk or retrieved from a disk. They could be stored to memory or retrieved from memory. In the first generation of blobs, each binary file consisted of a single type of data. The data represented either a sound or a graphic, but not both.

The second generation of blobs unfolded when word processing applications and desktop publishing applications started mixing text and graphics in a single medium, and storing these combinations in a single file. Although the term had not yet been introduced, files that contain both text and graphics were blobs.

Currently, digitized sound, voice, digitized video, graphics, textual data, and numerical data can all be combined into a single unit. This data can be stored and retrieved as a single unit. This complex combination of data, which can include sound, video, voice, graphics, textual, and numeric data, represents the third generation of the blob. The fourth generation is arriving. This generation of the blob adds applications to the mix! However, we will not discuss fourth-generation blobs in this book. We will focus our attention on blobs from the first, second, and third generations. Each generation of blobs has a file format. Next, we shall explore some of these formats.

Blob Classifications

The blobs we shall discuss can be categorized as either:

- *Graphics blobs*
- *Sound/Music blobs*
- *Video blobs*

Graphics Blobs

Graphics blobs are normally contained in files or memory in specific formats. Most of these formats were created to be used with a specific product. For example, the PCX format was created to store graphic images that were produced by the PC Paintbrush graphics editor software. When the PC Paintbrush product became popular, the file format associated with that product became popular also. Some graphics file formats were created to be used as standard file formats. GIF is an example of such a format. The GIF file format is a copyrighted format presently owned by CompuServe. The GIF format provides a standard format for storing and retrieving graphics. The GIF file format is heavily used as a form of graphics storage on BBs, and is well suited for use in telecommunications. Most graphics file formats are known by their extension. For example, graphics files stored with such filenames as picture.gif, picture.pcx, and picture.tif are typically referred to by the extension, for example, GIF, PCX, and TIF.

Table 9.1 lists some of the popular graphics file formats that the C++ programmer may encounter. The table divides the formats into simple, complex, raster, and vector. A file format is classified as simple if it supports only one type of data and one compression or decoding scheme. If the file format supports multiple types of data or multiple compression/decoding schemes, the file format is classified as complex.

Most of the file formats will compress the bitmaps representing the graphics image using RLE. RLE stands for *run-length encoding*. RLE is a method for compressing data that depends on data redundancy. For example, the string:

```
AAAABBBABBBBBBCCCCCCCDDDDABACCC
```

can be represented by the string:

```
4A3BA6B7C4DABA3C
```

The second string is almost 50 percent smaller than the first string. Bitmaps can be run-length encoded in the same way. The string:

Table 9.1   Some Popular Graphics File Formats Divided into Raster Simple and Complex, and Vector Simple and Complex Formats

	Simple	*Complex*
Raster	BMP	GIF
	PCX	TIF
	MSP	EPS
	PIC	TGA
	IMG	WPG
	LBM	
Vector	DRW	
	VECTOR	

```
00000011110000011100000001111
```

can be represented by the string:

```
604150316041
```

The second string is more than 50 percent smaller than the first string. This run-length encoding scheme is only one of many. The run-length encoding schemes depend on redundant patterns of data. If there is little redundancy, then the compression offers little space savings. However, if there are lots of contiguous 0s and 1s, then the RLE can save a considerable amount of space in both internal memory and external memory. Because the data to be processed for a graphics file is stored as a bitmap, the **ostrstream**, **istrstream**, and **strstream** classes are ideal candidates for blob stream modeling. The **seekp( )** and **tellp( )** member functions simplify processing streams of bytes. We will have more to say about **ostrstream** and **istrstream** in connection with bitmaps later.

Processing graphics blobs will involve reading a file containing a graphics bitmap, or series of records representing a graphics bitmap. Along with reading the file, a header describing the bitmap is usually contained within the file and, finally, the bitmap data is usually RLE. The header normally describes bitmap image dimensions, color representations, and file format version numbers. Some headers contain palette information. Sometimes, the palette is stored separately in another part of the file. The graphics blob will almost always consist of a number of components. As data structures require algorithms, graphics blobs require blob readers and blob writers. Components of the **iostream** classes can be used to model graphics blobs, and **iostream** member functions can aid in reading and writing blobs.

Popular Simple Graphics Blob Formats

There are a number of simple graphics blob formats that are in popular use.

IMG   The IMG file format is normally associated with the Ventura Publisher, or software from Digital Research that uses the Gem windowing environment. IMG is a simple format that has a header of 16 or 18 bytes. The IMG file format uses an RLE scheme for compression.

MSP   The MSP file format is created by the Microsoft Paint program that ran under Windows 2.0. Although completely overshadowed by its successor, the BMP format, the MSP format can still be found on BBs, CompuServe forums, and the Internet. The MSP format supports only monochrome images, and uses a form of RLE for compression. The basic structure of the MSP is header, a line length array, and the compressed image lines.

LBM   The LBM format is created by the Deluxe Paint graphics editor. The LBM is a derivative of the IFF (interchange format files) format. The basic IFF format allows for images of 2 to 256 colors. The IFF and the LBM file structures consist of series of chunks that describe the header, colors, and data. The LBM format is also capable of containing a preview. This allows the contents of the file to be viewed without loading the entire file. The LBM and IFF formats are on the border line between simple and complex file formats.

BMP   The BMP format is native to two environments: the Microsoft Windows environment and the OS/2 Presentation Manager environment. The Software Development tools that produce bitmaps in these environments produce BMP files. The Microsoft Windows Paintbrush program produces BMP files. As Microsoft Windows and OS/2 Presentation Manager become more popular, the BMP format is becoming more popular. This format has rivals only among the PCX and GIF formats. We discuss the BMP format in more detail later in this chapter.

PCX   Of the simple formats, the PCX format is the most popular. This format was created by the ZSoft corporation, and is used as the file format for the PC Paintbrush graphics editor, which is one of the most used graphics editors in the PC environment. Files produced by this editor can be found everywhere. Virtually all major raster import and export filters and conversion programs support the PCX file format. There are hundreds of thousands of files in this format on BBs. Much of the graphic art that can be found on such information services as CompuServe are in this format. As is the problem with most of the simple blob formats, the PCX format is device-dependent. Its structure is closely tied to underlying graphics adapter structures. Also, the PCX format is not extendible. It is not readily adapted to handle other types of graphics or compression schemes. However, because PCX file format is so pervasive, it warrants some further discussion.

The PCX structure consists primarily of a 128-byte header and an RLE-encoded bitmap. The structure could have a 256-color palette appended at the end, depending on what type of graphics are stored. The scan lines of the image are encoded as a series of runs and repeat counts. In essence, a PCX reader will extract the 128-byte header, and then start the decoding process on the bitmap. After the header is extracted, the first byte is examined; if the top two bits are set, that byte represents a repeat count and the lower six bits indicate the number of times the next byte in the data stream should be repeated. The encoded bitmap can cross bit planes and scan lines. Marv Muse's *Bitmapped Graphics in C++* offers an excellent treatment of decoding and encoding both the complex and simple bitmap graphics formats. The code excerpt in Listing 9.1 demonstrates how an **ostrstream** object can be used to aid in decoding a PCX image.

Four **ostrstream** objects were declared, representing the RGB color model. Each object was named after a component in the model: red, blue, green, and intensity. We discussed the RGB color model in Chapter 8. These four **ostrstream** objects represent the color planes for a VGA adapter card. There are four arrays that are declared of size 38,400. This is a magic number that is tied to VGA hardware. The standard VGA high-resolution is 640 pixels across by 480 pixels down. To get the total number of pixels per screen, multiply these two values: 640 pixels * 480 pixels = 307,200 pixels per screen. If the pixels are held in 1 byte (8-bit chunks), then we can divide 307,200 by 8 and get the number of bytes that it would take to store 1 bit plane. 307,200/ 8 = 38,400. Hence, we have four arrays that represent the color planes on the VGA adapter card. Each of the **ostrstream** objects was constructed using a pre-defined array that represented a color plane.

The constructors for the **ostrstream** object are discussed in Chapter 3. The constructor requires the name of the array and the size of the array. We used the **write( )** member function to store the bytes from the **Graphic** array. The **Graphic** array holds the entire PCX disk file.

Listing 9.1

```
void pcx_image::decodePcxImage(void)
{
    int count;
    int LineCount;
    int Duplicate;
    unsigned char ScanLine[320];
    memset (&ScanLine [0], ' ',320);
    unsigned char *Scan = ScanLine;
    unsigned char *Data;
    ostrstream Red(RedBitPlane,38400);
    ostrstream Blue(BlueBitPlane,38400);
    ostrstream Green(GreenBitPlane,38400);
    ostrstream Intensity(Intense,38400);

    Green = GreenBitPlane;
    Blue = BlueBitPlane;
    Intensity = IntensityBitPlane;
    Data = &Graphic[128];
    LineCount = 0;
    while(LineCount < Record.PcxHeader.Vres)
    {
        count = 0;
        while(count < 320)
        {
            if((*Data & 0xc0) == 0xc0){
                Duplicate = *Data & 0x3f;
                Data++;
                memset(Scan,*Data,Duplicate);
                Scan += Duplicate;
                count += Duplicate;
            }
            else{
                *Scan = *Data;
                Scan++;
                count++;
            }
            Data++;
        }
        Scan = &ScanLine[0];
        Blue.write(Scan,80);
        Scan += 80;
        Blue.seekp(Blue.tellp( ) + 80,ios::cur);
        Green.write(Scan,80);
        Scan += 80;
```

```
              Green.seekp(Green.tellp( ) + 80,ios::cur);
              Red.write(Scan,80);
              Scan += 80;
              Red.seekp(Red.tellp( ) +80,ios::cur);
              Intensity.write(Scan,80);
              Scan += 80;
              Intensity.seekp(Intensity.tellp( ) + 89,ios::cur);
              Scan = &ScanLine[0];
              memset(&ScanLine[0],' ',320);
              LineCount++;
          }
      }
```

The **filelength( )** member function in Listing 9.2 determines the file's size using the **filelength( ) stdio** function and the **fd( )** member function of **In**'s **filebuf** component. The **fd( )** member function returns the file descriptor of the PCX file. Once the file descriptor or file handle is obtained, the **filelength( )** function can get the size of the file. The **allocatePcxImage( )** member function in Listing 9.2 allocates enough memory to hold the entire PCX file. The **retrievePcxImage( )** member function reads the entire file into memory and stores in the array named **Graphic**.

Listing 9.2

```
long pcx_image::fileLength(char *PcxCompressedFile)
{
   int Result;
   ifstream In;

   In.open(PcxCompressedFile,ios::binary);
   if(!In){
      cerr << "could not open: " << PcxCompressedFile ;
      cin.get( );
      exit(0);
   }
   FileSize = filelength(In.rdbuf( )->fd( ));
   In.close( );
   return(FileSize);
}

int pcx_image::allocatePcxImage(void)
{

   Graphic = new (unsigned char [FileSize]);
   if(!Graphic){
      cout << "could not allocate graphic";
      cin.get( );
      return(NULL);
   }
   return(1);
}

void pcx_image::retrievePcxImage(char *PcxCompressedFile)
{
   ifstream In;
```

```
    In.open(PcxCompressedFile,ios::binary);
    if(!In){
        exit(0);
    }
    In.read(Graphic,FileSize);
    In.close( );
}
```

This technique is an improvement over many of the popular methods for obtaining and decoding a PCX file. The first improvement is that it takes advantage of some of the object-oriented features found in the IOSTREAMS. Second, instead of retrieving and decoding the file one byte at a time from a disk file, the **retrievePcxImage( )** reads the entire file into memory. The file is then decoded while in memory; this improves the speed of displaying this PCX image dramatically.

The four member functions contained in Listing 9.1 and Listing 9.2 represent the core of a PCX blob reader. Once the bitmaps are obtained, they can be displayed using bitmap functions that are supported by the Windows or OS/2 environment. For instance, the **GpiCreateBitmap( )** function found in the OS/2 Presentation Manager environment can take **Red.str( )**, **Blue.str( )**, **Green.str( )**, or **Intensity.str( )** as an argument. The bitmaps can then be copied into a memory device, and later **bitblt**ed to the screen to form a complete picture.

The simple graphics blobs can generally be approached in the same fashion. Therefore, a blob stream class can be constructed using **ostrstreams** and **istrstreams** to represent bitmap data, and using the stream position member functions from the **streambuf**, **istream**, and **ostream** classes to decode and encode the data bytes representing the bitmaps.

Popular Complex Graphics Blob Formats

The complex formats are not necessarily difficult. We use complex here to designate multiplicity of coding schemes or data type representation.

TIFF The TIFF (Tagged Information File Format) is a flexible format capable of storing images of any size in monochrome or in up to 24 bits of color. This format emphasizes the *structure* in the term data structure, because of its rich and powerful representational capabilities. TIFF files are, for the most part, device-independent. A TIFF data structure consists of a header followed by any number of *tags*. These tags are polymorphic in nature; that is, they mean different things under different circumstances. A tag could specify the physical dimensions of the image, or some commentary on the contained image. A tag could specify what type of encoding scheme was used to represent the image (yes, TIFF supports multiple encoding schemes!). A tag could specify whether the contained image is a facsimile. The tag concept means that the TIFF format is both open and extensible. The trade-off for this flexibility is the complexity of the algorithms used to access and manipulate TIFF files.

GIF The GIF (Graphics Interchange Format) is another flexible graphics blob format. This format is extensible. It was designed with the notion that hardware changes in mind. GIF is a complex counterpart of the PCX file format. Files stored in the GIF format can be found on networks and BBs all over the world.

The GIF file format uses LZW compression, named after Lempil-Ziv and Welch envisioned it. The LZW compression technique is essentially a string table compression. This compression technique works by storing the runs in the image and replacing those runs with tokens. The runs may be of variable length. GIF files can store graphics as well as text. A GIF format can contain control information. Some of the controls determine the duration that an image is displayed, or how an image can be displayed. The copyright to the GIF format is currently owned by CompuServe, and the file format specifications for GIF are available on CompuServe forums.

So far, the BMP format is the only format that has built-in support at the operating system level on PC desktop computers. Microsoft Windows, OS/2 Presentation Manager, and X Windows all have built-in support for reading and writing BMP blobs. Although the formats under each of these environments are not exactly the same, they share a large intersection of commonality. The trend for C++ programmers is moving toward the BMP format, mainly because the current operating system environments have API calls that greatly simplify using bitmaps in applications. Also, device-independent bitmaps are another aspect of program reusability, extensibility, and portability. The current trends in multiplatform applications dictate this kind of flexibility. We discuss the BMP format under Windows and OS/2 in more detail later in this chapter.

Sound Blobs

The new multimedia operating systems and multimedia applications have added a new dimension to I/O programming for the C++ programmer. Along with processing graphics files, sound file manipulation is becoming a regular programming requirement in the desktop environment. Sound files are digitized versions of analog sound waves. Sound files are made possible by digital sound processors that can be found in sound chips and sound adapter cards. The digital sound processor (DSP) has two fundamental components: the ADC and the DAC. Figure 9.1 shows the basic layout of a sound card adapter. The ADC is an analog to digital converter. The ADC is responsible for recording and storing sounds that it receives. The ADC receives the analog sound and tastes the sound over and over, each time taking a reading of the sound's volume and pitch. The ADC component converts the information that it gets from this process into numbers. By touching, or tasting, the sound repeatedly at thousands of times per second, the ADC is able to build up a digital representation of the analog sound. This digital representation of the analog sound is known as a *sample*. The process of obtaining samples is referred to as *sampling*. The higher the sampling rate, the better the quality of the sample. That is, the more times per second the ADC can access the analog sound wave, the more accurate readings it can make. Hence, the numbers that it uses to represent the sound will be more accurate. Once a digital representation is obtained, it can be manipulated and processed by a computer. This digitized sound can exist in memory as a data object or on an external storage medium as a file, resource, or persistent object. It is the digitized representation, or sample, the C++ programmer will be manipulating.

Once the sample has been obtained, the original sound can be reproduced by the second component of the digital sound processor, the DAC (digital to analog converter). The DAC converts a number to an analog signal, and a voltage sends this signal to the audio technology of the desktop computer. The voltage passes through the audio connection and finally reaches the speakers that can convert it to an audible vibration.

The higher the sampling rate, the closer the digitized representation is to the analog sound wave. The higher the sampling rate, the more information that is generated. The more information generated, the larger the file or memory requirements for the sample. As with the graphics blobs, sound blobs have specific formats. Also, as with their graphics counterparts, many of the formats are tied to particular software packages and hardware devices. Table 9.2 lists some of the sound file formats the C++ programmer is likely to encounter when programming sound I/O.

VOC

The VOC format originated at Creative Labs and is used with the Sound Blaster family of sound card adapters. The VOC format is capable of storing digitized sam-

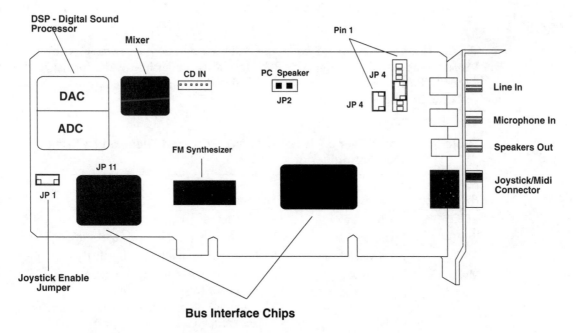

Figure 9.1 *Basic layout and components of a sound card.*

ples, representing almost any kind of sound. VOC files can contain music, sound effects, or even the human voice. VOC files contain a header and the raw digitized sample. The header contains information about the sample, such as the frequency at which the sample was recorded.

The raw digitized sample consists of a series of blocks.

MOD

MOD files are Amiga sound files. MOD files generally contain music. The music is usually divided by instrument and contained in four segments.

SND

Sound files with the extension SND are usually files that have been converted from the Macintosh to the PC environment. However, many PC applications that generated simple sounds also used this extension. The SND files consist of a header and digitized sound.

CMF

The CMF (Creative Music File) is used to contain synthesized music. The CMF file contains a list of notes, instrument changes, and tempos. These lists are sorted into the correct order for playing.

ROL

The ROL file format originated at the Adlib corporation, and was used by their Visual Composer application. The ROL format is similar in use and format to the CMF file. Both formats contain events that describe what is happening in the music, and when it is happening.

Table 9.2   Some Sound File Formats, Who Created Them, and a Brief Description

File Formats	Creator	Description
VOC	Creative Labs	Used for defining and storing digitized samples.
WAV	Microsoft	Used for defining and storing digitized samples.
SND	For a Macintosh	Header information followed by digitized samples.
MOD	For an Amiga	Has music separated into four segments, usually by instrument (digitized samples).
ROL	Visual Composer (Adlib)	Contains a list of notes, tempos, and instrument changes grouped together by type.
CMF	Creative Labs	Contains synthesized music consisting of a list of notes, instruments changes and tempos.

WAV

The WAV format is a Microsoft format. It is used almost exclusively in Microsoft Windows multimedia programming. The WAV format is similar in function to the VOC format in that it is capable of containing digitized sound representing music, sound effects, and the human voice. The MMPM/2 under OS/2 also supports the WAV format. Because of this built-in support for WAV files, the VOC digitized file format will most likely be replaced.

MID

The MID file is an extension for MIDI files. MIDI (Musical Instrument Digital Interface) is the industry standard for representing digitized music as well as commands to synthesized instruments. The MID file is a superset of the CMF and ROL type file. It stores music and commands. MMPM/2 for OS/2 and Microsoft Windows also have support for this file format.

Because of the built-in support for WAV and MIDI files under OS/2 and Windows, these file formats are likely to replace the other formats in desktop multimedia programming. The WAV file will contain the digitized sound, and the MID file will contain the music. The third category of blobs is the motion video blob.

Digital Video Blobs

The digital video blobs contain full-motion digitized video and sound. The digital video formats are the most complex and storage-intensive of the blobs. There are three popular movie platforms in the desktop multimedia environment: Apple's QuickTime for the Macintosh and Windows, Microsoft Video, and OS/2's Ultimotion. These three environments have built-in support among their respective operating systems. The AVI (Audio Visual Interleave) is the most popular on IBM-compatible computers. The AVI format has support under the Microsoft Windows environment and the MMPM/2 environment for OS/2. Both environments have multimedia developers' kits that support AVI reading and writing through the MCI (Media Control Interface) and the MMIO (Multimedia Input/Output) interface.

The suggested readings in Appendix E contain numerous references that can be used to explore the world of blob programming in greater detail. Because the techniques of graphics bitmap decoding and encoding, sound digitization, and full-motion video recording are not the subject matter of this book, we did not go into the detailed methods for this kind of programming. However, we wanted the C++ programmer who is using the IOSTREAMS classes to be aware of what blobs are and how they can be approached. The Windows for the NT and MMPM/2 for OS/2 both have built-in support for all three categories of blobs using the Windows GDI, OS/2 GPI, and MCI API. The C++ IOSTREAMS can be integrated with these environments, as demonstrated in Chapters 7 and 8. The simplest method for accessing graphics blobs in these environments is with the graphics APIs and the BMP format. The simplest method for accessing sound and video blobs is through the MCI.

Operating System Support for Graphics Blobs

The Windows environment and the Presentation Manager both support graphics blobs. Starting with Windows 3.0., the GDI supports the notion of a DIB (Device Independent Bitmap). OS/2 Presentation Manager does not yet support DIB's but does offer support for BMP file formats by calls to the GPI.

Windows BMP Blob

Windows' BMP Blob, DIB, does not depend on the structure of the underlying graphics adapter for its structure. Prior to Windows 3.0, the bitmaps used in the GDI were device-dependent. These bitmaps had structures that depended on the attached graphics adapter. If the bitmap was intended for a VGA display, the bitmap would contain the RGBI color planes. The new DIB contains a header and a bitmap that are self-contained and device-independent.

DIBS can be created using the resource tools that accompany most C++ compilers for Windows. For instance, Borland's resource workshop can create BMP files. PC Paintbrush for Windows also can save graphic images in the BMP format. The GDI can also produce a DIB. The DIB has four basic components. The DIB will have two headers, the BITMAPFILEHEADER and the BITMAPINFOHEADER or BITMAP-COREHEADER, a color table, and the bitmap bits. So, a BMP file can start out with two possible combinations:

```
BITMAPFILEHEADER
BITMAPINFOHEADER
```

or

```
BITMAPFILEHEADER
BITMAPCOREHEADER
```

The first combination represents the latest structure of BMPs. The second combination is used for BMPs that are supported under OS/2 1.1 and 1.2. Some of the Microsoft documentation calls this bitmap the Microsoft OS/2 Presentation Manager bitmap! Therefore, in designing BMP readers and writers, the C++ programmer must specifically choose one or the other. The BMP format does not support both formats simultaneously. Although the color table component is optional for the 1-bit-per-pixel, 4-bits-per-pixel, and 8-bits-per-pixel bitmaps, it is normally contained in the BMP file, so be prepared to read it. Because of the direct representational aspects of the 24-bit-per-pixel bitmap, a color table is not required.

Table 9.3   Five Fields of the BMP Format BITMAPFILEHEADER

Size	Description	Field
bfType	UNIT	The bytes BM (bitmap)
bfType	DWORD	Total size of the file
bfReserved1	UNIT	Set to 0
bfreserved2	UNIT	Set to 0
bfOffBits	DWORD	Offset to bitmap bits from beginning of file

Headers

The BMP format, BITMAPFILEHEADER, has five fields. Table 9.3 shows the fields and their descriptions. The BITMAPFILEHEADER precedes the BITMAPINFO-HEADER. Table 9.4 shows the fields of the BITMAPINFOHEADER structure. The BITMAPCOREHEADER has five fields. Table 9.5 shows the fields and their descriptions.

Bitmap Bits

The bitmap bits have three interpretations, depending on whether the pixel is represented by 1, 4, 8, or 24 bits. If the pixel is represented by 1 bit, then the bitmap is a monochrome picture, and the colors for the bitmap can be obtained from an RGBQUAD structure in the color table. If the pixel is represented by 4 or 8 bits, then the bits representing the pixel indicate an index into the color table for that bitmap. If the pixel is represented by 24 bits, each of the three bytes (24/8) represents an RGB value. When a bitmap has a 24-bit pixel, there is no color table involved.

The bits for the BMP format are stored in the file by the scan line, with the bottom row of the scan line at the top of the file. The bitmap is actually stored upside down, and the most significant byte occurs at the left top. The BMP format does support image compression using RLE; however, it is rarely used. There is a good reason for this. The RLE compression schemes rely on data redundancy. If there are long sequences on contiguous 1s or 0s, then the RLE represents these strings as runs and repeat counts. However, as the bitmap gets more complex, there are fewer long sequences of repeats. Under these circumstances, the RLE compression may actually result in a file that is larger than the original BMP. As 24-bit BMPs gain in popularity, other encoding schemes will have to be introduced. The basic RLE scheme is simply not useful in this context. Scan lines in the BMP format are padded at the end so that their length is a number easily divisible by 4. Table 9.6 lists the bitmap functions and their uses.

Because built-in support is provided for the BMP format by the Windows environment, and the Windows environment is one of the most popular environments for desktop computers, the BMP format will most likely supplant such formats as the LBM, IFF, and even the infamous PCX.

Table 9.4   Fields of the BITMAPINFOHEADER Structure

Field	Size	Description
bfSize	DWORD	Size of structure in bytes
bfWidth	LONG	Width of bitmap in pixels
bfHeight	LONG	Height of the bitmap in pixels
bfPlanes	WORD	Set to 1
biBitCount	WORD	Color bits per pixel (1, 4, 8, or 24)
biCompression	DWORD	Compression scheme (0 for none)
biSizeImage	DWORD	Size of bitmap bits in bytes (required only if compression is used)
biXpelsPerMeter	LONG	Horizontal resolution in pixels per meter
biXPelsPerMeter	LONG	Vertical resolution in pixels per meter
biCirUsed	DWORD	Number of colors used in image
biCirImportant	DWORD	Number of important colors in image

OS/2 Presentation Manager BMP Blob

Unlike its Windows counterpart, the OS/2 Presentation Manager (PM) does not yet support DIBs. The BMP files in OS2 are device-dependent. However, the fact that they are supported by GPI calls is justification enough to use them. Because the BMP format is supported by PM, the C++ programmer does not have to write blob readers or blob writers. The C++ programmer does not have to decode or encode the BMP format. This is done by the operating system if necessary. The most recent format for the PM bitmap is very similar to the Windows BMP format. The PM bitmap contains three basic components:

Table 9.5   Five Bitmap Format Core Header Fields

The BITMAPCOREHEADER structure contains information about the dimensions and color format of a device-independent bitmap that is compatible with OS/2 Presentation Manager versions 1.1 and 1.2 bitmaps.

```
typedef struct tagBITMAPCOREHEADER {
    DWORD    bcSize;
    WORD     bcWidth;
    WORD     bcHeight;
    WORD     bcPlane;
    WORD     bcBitCount;
}   BITMAPCOREHEADER;
```

Table 9.6   Bitmap Functions and Their Uses

Function	Description
CreateDIBitmap	Creates a device-specific memory bitmap from a device-independent bitmap (DIB) specification and optionally initializes bits in the bitmap. This function is similar to **CreateBitmap.**
GetDIBits	Retrieves the bits in memory for a specific bitmap in device-independent form. This function is similar to **GetBitmapBits.**
SetDIBits	Sets a memory bitmap's bits from a DIB. This function is similar to **SetBitmapBits.**
SetDIBitsToDevice	Sets bits on a device surface directly from a DIB.
StretchDIBits	Moves a device-independent bitmap (DIB) from a source rectangle into a destination rectangle, stretching or compressing the bitmap as required.

- *The Bitmap File Header*
- *The Bitmap Information Header*
- *The Bitmap Bits*

Because the Bitmap Information Header can also contain the color table information, the PM bitmap structure could be considered to consist of four components: The bitmap file header is represented by the BITMAPFILEHEADER2 structure. The bitmap information header is represented by two structures: the BITMAPINFO-HEADER2 structure and the BITMAPINFO2 structure. The BITMAPINFO-HEADER2 and the BITMAPINFO2 structures overlap in memory and are distinguished only by the RGB field.

Although the OS/2 BMP format is device-dependent, it relieves some of the dependence by representing the BMP as a single-plane bitmap. Some bitmaps, such as the PCX format, store bitmap information according to the color planes of the VGA adapter. In this instance, a PCX format can be considered to be more device-dependent than an OS/2 BMP format. The advantage of using the latter is that it has built-in support by the operating system. Even though the bitmap is stored as a single plane, the image can be subdivided to represent the four color planes of the image. In fact, one method of creating a PCX reader under the OS/2 or Windows environment involves performing just the opposite of converting one color plane to four. Instead, a PCX reader could convert the four color planes into the single bitmap structure that is supported under OS/2, thus allowing PCX images to be viewed in a Presentation Manager environment. The **decodePcxImage( )** member function in Listing 9.1 separates a 16-color PCX image into four **ostrstream** objects—*red, green, blue,* and *intensity*—representing the color planes of a VGA adapter. These **ostrstream** objects can be recombined into a single **ostrstream** object representing an OS/2 bitmap.

Bitmap Formats

A bit count is a value that specifies how many adjacent bitmap bits correspond to each pixel in a bitmap image. Table 9.7 shows the bitmap uncompressed sizes corresponding to the number of bits per pixel. The bits are stored contiguously in the bitmap plane. If there are 4 bits for each pixel, then 4 bits for pixel 1 are immediately followed by the 4 bits for pixel 2, and the 4 bits for pixel 2 are immediately followed by the 4 bits for pixel 3, and so on. As in the case with the Windows BMP, the bottom scan line appears first in memory with the leftmost byte at the start of the bitmap image. Table 9.8 lists the important bitmap functions used in Presentation Manager, and their descriptions.

Operating System Support for Other Blobs

Both Windows for the NT and the MMPM/2 for OS/2 support multimedia blobs, using the MCI (Media Control Interface) and the RIFF file format. The C++ programmer can access this support using the multimedia developer's toolkit available from IBM and Microsoft. The toolkit includes the libraries and header files that support the MCI, as well as the MMIO file routines that allow access to the RIFF format.

RIFF and the MMIO

The RIFF (Resource Interchange File Format) can be used to store sound blobs, such as WAV files, graphics blobs, and even AVI blobs. However, the most popular use of the RIFF is to store audio information. The RIFF file is considered a complex type format because it allows for multiple types of data in a single file. The file could contain AVI type information, as well as WAV type information.

The basic component of the RIFF file format is the *chunk*. The RIFF file format is a data structure that exists on disk and consists of a series of chunks. Each chunk is started with a header that has a code identifying the chunk. The similarities between TIFF and RIFF are not coincidental! As mentioned earlier in this chapter, blobs are data structures and data structures require algorithms. The RIFF data structure is no exception. It is recursive in nature and can contain chunks within chunks. The Win-

Table 9.7   Bitmap Uncompressed Sizes and Their Corresponding Number of Bits

Format	Bits per Pel	Size of 640 × 480 Image in Bytes (Uncompressed)
Monochrome	1	38,400
16-color	4	153,600
256-color	8	307,200
16.7-million-color	24	921,600

Table 9.8   Important Bitmap Functions Used in the Presentation Manager's GPI, and Their Descriptions

Function	*Description*
GpiCreateBitmap	Creates a bitmap that is compatible with a device associated with a presentation space.
GpiDrawBits	Copies bitmap image data from storage to a bitmap that has been selected into a device context.
GpiImage	Draws an image primitive.
GpiLoadBitmap	Loads a bitmap from a resource file or application EXE file.
GpiQueryBitmapBits	Translates data from a bitmap to application storage.
GpiQueryBitmapDimension	Determines the width and height of a bitmap in units of 0.1 mm.
GpiQueryBitmapHandle	Determines the handle of a bitmap with a specific local ID.
GpiQueryBitmapInfoHeader	Determines information about a particular bitmap, then transfers the information to the BITMAPINFOHEADER structure.
GpiQueryBitmapParameters	Determines information about a particular bitmap, then transfers the information to the BITMAPINFOHEADER structure. Use **GpiQueryBitmapInfoHeader** whenever possible.
GpiQueryDeviceBitmap Formats	Determines the device bitmap formats (number of planes and number of bits per pel) supported by the device, with the format that most closely matches the device returned first.
GpiQueryPel	Determines the color index of RGB value for a specific pel, whose location is specified in world coordinates.
GpiSetBitmap	Selects a bitmap into a memory device context.
GpiSetBitmapBits	Transfers standard-format bitmaps from a buffer into a bitmap, associated with a memory device context.
GpiSetBitmapDimension	Defines the height and width of a bitmap, in units of 0.1 mm.
GpiSetBitmapID	Assigns a local identifier to a bitmap.
GpiSetPel	Draws a pel using the current line bundle color and mix attributes at a specified position in world coordinates.
WinDrawBitmap	Draws a bitmap in a display window.

dows Multimedia API contains the MMIO file access functions. These functions support the reading, writing, and creation of RIFF files. The storage and retrieval algorithms for RIFF files should take advantage of the MMIO functions. Three of the primary functions used with the RIFF format are **mmioCreateChunk( )**, **mmioAscend( )**, and **mmioDescend( )**. The **mmioDescend( )** function is used to locate chunks within a RIFF file. This function is useful because the chunks can be embedded within chunks, and require a kind of recursive processing. The **mmiosAscend( )** moves to a previous level chunk in a RIFF file. The **mmiosDescend( )** and **mmiosAscend( )** functions allow the programmer to move up and down the hierarchy of chunks within the RIFF file. The **mmioCreateChunk( )** is used to add new chunks to a RIFF file. Table 9.9 lists the basic MMIO functions and their descriptions.

Table 9.9   Basic MMIO Functions and Their Descriptions

Function	Description
mmioAdvance	Fills and empties the contents of an I/O buffer of a file set up for direct I/O buffer access.
mmioAscend	Ascends out of a chunk in a RIFF file that was descended into by **mmioDescend** or created by **mmioCreateChunk.**
mmioCFAddElement	Adds an element to the CGRP chunk of an open RIFF compound file.
mmioCFAddEntry	Adds an entry to the CTOC chunk of an open RIFF compound file.
mmioCFChangeEntry	Changes a CTOC entry in an open RIFF compound file.
mmioCFClose	Closes a RIFF compound file that was opened by **mmioCFOpen.**
mmioCFCompact	Compacts the elements of a RIFF compound file.
mmioCFCopy	Copies the CTOC and CGRP chunks from an open RIFF compound file to another RIFF compound file.
mmioCFDeleteEntry	Deletes a CTOC entry in an open RIFF compound file.
mmioCFFindEntry	Finds a CTOC entry in an open RIFF compound file.
mmioCFGetInfo	Retrieves the CTOC header of an open RIFF compound file.
mmioCFOpen	Opens a RIFF compound file by name.
mmioCFSetInfo	Modifies information that is stored in the CTOC header of an open RIFF compound file.
mmioClose	Closes a file opened by **mmioOpen.**
mmioCreateChunk	Creates a chunk in a RIFF file that was opened by **mmioOpen.**
mmioDescend	Descends into a RIFF file chunk beginning at the current file position, or searches for a specified chunk.
mmioDetermineSSIOProc	Determines the storage system of the media data object.
mmioFindElement	Enumerates the entries of a compound file.
mmioFlush	Forces the contents of an I/O buffer to be written to disk.
mmioFOURCC	Converts four characters to a four-character code (FOURCC).

Table 9.9 (*Continued*)   **Basic MMIO Functions and Their Descriptions**

Function	Description
mmioGetFormatName	Provides the descriptive name of the format supported by the IOProc.
mmioGetFormats	Provides a list of all format I/O procedures available for use.
mmioGetHeader	Obtains media-specific information about data in a file, such as the media type, media structure, and the size of the media structure.
mmioGetInfo	Retrieves information from the file I/O buffer to a file opened for buffered I/O.
mmioGetLastError	Returns the last error condition stored in **dwErrorRet** that might contain additional information for the analysis of the last error routine.
mmioIdentifyFile	Determines (if possible) the format of a file by either using the filename or querying currently installed I/O procedures to see which IOProc can understand and process the specified file.
mmioIdentifyStorageSystem	Identifies the storage system that contains the media data object.
mmioIniFileCODEC	Modifies the initialization file (MMPMMMIO.INI) for MMIO services. It adds, replaces, removes, or finds a CODEC procedure in the MMPMMMIO.INI file.
mmioIniFileHandler	Adds, replaces, removes, or finds an I/O procedure in the initialization file (MMPMMMIO.INI).
mmioInstallIOProc	Installs an I/O procedure in the MMIO IOProc table, removes an IOProc from the table, or finds a procedure when given its FOURCC identifier.
mmioLoadCODECProc	Loads the CODEC Proc and returns the entry point.
mmioOpen	Opens a file and returns an MMIO handle.
mmioQueryCODECName	Returns the CODEC Proc name.
mmioQueryCODECNameLength	Returns the length of the CODEC Proc name.
mmioQueryFormatCount	Provides the number of IOProcs that match the requested format.
mmioQueryHeaderLength	Determines the size of the header for a specified file.
mmioQueryIOProcModuleHandl	Provides the module handle of an IOProc's DLL. This handle must be used to retrieve

Table 9.9 (Continued)   Basic MMIO Functions and Their Descriptions

Function	Description
	resources from the DLL. This function provides the handle of the DLL only if it was loaded by MMIO from the MMPMMMIO.INI file.
mmioRead	Reads a specified number of bytes from a file opened by mmioOpen.
mmioRemoveElement	Removes the specified element in a compound file.
mmioSeek	Changes the current position for reading, writing, or both in a file opened by mmioOpen.
mmioSendMessage	Sends a message to the I/O procedure associated with a file that was opened with mmioOpen.
mmioSet	Sets or queries extended file information.
mmioSetBuffer	Enables or disables buffered I/O, or changes the buffer or buffer size, for a file that was opened using mmioOpen.
mmioSetHeader	Sets media-specific information for data to be written to a file.
mmioSetInfo	Changes information on the file I/O buffer of a file opened for buffered I/O.
mmioStringToFOURCC	Converts a null-terminated string to a four-character code (FOURCC).
mmioWrite	Writes to a file that was opened using mmioOpen.

The MMPM/2 for OS/2 also supports the RIFF format and the MMIO file interface. The MMIO file interface serves as a multimedia file extension to the regular file functions found in Windows and OS/2. The MCI can be used to access WAV, AVI, and MID blobs. The MCI is also supported by both Windows and OS/2. Here again is a logical place to integrate the IOSTREAM classes with the multimedia blobs. The **ifstream** and **ofstream** classes can be extended to encapsulate the MMIO functionality.

CHAPTER 10

Communications Ports

There is no antiplace, since we are all consumers of space and time. There is, of course, the unknown that we only presume is out there until we know it by being there. . . .

MOLEFI KETE ASANTE—INSIDE PLACE

Asynchronous Serial Transmission

The communication ports connected to the basic IBM-compatible computer allow *asynchronous data transmission*. A port has a group of connectors in the form of pins, sockets, or edges. A port is a device on the computer that is capable of sending and receiving signals. Asynchronous data transmission is a method of transmitting data in which each transmitted character is preceded by a start bit and followed by a stop bit. The data between the start and stop bit form a package of sorts. Asynchronous transmission is advantageous when the transmission is irregular. Asynchronous transmission is practically the opposite of its counterpart—*synchronous transmission*. Synchronous transmission calls for the sending and receiving devices to be operating continuously at the same frequency, and usually implies a constant time interval between successive bits, characters, or events. Synchronous communications support higher rates of transmission; however, synchronous communications are more expensive to implement in terms of time and effort.

The asynchronous port is usually called the *serial port* or *com port*. The serial port or com port on the desktop computer is an asynchronous transmitter. Data is transmitted through a serial port one bit at a time. This is in contrast to how data is transmitted through the *parallel port*. The parallel port sends data one

285

byte at a time, or 8 *parallel bits* at a time. The fundamental sequence of bits moving through the serial port is:

1 start bit

8 data bits

Optional parity bit

1 or 2 stop bits

Between the transmission of each byte, a nonspecified amount of time may pass. The configurations of most serial ports are tied to the RS-232 standard.

The RS-232C Standard

The RS-232C is the *recommended standard* for how a serial port should physically communicate. The RS-232C is the design standard for the interface between a computer and its communications port. This recommended standard was established by the Electronics Industry Association (EIA) in 1969 to provide a standard for manufacturers of data communications.

The RS-232 provides an interface between DTE (Data Terminal Equipment) and DCE (Data Communications Equipment). The RS-232C interface specifies both the electrical and mechanical characteristics of the connection between two devices. The standard includes specifications for how to deal with voltage levels; which pins on the port are used to send and receive data; which pins detect various status signals; and so on. Figure 10.1 shows what the visible back ends of two typical communications ports look like. There are 25-pin and 9-pin connections. Figure 10.2 depicts the RS-232C pin assignments that refer to the communications port connected to the computer. The RS-232 also specifies that DCE devices use a female RS-232C connector, and that DTE devices use a male connector. DTE and DCE devices recognizing the RS-232 recommendation can communicate based on this agreed-upon specification. The computer is normally the DTE device, and the modem is a DCE device. However, there is nothing to stop communications between computers and any kind of device that can be connected to the RS-232 port or serial port.

Devices Connected to the Communications Port

Any device that is capable of serial communications, and that has physical connections that allow interfacing to the serial port, can be accessed by the serial port. If the device adheres to the RS-232 standard, the communication can occur in a straight-

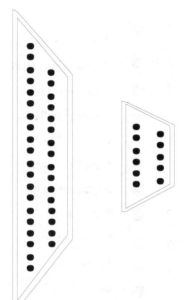

Figure 10.1 *Visible back ends of two typical communication ports.*

forward manner. Modems, fax cards, data acquisition, devices, and even robots can be connected to the communications port. Besides the physical and logical recommendations of the RS-232, there are no software requirements that must be met between two devices. This means that how one device interacts with another depends solely upon the application. Normally, all that is required besides the physical ports on both devices is a cable to connect the devices. Figure 10.3 shows a computer connected to my favorite device. Two computers can also be connected together through the serial port. In fact, this is an inexpensive way to implement a local area network.

Com1, Com2, Com3, and Com4

The typical IBM PC, AT, or RT has at least one com port, and can usually access as many as four com ports. The com ports are normally referred to as *com1, com2, com3,* and *com4*. These are the logical names recognized by the operating system. Sometimes AUX is a logical alias for a com port. The com port is treated as a special type of file by the operating system. The com port can be opened using the **open( )** member function of an **ofstream** or **ifstream** class. This means that IOSTREAM classes can be used to send bytes and retrieve bytes from the com port. The **streambuf** class and its derivatives, **filebuf** and **strstreambuf**, are ideally suited to processing

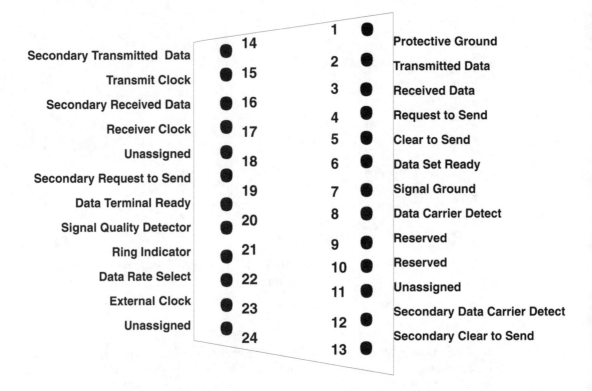

Figure 10.2 *Depiction of the RS-232C pin assignments referring to the communications port connected to the computer.*

data bytes that reside in a buffer that is connected to a communications session. The program in Listing 10.1 uses the **ifstream** class to access the com1 port.

Listing 10.1

```
// This program uses the open( ) member function to open
// com1, and the << inserter to insert a byte into com1.

#include <fstream.h>
#include <stdlib.h>

void main(void)
{

    ifstream ComPort;

    ComPort.open("com1");
    if(!ComPort){
        cerr << " Did not open com 1";
```

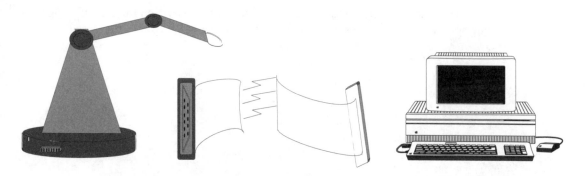

Figure 10.3 *A connection between a robot and a computer via the RS-232C cable.*

```
    exit(0);
  }
  ComPort << '\F';
  ComPort.close( );
}
```

The simple program in Listing 10.1 sends a form feed control character to com1. Then, using the **close( )** member function, the com port is closed. If only all communications programming was this simple! The meaning of bytes sent to and received from the communications port are application-dependent. However, some kind of communications protocol is usually necessary. For example, the baud rate (speed) at which the communications port sends and receives data must be the same for devices on both ends of the communication session. The flow of control involves the regulation of data transferred between two devices. If no agreed-upon flow of control is established, data can be lost or garbled. Examples of flow control protocols are EON/XOFF and ETX/ACK. Stop bits and start bits can be used to establish the boundaries of a packet of data. Although the **<<,>>**, **open( )**, **read( )**, **write( )**, and **close( )** member functions of the **ifstream** and **ofstream** classes can be used to access the com ports, the core IOSTREAM classes cannot set the baud rate or packet size of the com port.

The IOSTREAM classes can be extended to include port setting functionality. For instance, the **ios** class could be extended to include the baud rate state of the com port. However, the IOSTREAM classes basically model streams of data to and from devices. It may not be in the best interest of the application to extend the IOSTREAM classes to model the actual device. A device can be modeled using the C++ object-oriented capabilities and then, through the containment relationship, IOSTREAM classes can be connected to the device.

The simple program in Listing 10.2 shows how a device can be modeled by encapsulating the **DosDevIOCtl** functionality, and connecting the device to an

ifstream class through containment. This program was written for the OS/2 operating system. MS-DOS also has IOCTL functionality.

Listing 10.2

```
#define INCL_DOSFILEMGR
#define INCL_DOSDEVIOCTL
#define INCL_DOSDEVICES
#include <os2.h>
#include <fstream.h>

class device{
protected:
    HFILE Handle;
    USHORT BaudRate;
    ULONG PacketSize;
    ULONG Action;
    APIRET Code;
public:
    device(char *Com,USHORT Baud, ULONG Packet);
    ofstream DeviceStream;
    int action(ULONG Command);
}

device::device(char *Com,USHORT Baud, ULONG Packet)
{

    DeviceStream.open(Com);
    if(!DeviceStream){
        return;
    }
    BaudRate = Baud;
    PacketSize = Packet;
    Code = DosDevIOCtl(DeviceStream.fd( ),
                    ASYNC_SETBAUDRATE,
                    (PULONG) &BaudRate,
                    sizeof(BaudRate),
                    &PacketSize,
                    NULL,
                    0,
                    NULL);
}

void main(void)
{
  device C4PO("com1",9600,2);
  if(C4PO.DeviceStream.fail( )){
     cerr << "device initialization failed"
     exit(0);
  }
  C4PO.DeviceStream << "\f";
  C4PO.DeviceStream.close( );
}
```

The program in Listing 10.2 initializes the com1 to 9600 baud using the constructor of the device class. The device class has an **ofstream** object that will be used to handle the communications stream between the two devices. Once the **C4PO** device is constructed, the **DeviceStream** is tested. A form feed is sent to the **C4PO** device, causing it to stand to attention. Then, com1 is closed using the **close( )** member function of the **ofstream** object contained in the device object. Although this is an oversimplification of the process of connecting IOSTREAM classes to a com device, it serves to demonstrate the basic components involved, and how they can be constructed to access a com port.

IOCTL Interface

Unlike the high-level MCI, GDI, GPI, and MMIO interfaces that can be used to access multimedia devices, the IOCTL is a low-level interface. The IOCTL interface is a layer of abstraction between the operating system and the device driver. This layer of abstraction allows the operating system to control devices through the device drivers. The IOCTL interface allows an application or subsystem to send device-specific control commands to a device driver. In the program in Listing 10.2, the constructor for the device object sent the ASYNC_SETBAUDRATE command through the **DosDevIOCtl( )** function to the communications port device driver. The ASYNC_SETBAUDRATE command sets the com port transmission rate. Programming modems and fax cards can be accomplished in this manner.

The **DosDevIOCtl( )** function under OS/2 has many subfunctions. The functions are used to send data to and retrieve data from device drivers. The data can represent device status or command sequences. The programmer uses the IOCTL functions for device operations that are not built into the operating system API. The **DosDevIOCtl( )** function offers a compromise between having full support for a device's operation and having no support at all. This gives the operating system the flexibility to support any device that has a device driver installed in the system.

In OS2 and MS-DOS, the IOCTL functions require the file handle of the device that is to be controlled. For a device to have a file handle, it must be opened as a file. This means that the device must be recognized as a file to the operating system. If the device is recognized as a file by the operating system, then the **ifstream**, **ofstream**, and **fstream** classes can be used to read and write data to that device. Because the **ifstream** and **ofstream** classes contain the file handle or file descriptor, they should naturally be connected to the device model. We show another approach to accessing the serial port using a user-defined class derived from IOSTREAM classes. The **siostream** class represents the asynchronous stream, and the **siobuf** represents the buffer for **siostream**.

The siostream Class

Attempting to reuse the ANSI C **stdio** library to access nonfile I/O requires the creation of a file type device driver. This driver would permit the operating system to access the device through its low-level system calls, such as the UNIX-style **read( )** and **write( )** functions. To do this requires considerable understanding of the operating system's I/O operation. Another option is to change the interface between the operating system and the library. Besides adding additional overhead to each I/O call, this choice would require complete recompilation of the **stdio** library. The final choice is to keep calls to nonfile type devices separate from existing I/O routines. That is, maintain separate interfaces for each unique I/O device. This is a safer approach that generally results in the duplication of much existing code.

By inheriting a special class from the **iostream** library for new I/O devices, we can avoid these restrictions while still maintaining a common interface for I/O access. Accessing the device requires knowledge of only the new device, or system calls for it. There is no degradation of existing I/O performance, since the original code is never modified. All functionality, primarily data formatting, is preserved. The only requirement is understanding how to derive a class properly from the IOSTREAM classes.

The need for a derived class for asynchronous communication may be questioned. The use of a *friend* keyword in a new class can supply most of the desired functionality without the complexity of a class derived from **iostream**. *Friend* directives are quick patches for affixing new objects into the IOSTREAM classes. However, deriving a new class by inheritance from the IOSTREAM classes permits a richer and more robust class for new types of streams.

Generally, a class that uses the *friend* keyword for streaming data is restricted to streaming a single data type. Such a class loses all the formatting functionality supplied by the **ios** class. It also lacks the formatting states that follow from the **ios** class. This may not be a great restriction when retrieving data in a text mode. On the other hand, it is desirable to maintain the formatting ability of a stream when storing data. For example, take a section of code that has an output stream accepting different types of source data:

```
os << "The value of PI to " << 2 << " decimals = " << 3.14 << endl;
```

The destination stream, *os*, may start out as an alias for **cout.** Later in the code's life, it may be used with another object stream class. If this object cannot handle the formatting it has inherited from the new class, then a temporary stream class may be created, the code's compilation could fail, or the program may crash on execution.

The design goal for our class derived for asynchronous modeling is to show how a class that accesses an asynchronous device driver can be integrated with IOSTREAM classes. This class is only a skeleton of an asynchronous class. It should be viewed only as a template for any future design. The Windows API asynchronous communication calls are used. A Hayes-compatible modem is the target for our example. Listing 10.3 is a program that confirms that such a device is accessible.

Listing 10.3

```
// This is a nonobject-oriented modem access. This program uses the
// Window API functions OpenComm( ), WriteComm( ), ReadComm( ), and
// CloseComm( ).

#define INBUF        80
#define MAX_POLL 100000L
#define INQUEUE     1024
#define OUTQUEUE     128

int modem_test (void)
{
    int i;
    char szBuf[INBUF];
    int idComDev;
    WORD cbRead;
    DCB dcb;

    cout << "TESTING MODEM ACCESS\n";
    if((idComDev = OpenComm ("COM1", INQUEUE, OUTQUEUE)) < 0)
      return -1;
    if((BuildCommDCB ("COM1:9600,N,8,1", &dcb) < 0))
      return -1;
    if(SetCommState (&dcb) < 0)
      return -1;
    strcpy(szBuf, "ATV1\r\n");
    WriteComm(idComDev, szBuf, strlen (szBuf));
    i = MAX_POLL;
    do{
        cbRead = ReadComm(idComDev, szBuf, INBUF);
        if(cbRead > 0){
          szBuf[cbRead] = '\0';
          cout << szBuf;
          i = MAX_POLL;
        }
    }
    while(i-);
    CloseComm(idComDev);
    cout << "END OF MODEM ACCESS TEST" << endl;
    return 0;
}
```

It establishes a communication device's queues, builds a device control block for the device, and initializes the modem with the string **ATV1\r\n**. Then, a polling loop begins to wait for a response. If everything is working, the output should be:

```
TESTING MODEM ACCESS

ATV1

OK

END OF MODEM ACCESS TEST
```

Listing 10.4 contains the definitions and declarations for our **siobuf** class and **siostream** class.

Listing 10.4

```
#ifndef _SIOSTREAM_H
#define _SIOSTREAM_H

#include <iostream.h>
#include <strstream.h>
#include <windows.h>

#define siobuf_inherited strstreambuf

class siobuf : public siobuf_inherited {
public:
    siobuf ( );
    siobuf (LPSTR);
    ~siobuf( );
    int    open      (LPSTR);
    void   close     ( );
    int    is_open   ( );
protected:
    virtual  int   doallocate  ( );
    virtual  int   underflow   ( );
    virtual  int   overflow    (int = EOF);
    virtual  int   sync        ( );
private:
    int   fOpened;
    int   idComDev;
    WORD  cbOutQueue;
    WORD  cbInQueue;
    DCB   dcb;
    };
inline int siobuf::is_open ( ) { return fOpened; }

class siostream : public iostream {
public:
    siostream ( );
    siostream (LPSTR);
    ~siostream ( );
    siobuf * rdbuf ( );
private:
    siobuf buf;
};

inline siobuf * siostream::rdbuf( ) { return &this->buf; }

#endif // _SIOSTREAM_H

siostream::siostream( ) : iostream (rdbuf( ))
{
}
```

```
siostream::siostream (LPSTR mode) : iostream (rdbuf( ))
{
   rdbuf( )->open (mode);
}

siostream::~siostream( )
{
}

#define MAX_POLL_CNT    10000L
#define INQUEUE_SIZE    1024
#define OUTQUEUE_SIZE    128

siobuf::siobuf( ) : siobuf_inherited( )
{
   fOpened     = FALSE;
   cbInQueue  = INQUEUE_SIZE;
   cbOutQueue = OUTQUEUE_SIZE;
}

siobuf::siobuf (LPSTR mode)
{
   siobuf( );
   fOpened = open (mode);
}
siobuf::~siobuf( )
{
   close ( );
}

int siobuf::open (LPSTR mode)
{
   LPSTR pszColon;

   if(fOpened)
      return FALSE;

   pszColon = strchr (mode, ':');
   if(pszColon == NULL)
      return FALSE;

   *pszColon = '\0';
   idComDev = OpenComm (mode, cbInQueue, cbOutQueue);
   *pszColon = ':';
   if (idComDev < 0)
      return FALSE;
   fOpened = TRUE; // assume success
   if(BuildCommDCB(mode, &dcb) < 0)
      fOpened = FALSE;
   else if(SetCommState(&dcb) < 0)
      fOpened = FALSE;
   if(!fOpened)
      CloseComm(idComDev);
   return fOpened;
}
```

```
void siobuf::close ( )
{
   if(fOpened)
      CloseComm(idComDev);
}

int siobuf::doallocate( )
{
   if(!fOpened)
      return EOF;
   return siobuf_inherited::doallocate( );
}

int siobuf::underflow( )
{
   LPSTR base_;
   int cb = out_waiting( );
   long cpoll = MAX_POLL_CNT;
   if(!fOpened)
      return EOF;
   if(in_avail( ))
      return (BYTE) *gptr( );
   if(cb && (WriteComm(idComDev, pbase( ), cb) != cb))
      return EOF;
   base_ = base( );
   do
   {
      cb = ReadComm(idComDev, base_, blen( ));
      if(cb > 0)
         cpoll = 0;
      else if (!cpoll-)
         return EOF;
   }
   while (cpoll);
   // set up get and put areas
   setg(base_, base_, base_+cb);
   setp(base_, base_);
   return cb ? (BYTE) *gptr( ) : EOF;
}

int siobuf::overflow (int c)
{
   // allocate put area as needed
   if(!base( ))
      doallocate( ); // if doallocated fails then base will remain NULL
   if(!pbase( ))
      setp (base( ), ebuf( ));
   if(pbase( )){
      if (pptr( ) >= epptr( )){
         LPSTR pOldBase = base( );

         if (siobuf_inherited::doallocate( ) == EOF)
            return EOF;
```

```
            // After reallocation setup put and (if necessary) get area
            // indicators. doallocate only guarantees that setb( ) is
            // called. But both Borland and Microsoft appear to take
            // care of the put area indicators.
            if(gptr( ) != NULL){
                int ebOfs = (int) (eback( ) - pOldBase);
                int gOfs = (int) (gptr( ) - pOldBase);
                int egOfs = (int) (egptr( ) - pOldBase);
                LPSTR pBase = base( );
                setg (pBase+ebOfs, pBase+gOfs, pBase+egOfs);
            }
        }
        if(pptr( ) < epptr( ))
        return sputc(c); //now there is room in the put area
    }
    return EOF; //could not make more space
}

int siobuf::sync( )
{
    if(out_waiting( ) && (overflow (EOF) != EOF))
        return EOF;
    return in_avail( ) ? EOF : 0;
}
```

The following is the class interface specification for the asynchronous access classes **siobuf** and **siostream**:

Class Interface Specification:
```
siobuf
```

Declared in:
```
<siostream.h>
```

Derived from:
```
streambuf
```

Base Class for:
None

Contains:
None

Constructors:
```
siobuf::siobuf( );
siobuf::siobuf(LPSTR);
```

Destructors:

```
virtual siobuf::~siobuf( );
```

Protected Data Members:

None

Protected Member Functions:

```
virtual int doallocate( );
virtual int underflow( );
virtual int overflow (int = EOF);
virtual int sync( );
```

Public Member Functions:

```
void close( );
int is_open( );
int open (LPSTR);
```

DESCRIPTION A **siobuf** can be implemented in a closed or opened mode. Both constructors will create an empty **siobuf** whose buffer will be dynamically allocated. Actual memory will not be allocated until needed.

The siobuf Constructors and Destructors

The constructor:

```
siobuf::siobuf ( );
```

creates an empty **siobuf** in dynamic mode. The reserve area is not allocated until needed. This allocation size is an implementation-specific minimum inherited from **streambuf** through its **doallocate( )** member function.

The constructor:

```
siobuf::siobuf (LPSTR mode);
```

is similar to the first constructor, except that here the programmer may specify the communication port to open, and the mode to open the port. The ASCIZ string **mode** follows the format used by the Windows API **BuildCommDCB( )** function. The constructor call:

```
siobuf siob ("COM2:2400,E,7,2");
```

is equivalent to:

```
siobuf siob;
siob.open("COM2:2400,E,7,2");
```

The destructor:

```
siobuf::~siobuf( );
```

deletes a **siobuf.** If the port has been opened, it will be closed by the **CloseComm( )** function. It will finally call its inherited destructor to delete its reserve area. This destructor must be virtual, since it is normally destroyed when a **siostream** using it is destroyed.

The Protected siobuf Member Functions

The **doallocate( )**, **overflow( )**, **underflow( )**, and **sync( )** member functions take over the default behavior for **siobuf** that is specific to it. Of primary concern is the **underflow( )** and **overflow( )** member functions. These member functions provide the main interface between the Windows API calls and the **siobuf** class. The other member functions provide additional support for the class. These member functions are incomplete. Error handling and response were left out for brevity of the example.

The member function:

```
int doallocate( );
```

should call its inherited **doallocate( )** function if a com port has been successfully opened and returns its results. If a com port has not been successfully opened, it should return EOF to indicate failure.

The member function:

```
int underflow( );
```

will be called when there is no data waiting in the **get** area. It first attempts to free up some of the reserve space by sending any data in the **put** area to the communication device through the **WriteComm( )** API function. It will then perform a poll for waiting data. If any data is available, it will be retrieved using the **ReadComm( )** API function. If no data arrived by the end of the polling loop, then EOF will be returned. If data was retrieved, then the area indicators will be adjusted using the inherited **setg( )** and **setp( )** member functions, and will return the first character read into the **get** area.

The member function:

```
int overflow(int = c);
```

is the complement to the **underflow( )** member function. It is called when data is written to the buffer's **put** area, and the **put** area has become full. It first calls the **doallocate( )** member function. If this succeeds, it recopies the data into the new reserve area and adjusts the area indicators through the **setb( )** and **setp( )** member functions. If reallocation is successful, then the character *c* is added to the put area and returned. Otherwise, EOF is returned.

The member function:

```
int sync( );
```

calls the **out_waiting( )** member function to see if any data is in the **put** area, and calls the **overflow( )** member function to force it out. If it cannot send waiting data, then EOF is returned; then it checks to see if there is any waiting data by using the **in_avail( )** member function. If there aren't any characters in the **get** area, then zero is returned. Otherwise, EOF is returned, since we don't restore unfetched characters to the com device. This restriction is only to simplify the example.

The Public siobuf Member Functions

The member function:

```
void close( );
```

will call the Windows **CloseComm( )** API function if a com port has been successfully opened. Then it will always be called by the **siobuf** destructor.

The member function:

```
int is_open( );
```

is an inline member function that returns the TRUE (!FALSE) if the **siobuf** com device has been successfully opened. It returns FALSE (0) if the com device has not been opened or if the **close( )** member function has been called.

The member function:

```
int open (LPSTR mode);
```

opens and initializes the com port using the **OpenComm( )**, **BuildCommDCB( )**, and **SetCommState( )** Windows API functions. It will return FALSE (0) if any of these functions fails. It will make certain that the com port is closed if the latter two functions fail.

The siostream Class for the Asynchronous Access Class

The following is the class interface specification for the **siostream** class.

Class Interface Specification:

```
siostream
```

Declared in:

```
<siostream.h>
```

Derived from:

```
iostream
```

Base Class for:

None

Contains:

```
siobuf
```

Constructors:

```
siostream( );
siostream(LPSTR);
```

Destructors:

```
siostream::~siostream( );
```

Protected Member Functions

None

Public Member Functions:

```
siobuf * rdbuf ( );
```

DESCRIPTION **siostream** is a type of **iostream** that uses a **siobuf** to buffer I/O data and interface to an asynchronous device. Practically all of its behavior is inherited from the **iostream** class. It differs only in its means of construction and the addition of a **rdbuf( )** member function that can return its buffer as a type of **siobuf.**

The siostream Constructors and Destructors

The constructors:

```
siostream( );
siostream(LPSTR mode);
```

are comparable to the two **siobuf** constructors. The first permits the programmer to open the **siostream** at a later point through a call to its buffer. For example:

```
siostream sio;
sio.rdbuf( )->open ("COM1:1200,E,8,1");
```

is equivalent to:

```
siostream sio ("COM1:1200,E,8,1");
```

The bodies of these two constructors are empty. They rely on the inherited constructors to do the actual work.

The destructor:

```
siostream::~siostream( );
```

deletes a **siostream.** As with **siostream**'s constructors, the body of its destructor is empty and the inherited destructors will perform the actual work.

The Public siostream Member Functions

The member function:

```
siobuf * rdbuf( );
```

is a static polymorphism of the inherited **rdbuf( )** member function. The inherited member function will return the used **siobuf** typed to its ancestor **streambuf** class. Overloading this member function permits access to the **siobuf** in a type-safe manner. Any incorrect use of these member functions will be caught at compile time. For example:

```
siobuf * psiob;
streambuf * psb;
siostream sio;

psiob = sio.rdbuf( );   // ok, the new rdbuf( ) member function used
psb = sio.rdbuf( );     // ok, the inherited rdbuf( ) member function used
psiob = cout.rdbuf( );  // error, ostream doesn't have a rdbuf( )
                        // member function that returns a siobuf pointer.
```

The **siobuf** and **siostream** classes can be further developed and used to do simple asynchronous port access. We have left out many of the details so that the reader can understand the outline of what an asynchronous class would require. This template represents only one of many possibilities of design choices.

The Class Relationship Diagram Specification

The class relationship diagram is a design and documentation technique that originated at Ctest Laboratories. The class relationship diagram can be used to show whether classes are related through inheritance, containment, or some other method. The class relationship diagram can show whether the class is a product of single inheritance, multiple inheritance, or aggregation.

The class relationship diagram can show any level of relational detail in a set of classes. A high-level overview of the relationship can be diagrammed, or a low-level relationship can be telescoped to the source code level.

The diagram consists of four basic components:

- A relation operator symbol
- Flow lines
- A vertical and horizontal specification
- A class grouping symbol

The diagramming technique introduces the protoclass abstraction to the object-oriented paradigm. The protoclass is the set difference between n classes. For example, given two classes A and B, the protoclass is the set difference between A and B. If class A contains the members $\{1,2,3,4\}$, and class B contains the members $\{1,2,3,4,5\}$, the protoclass for the combination of A and B is $\{5\}$, and the protoclass would belong to the class B. The class A and class B need not refer to different classes.

Every class relationship includes a NULL class. Although it is not shown in the diagram, it is understood to be present. For example, in describing the relationship between a single class and itself, we show the existence of the protoclass. Given a single class A with members $\{1,2,3,4\}$, to get the protoclass for A,

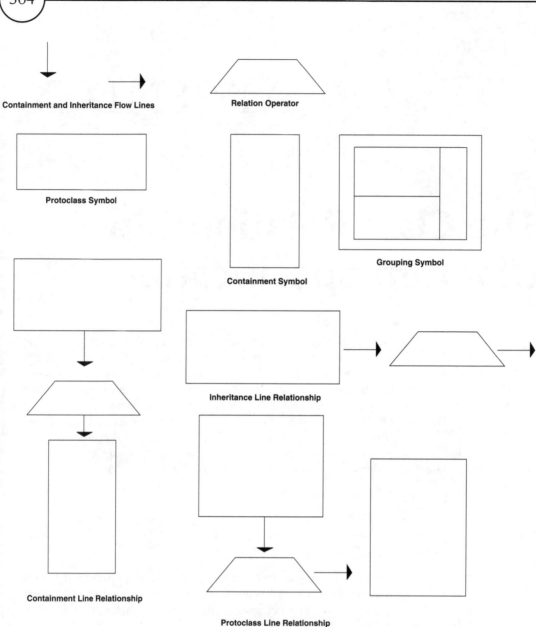

Figure A.1   *Class relationship diagrams symbols and relationship lines.*

perform the set difference between A and the Null Class { }. Hence, {1,2,3,4} / { } is {1,2,3,4}. The protoclass for the base class A is exactly its member functions. The implication of this is that every class has a protoclass and a NULL class.

The relationship symbol shows how classes are related. Whatever relationship exists between the classes is expressed within the relationship symbol. The flow lines show which classes are combined together in a relationship. The flow lines state that the classes connected between the two end points are related. The relation symbol tells how they are related. There are no assumptions about the types of relationships that can be contained in the relationship symbol. Therefore, the CRD (Class Relationship Diagram) can show any kind of relationship between classes. The flow lines have the semantic that "A is related to B" by the relationship contained in the relationship symbol.

The horizontal and vertical specifications designate the two fundamental relationships that exist in all object-oriented paradigms: inheritance and containment. If two classes are related by inheritance, they will be separated by a horizontal line in the class grouping symbol. When classes are related by containment, they are separated by a vertical line in the class grouping symbol.

The class grouping symbol is used to show the collection of classes under consideration in a relational analysis. The class grouping symbol may show the highest representation of a class (i.e., the class name) or the lowest representation of a class (i.e., source code specifying data members and member functions). Although the class grouping symbol depicts the basic inheritance and containment relationship that exists between a set of classes, the entire class relationship diagram specifies the total relationship that exists between the classes. Figure A.1 shows the symbols for the CRD, and their purpose.

Stream Class Hierarchy Charts

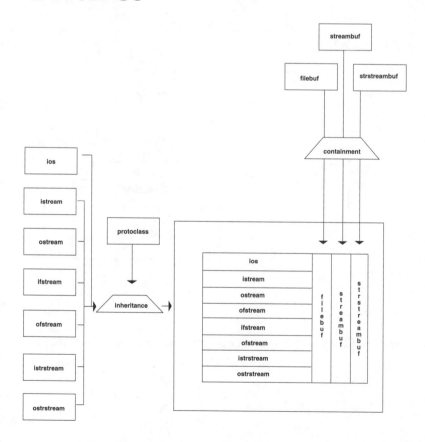

Figure B.1 *The class relationship diagram of the IOSTREAM family of classes.*

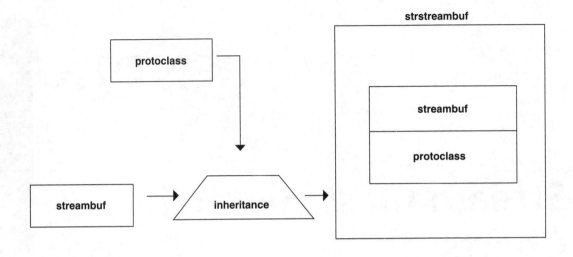

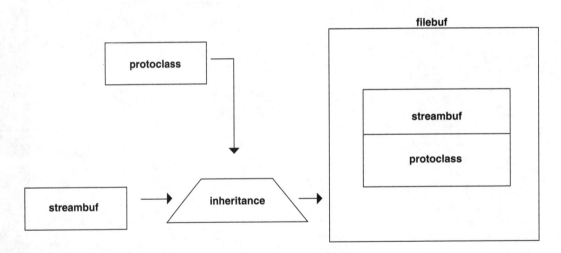

Figure B.2   *Buffer classes: The class relationship diagram for the **strstreambuf** and **filebuf** classes.*

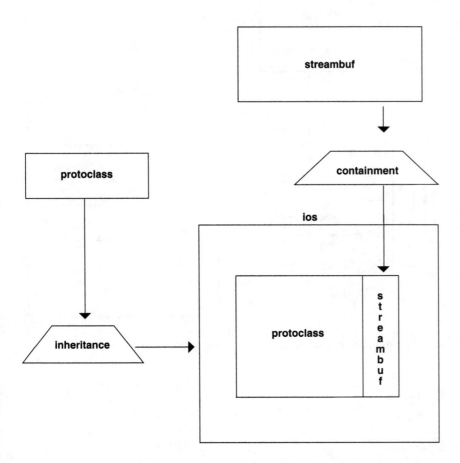

Figure B.3 *Formatting class: The class relationship diagram for the **ios** class.*

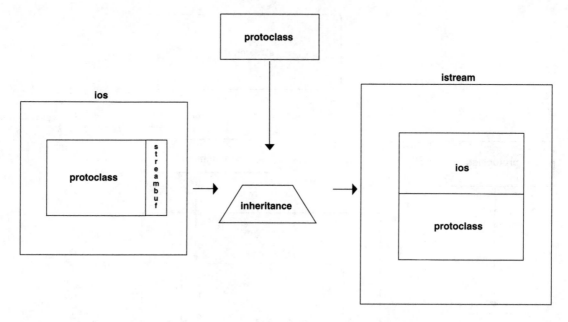

Figure B.4   *Input class: The class relationship diagram for the **istream** class.*

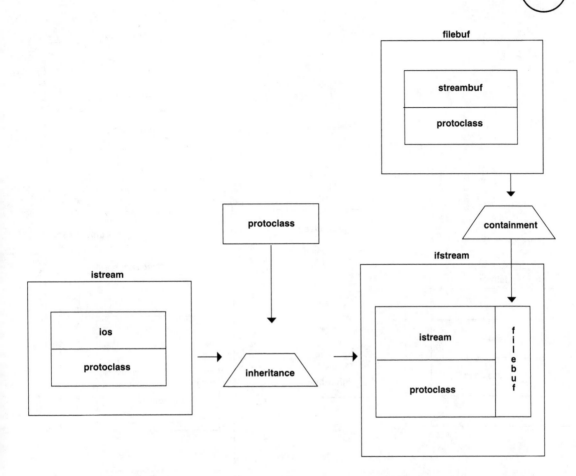

Figure B.5 *Input class: The class relationship diagram for the **ifstream** class.*

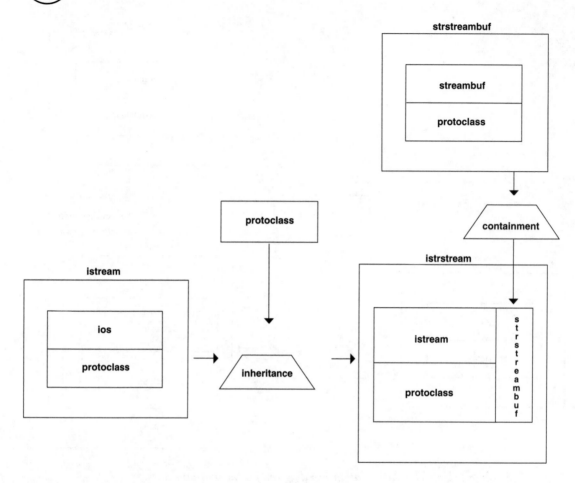

Figure B.6   *Input class: The class relationship diagram for the **istrstream** class.*

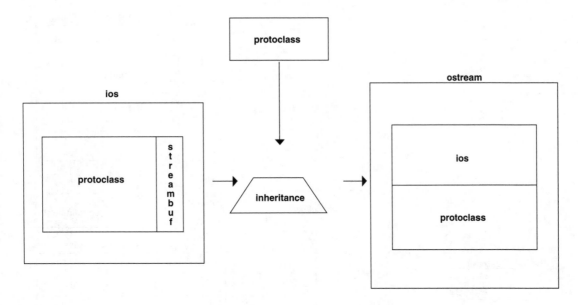

Figure B.7 *Output class: The class relationship diagram for the **ostream** class.*

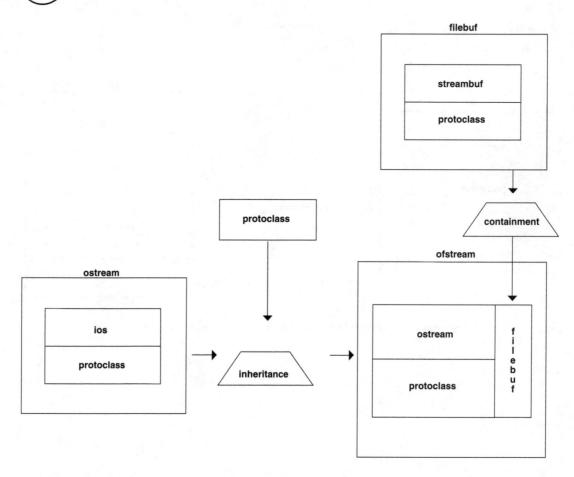

Figure B.8   *Output class: The class relationship diagram for the **ofstream** class.*

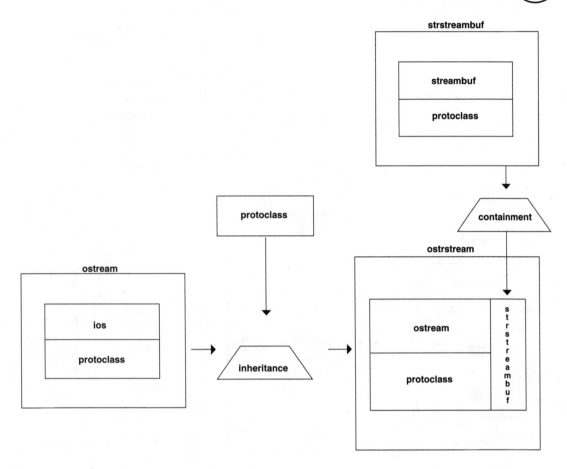

Figure B.9 *Output class: The class relationship diagram for the **ostrstream** class.*

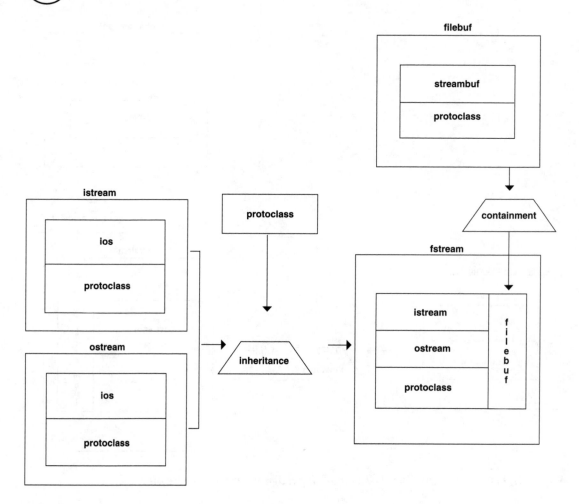

Figure B.10   *Bidirectional class: The class relationship diagram for the **fstream** class.*

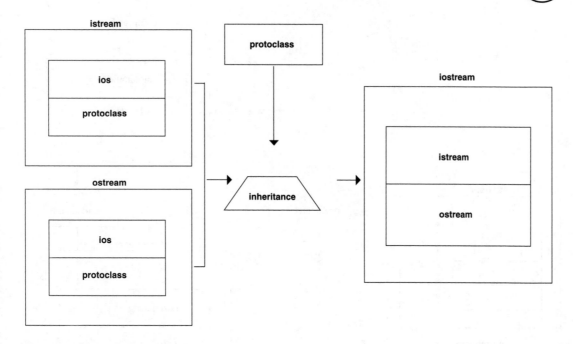

Figure B.11   *Bidirectional class: The class relationship diagram for the **iostream** class.*

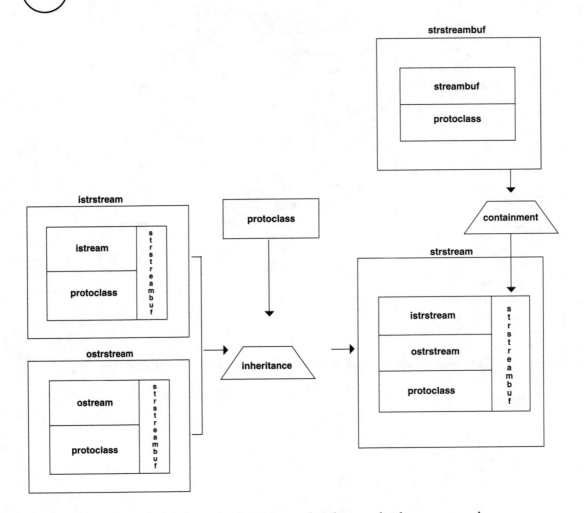

Figure B.12   *Bidirectional class: The class relationship diagram for the **strstream** class.*

IOSTREAM Classes Quick Reference

Buffering Classes

Class Interface Specification:

streambuf

Declared in:

<iostream.h>

Derived from:

None

Base for:

filebuf
strstreambuf
stdiobuf

Contains:

None

Constructors:

```
streambuf( )
```
Creates an empty buffer object.
```
streambuf(char *, int)
```
Uses the specified array and size as the buffer.

Destructors:

```
virtual ~streambuf( )
```

Protected Data Members:

None

Protected Member Functions:

```
int allocate( )
```
Sets up a buffer area.
```
char *base( )
```
Returns the start of the buffer area.
```
int blen( )
```
Returns the length of the buffer area.
```
char *eback( )
```
Returns the base of **putback** section to **get** area.
```
char *ebuf( )
```
Returns the end+1 of the **get** area.
```
char *egptr( )
```
Returns the end+1 of the **put** area.
```
char *epptr( )
void gbump(int)
```
Advances the **get** pointer.
```
char *gptr( )
```
Returns next location in **get** area.
```
void pbump(int n)
```
Advances the **put** pointer.
```
*char pptr( );
```
Returns the next location in the **put** area.
```
int sbumpc( );
```

Returns the current character from the input buffer, then advances.

```
virtual streampos seekpos(streamoff, ios::seek_dir,int = (ios::in. |
    ios::out))
```

Moves the **get** or **put** pointer and the third parameter, and determines which one or if both, relative to current position.

```
virtual streampos seekpos(streampos, int = (ios::in | ios::out))
```

Moves the **get** or **put** pointer to an absolute value.

```
void setb(char *, char*, int = 0)
```

Sets the buffer area.

```
virtual streambuf* setbuf(signed char *, int)
streambuf* setbuf(unsigned char*, int)
```

Connects to a specified buffer.

```
void setb(char *, char *, int = 0)
```

Sets the buffer area.

```
void setg(char * char *, char *)
```

Initializes the **get** pointers.

```
void setp(char *, char *)
```

Initializes the **put** pointers.

```
void unbuffered(int);
```

Sets the buffering state.

```
int unbuffered( );
```

Returns nonzero if not buffered.

Public Data Members:

None

Public Member Functions:

```
int in_avail( )
```

Returns the number of characters remaining in the input buffer.

```
int out_waiting( )
```

Returns the number of characters remaining in the output buffer.

```
int sgetc( )
```

Peeks at the next character in the input buffer.

```
int sgetn(char*, int n)
```

Gets the next *n* character in the input buffer.

```
int snextc( )
```

Advances to and returns the next character from the input buffer.

```
int sputbackc(char)
```

Returns a character to input.

```
int sputc(const char*, int n)
```

Puts *n* characters into the output buffer.

```
void stossc( );
```

Advances to the next character in the input buffer.

DESCRIPTION streambuf is a class that models a buffer. It provides access to the buffer, along with position designators for the buffer.

Class Interface Specification

```
filebuf
```

Declared in:

```
<fstream.h>
```

Derived from:

```
streambuf
```

Base for:

None

Contains:

None

Constructors:

```
filebuf( )
```

Creates a **filebuf** that isn't attached to a file.

```
filebuf(int fd)
```

Creates a **filebuf** that is attached to a file as specified by file descriptor *fd.*

```
filebuf(int fd, char*, int n)
```

Creates a **filebuf** that is attached to a file and uses a specified *n* character buffer.

```
filebuf(int fd, unsigned char*, int n);
```

Creates a **filebuf** attached to a file and uses a specified *n* character buffer.

Destructor:

`~filebuf( )`

Protected Data Members:

`int xfd`

A file descriptor.

`int mode`

The open mode for the **filebuf.**

`short opened`

Value is nonzero if the file is opened.

`char lahead[2]`

An array that stores the current input characters.

Protected Member Functions:

None

Public Data Members:

`static const int openprot`

The default file projection.

Public Member Functions:

`filebuf* attach(int)`

Attaches this closed **filebuf** to opened file descriptor.

`filebuf* close( )`

Flushes and closes the file and returns 0 if an error occurs.

`int is_open( )`

Returns nonzero if the **filebuf** is attached to file descriptor.

`filebuf* open (const char *name, int mode, int prot = filebuf::openprot)`

Opens the file specified by **name** and connects to it. The file opening mode is specified by **mode.**

`virtual int overflow (int = EOF)`

Flushes a buffer to its destination. Every derived class should define the implementation of this function.

`virtual streampos seekoff(streamoff, ios::seek_dir, int)`

Moves the file pointer relative to the current position.

```
virtual streambuf* setbuf(char*, int);
```
Specifies a buffer for this **filebuf.**

```
virtual int sync( )
```
Establishes consistency between internal data structures and external stream representation.

```
virtual int underflow( )
```
Makes input available. This is called when no more data exists in the input buffer. Every derived class should define the implementation of this function.

DESCRIPTION filebuf specializes the **streambuf** to work with files.

Class Interface Specification:

```
strstreambuf
```

Declared in:

```
<strstreambuf.h>
```

Derived from:

```
streambuf
```

Base for:

None

Contains:

None

Constructors:

```
strstreambuf( )
```
Creates a dynamic **strstreambuf.** Memory will be dynamically allocated as needed.

```
strstreambuf (void * (*) (long), void (*) (void *))
```
Creates a dynamic buffer with specified allocation and free functions.

```
strstreambuf (int n)
```
Creates a dynamic **strstreambuf**, initially allocating a buffer of at least *n* bytes.

```
strstreambuf (char*, int, char *strt = 0)
strstreambuf (signed char *, int, signed char *strt = 0)
strstreambuf (unsigned char *, int, unsigned char *strt = 0)
```

Creates a static **strstreambuf** with a specified buffer. If *strt* is not null, it delimits the buffer.

Destructors:

```
~strstreambuf( )
```

Protected Data Members:

None

Protected Member Functions:

None

Public Data Members:

None

Public Member Functions:

```
virtual int doallocate( )
```
Performs low-level buffer allocation.

```
void freeze(int = 1)
```
If the input parameter is nonzero, disallows storing any characters in the buffer. Unfreeze by passing a zero.

```
virtual int overflow(int)
```
Flushes a buffer to its destination. Every derived class should define the implementation.

```
virtual streampos seekoff(streamoff, ios::seek_dir, int);
```
Moves the pointer to the current position.

```
virtual streambuf* setbuf(char*, int);
```
Specifies the buffer to use.

```
char *str( )
```
Returns a pointer to the buffer and freezes it.

```
virtual int sync( )
```
Returns an EOF if an error occurs.

```
virtual int undeflow( )
```
Creates input available. This is called when a character is requested and **strstreambuf** is empty. Every derived class should define the implementation.

DESCRIPTION **strstreambuf** is a specialized **streambuf** for in-memory formatting.

Formatting Classes

Class Interface Specification:

```
ios
```

Declared in:

```
<iostream.h>
```

Derived from:

None

Base for:

```
istream
ostream
strstreambase
fstreambase
```

Contains:

```
streambuf
```

Constructors:

```
ios( )
```
Creates an **ios** object that has no **streambuf.**
```
ios(streambuf *)
```
Associates the specified **streambuf** with the stream.

Destructors:

```
~ios( )
```

Protected Data Members:

`streambuf_FAR *bp`

A pointer to the associated **streambuf.**

`ostream _FAR *x_tie`

The tied **ostream.**

`int state`

The current state of the **streambuf.**

`int x_fill;`

The padding character for output.

`long x_flags`

The formatting flag bits.

`int x_precision`

The floating-point precision on output.

`int x_width`

The field width on output.

Protected Member Functions:

None

Public Data Members:

`enum seek_dir { beg=0, cur=1, end=2 }`

The stream seek direction.

`enum open_mode`

app—append data; always writes at end of file.

ate—seeks to end of file upon open.

in—open for input.

out—open for output.

binary—opens file in binary mode.

trunc—discards the contents if file exists.

nocreate—if the file does not exist, **open( )** a file for output, fails unless **ate** or **app** is set.

`enum`

skipws—skips the white space on input.

left—left adjustment of output.

right—right adjustment of output.

internal—pads after a sign or base indicator.

dec—decimal conversion.

oct—octal conversion.

hex—hexadecimal conversion.

showbase—shows the base indicator on output.

showpoint—shows the decimal point for floating output.

uppercase—uppercase base letter indicators, hex digits, and *e* notation.

showpos—shows + with positive integers.

scientific—suffix floating-point numbers with exponential *e* notation on output.

fixed—uses fixed decimal point for floating-point numbers.

unitbuf—flushes all streams after insertion.

stdio—flushes **stdout, stderr** after insertion.

```
static const long adjust field
```

Left, right, internal values.

```
static const long basefield
```

Dec, oct, hex values.

```
static const long floatfield
```

Scientific, fixed values.

```
enum io_state
```

goodbit—value set when stream is in good state.

eofbit—value set when end of file has occurred.

failbit—value set when stream in fail state.

badbit—value set when stream in bad state.

hardfail—unrecoverable error.

Public Member Functions:

```
int bad( )
```

Nonzero if error occurred.

```
static long bitalloc( )
```

A user-defined formatting flag. It acquires a new flag bit set. The return value can be used to set, clear, and test the flag.

```
void clear (int = 0)
```

Sets the stream state to the given value.

```
int eof ( )
```

Nonzero on end of file.

`int fail( )`

Nonzero if an operation failure occurs.

`char fill( )`

Returns the current fill character.

`char fill (char)`

Sets the fill character; returns the previous one.

`long flags( )`

Returns the current format flags.

`long flags(long)`

Sets the format to the value specified as a **long**; returns previous flags.

`int good( )`

Nonzero if no state bits, no error bits set.

`void init (streambuf *)`

Provides the actual initialization.

`int precision( )`

Returns the current floating-point precision.

`int precision (int)`

Sets the floating-point precision; returns previous setting.

`streambuf* rdbuf( )`

Returns the pointer to this stream's assigned **streambuf.**

`int rdstate ( )`

Returns the stream state.

`long setf(long)`

Sets the flags marked by the specified **long**; returns previous settings.

`long setf(long_setbits, long_field)`

The bits corresponding to those specified in **_field** are cleared, and then resets those specified in **_setbits**.

`void setstate(int)`

Sets all status bits.

`static void sync_with_stdio( )`

Mixes **stdio** files and **iostreams.**

`ostream* tie( )`

Returns the tied stream, or zero if none.

`ostream* tie(ostream*)`

Ties another to this one and returns the previous tied stream.

```
long unsetf(long)
```

Clears the bits corresponding to those specified by **long**; returns previous settings.

```
int width( )
```

Returns the current width settings.

```
int width(int)
```

Sets the width as given; returns the previous width.

```
static int xalloc( )
```

Returns an array index of previous unused words that can be used as user-defined format.

DESCRIPTION The **ios** class encapsulates the stream state and the buffer. It represents the format and condition of the stream and any objects that have been inserted in or extracted from the stream. The **ios** class provides the **istream** class and **ostream** class with a buffer.

Input Classes

Class Interface Specification:

```
istream
```

Declared in:

```
<iostream.h>
```

Derived from:

```
ios
```

Base for:

```
ifstream
istrstream
iostream
istream_withassign
```

Contains:

```
streambuf *
```

Constructors:

```
istream(streambuf*)
```

Associates the specified **streambuf** with the stream.

Destructors:

```
virtual ~istream( )
```

Destroys an **istream** object.

Protected Data Members:

None

Protected Member Functions:

```
void eatwhite( )
```

Extracts consecutive white spaces.

```
int gcount( )
```

Returns the number of characters extracted last.

Public Data Members:

None

Public Member Functions:

```
int ipfx(int = 0)
```

Prefix function.

```
int sync( )
```

Returns a nonzero if the **filebuf** is attached to a file descriptor.

```
void isfx( ) {}
```

Suffix function.

```
istream& get(char*, int len, char = '\n')
istream& get(signed char*, int len, char = '\n')
istream& get(unsigned char*, int len, char = '\n')
```

Extracts characters into the given **char*** until the delimiter, third parameter, or end of file is encountered, or until **(len-1)** bytes have been read. The delimiter remains in the stream. It fails only if no characters were extracted.

```
istreams& get (char&)
istreams& get (signed char&)
istreams& get (unsigned char&)
```

Extracts a single character into the specified character reference.

```
istream& get(streambuf&, char = '\n')
```

Extracts characters into the specified **streambuf** until the delimiter is encountered.

```
istream& getline(char*, int, char)
istream& getline(signed char *buffer, int, char = '\n')
istream& getline(unsigned char *buffer, int, char = '\n')
```

Same as **get( )** function, except the delimiter is also extracted. The delimiter is not copied to buffer.

```
istream& ignore(int n = 1, int delim = EOF)
```

Causes up to *n* characters in the input stream to be skipped; stops if the delimiter is encountered.

```
int peek( );
```

Returns next character without extraction.

```
istream& putback(char)
```

Pushes back a character into the stream.

```
istream& read(char*, int)
istream& read(signed char*, int)
istream& read(unsigned char*, int)
```

Extracts a specified number of characters into an array. Use **gcount( )** for the number of characters actually extracted if an error occurred.

```
istream& seekg(streamoff, seek_dir)
```

Moves to position relative to the current position, following the definition: **enum seek_dir {beg,cur,end}.**

```
streampos tellg( )
```

Returns the current stream position.

```
istream& operator>>( )
```

Extracts the specified built-in data type from a stream.

DESCRIPTION istream is a class that models the input stream. The **istream** class recognizes binary and text strings. The **istream** class is a member function that translates generic streams of bytes into objects that can be extracted from the input stream.

Class Interface Specification:

```
ifstream
```

Declared in:

`<fstream.h>`

Derived from:

`istream`

`fstreambase`

Base for:

`filebuf`

Constructors:

`ifstream( )`

Creates an **ifstream** that isn't attached to a file.

`ifstream (const char *name, int mode = ios::in, int =`
`    filebuf::openprot)`

Creates an **ifstream** object, opens a file for input in protected mode, and connects to it. The already existing file is preserved; new writes are appended.

`ifstream(int fd, char *buf,int buf_len)`

Creates an **ifstream** connected to an open file. The file is specified by its descriptor, *fd*. The ifstream object uses the buffer specified by *buf* of length *buf_len*.

`ifstream(int fd)`

Creates an **ifstream**, connects to an open filedescriptor *fd.*

Destructors:

`~ifstream( )`

Protected Data Members:

None

Protected Member Functions:

None

Public Data Members:

None

Public Member Functions:

```
void open (const char*, int, int = filebuf::openprot)
```
Opens a file for **ifstream.**

```
filebuf* rdbuf( )
```
Returns the **filebuf** used.

```
setbuf(char *, int)
```
If fails, returns zero, sets **failbit.**

```
attach(int)
```
Attaches a specified file to an **ifstream** object.

DESCRIPTION ifstream class, derived from **fstreambase** and **istream,** provides input operations on a **filebuf.**

Class Interface Specification:

```
istream_withassign
```

Declared in:

```
<iostream.h>
```

Derived from:

```
istream
```

Base for:

None

Contains:

None

Constructors:

```
istream_withassign( )
```
Default constructor, calls **istream**'s constructor.

Destructors:

```
~istream_withassign
```

Protected Data Members:

None

Protected Member Functions:

None

Public Data Members:

None

Public Member Functions:

None

DESCRIPTION This is the **istream** class with an assignment operator.

Class Interface Specification:

istrstream

Declared in:

<strstrea.h>

Derived from:

istream
strstreambase

Base for:

None

Contains:

strstreambuf

Constructor:

istrstream(unsigned char *)
istrstream(char *)
istrstream(signed char *)
istrstream(const char *)

```
strstream(const signed char *)
strstream(const unsigned char *)
```

Creates an **istrstream** with a specified string. A null is never extracted.

```
istrstream(signed char *, int n)
istrstream(char *, int n)
istrstream(unsigned char *, int n)
istrstream(const char *, int n)
istrstream(const signed char *, int n)
istrstream(const unsigned char *, int n)
```

Creates an **istrstream** using up to *n* bytes of a specified string.

Destructors:

```
~istrstream( )
```

Protected Data Members:

None

Protected Member Functions:

None

Public Data Members:

None

Public Member Functions:

```
strstreambuf* rdbuf( )
```

Returns a pointer to the **streambuf**.

DESCRIPTION **istrstream** is a class that models the input memory stream or character array. The **istrstream** class recognizes binary and text strings. The **istrstream** class has a member function that translates generic streams of bytes into objects that can be extracted from the input stream.

Output Classes

Class Interface Specification:

```
ostream
```

Declared in:

`<iostream.h>`

Derived from:

`ios`

Base for:

`ofstream`

`ostrstream`

`iostream`

`ostream_withassign`

Contains:

`streambuf*`

Constructors:

`ostream(streambuf *)`

Associates a specified **streambuf** with the stream.

Destructors:

`virtual ~ostream`

Protected Data Members:

None

Protected Member Functions:

None

Public Data Members:

None

Public Member Functions:

`int opfx( )`

Prefix function.

```
void osfx( )
```
Suffix function.
```
ostream& flush( )
```
Flushes the stream.
```
ostream put(unsigned char)
ostream put(char)
ostream put(signed char)
```
Inserts the character.
```
ostream& seekp(streampos)
```
Moves to an absolute position.
```
ostream& seep(streamoff, seek_dir)
```
Moves a position relative to the current position, following the definition:
enum seek_dir {beg, cur, end}.
```
streampos tellp( )
```
Returns the current stream position.
```
ostream& write(const signed char*, int n)
ostream& write(const unsigned char*, int n)
ostream& write(const char*, int n)
```
Inserts *n* characters with the null character.
```
ostream& operator<<( )
```
Inserts built-in data type into a stream.

DESCRIPTION ostream provides a formatted and unformatted output to a **streambuf.**
The insertion operator (**<<**) is overloaded for all built-in data types.

Class Interface Specification:
```
ostream_withassign
```

Declared in:
```
<iostream.h>
```

Derived from:
```
ostream
```

Base for:
None

Contains:

None

Constructors:

```
ostream_withassign( )
```
Default constructor that calls **ostream**'s constructor.

Destructors:

```
~ostream_withassign( )
```

Protected Data Members:

None

Protected Member Functions:

None

Public Data Members:

None

Public Member Functions:

```
ostream_withassign_FAR &_Cdecl operator = (ostream_FAR *)
```
Gets the buffer from **istream** and does an entire initialization.
```
ostream_withassign_FAR & _Cdecl operator = (streambuf _FAR *)
```
Associates **streambuf** with the stream and does an entire initialization.

DESCRIPTION This is an **ostream** class with added assignment function.

Class Interface Specification:

```
ofstream
```

Declared in:

```
<fstream.h>
```

Derived from:

```
fstreambase
ostream
```

Base for:

None

Contains:

```
filebuf
```

Constructors:

```
ofstream( )
```
Creates an **ofstream** that isn't attached to a file.
```
ofstream(const char *name, int mode = ios::out, int prot =
    filebuf::openprot)
```
Creates an **ofstream**, opens a file, and connects to it.
```
ofstream(int fd)
```
Creates an **ofstream**, connects to an open file descriptor by *fd.*
```
ofstream(int fd, char *buf, int len)
```
Creates an **ofstream** connected to an open file descriptor specified by *fd.*
The buffer specified by *buf* of *len* is used by the **ofstream.**

Destructors:

```
~ofstream( )
```

Protected Data Members:

None

Protected Member Functions:

None

Public Data Members:

None

Public Member Functions:

```
void open(const char*, int =ios::out, int = filebuf::openprot)
```
Opens a file for an **ofstream** object.
```
filebuf* rdbuf( )
```
Returns the **filebuf** used.

DESCRIPTION The **ofstream** provides input operations on a **filebuf.**

Class Interface Specification:

ostrstream

Declared in:

<strstrea.h>

Derived from:

ostream
strstreambase

Base for:

None

Contains:

strstreambuf

Constructors:

ostrstream( )

Creates a dynamic **ostrstream** object.

ostrstream(signed char*, int, int)

ostrstream(char *buf, int len, int mode = ios::out)

ostrstream(unsigned char*, int, int)

Creates an **ostrstream** with a specified *len*-byte buffer. If the file-opening mode is **ios::app** or **ios::ate**, the **get/put** pointer is positioned at the null character of the string.

Destructors:

~ostrstream( )

Protected Data Members:

None

Protected Member Functions:

None

Public Member Functions:

```
int pcount( )
```
Returns the number of bytes currently stored in the buffer.

```
char *str( )
```
Returns and freezes the buffer. It must **deallocate** it if it was dynamic.

DESCRIPTION ostrstream is a class that models the output memory stream of character array. The **ostrstream** class has a member function that translates objects into a generic stream of bytes that can be inserted into an output stream.

Bidirectional Classes

Class Interface Specification:

```
fstream
```

Declared in:

```
<fstream.h>
```

Derived from:

```
fstreambase
iostream
```

Base for:

None

Contains:

```
filebuf
```

Constructors:

```
fstream( )
```
Creates an **fstream** that isn't connected to a file.

```
fstream (int fd, signed char *buf, int buf_len)
```
Creates an **fstream**, opens a file, connects to it. The buffer length is specified in **len**. In this case, the **buf** pointer is signed **char.**

```
fstream (int fd, unsigned char *buf, int buf_len)
```

Creates an **fstream**, opens a file, connects to it. The buffer length is specified in **len**. In this case, the **buf** pointer is unsigned **char**.

```
fstream(const signed char *buf, int, int = filebuf::openprot)
```

Creates an **fstream** object, opens a file, and connects to it. In this case, the **buf** pointer is an unsigned **char**.

```
fstream(const signed char *buf, int, int = filebuf::openprot)
```

Creates an **fstream** object, opens a file, and connects to it. In this case, the buffer is an unsigned **char**.

```
fstream(int)
```

Creates an **fstream** connected to an open file handle specified by **int**.

Destructors:

```
~fstream( )
```

Protected Data Members:

None

Protected Member Functions:

None

Public Data Members:

None

Public Member Functions:

```
void open (const char *name, int mode = ios::in, int prot =
  filebuf::openprot)
```

Opens a file specified by **name** for an **fstream**. The file-opening mode is specified by the variable **mode**.

```
void open (const unsigned char *name, int mode = ios::in, int prot =
  file buf::openprot)
```

Opens a file specified by **name** for an **fstream**. The file-opening mode is specified by the variable **mode**.

```
filebuf* rdbuf( )
```

Returns the **filebuf** used.

DESCRIPTION fstream provides simultaneous input and output on a **filebuf**.

Class Interface Specification:

fstreambase

Declared in:

<fstream.h>

Derived from:

ios

Base for:

fstream
ifstream
ofstream

Contains:

filebuf

Constructors:

fstreambase( )

Creates an **fstreambase** that isn't attached to a file.

fstreambase(int fd)

Creates an **fstreambase**, connects to an open file descriptor specified by *fd.*

fstreambase(int fd, char *buf, int len)

Creates an **fstreambase** connected to an open file descriptor specified by *fd.* The buffer is specified by *buf* of a length specified by *len.*

fstreambase(const char *, int mode, int = filebuf::openprot)

Creates an **fstreambase**, opens a file in mode specified by *mode*, and connects it.

Destructors:

~fstreambase( )

Protected Data Members:

None

Protected Member Functions:

None

Public Data Members:

None

Public Member Functions:

```
void attach(int)
```
Connects to an open file descriptor.
```
void close( )
```
Closes the associated **filebuf** and file.
```
void open(const char *name, int mode prot = filebuf::openprot)
```
Opens a file for an **fstreambase**. The file-opening mode is specified by *mode.*
```
filebuf* rdbuf( )
```
Returns the **filebuf** used.
```
void setbuf (char*, int)
```
Uses a buffer specified.

DESCRIPTION fstreambase provides operations common to file streams.

Class Interface Specification:

```
iostream
```

Declared in:

```
<iostream>
```

Derived from:

```
istream
ostream
```

Base for:

```
fstream
strstream
```

Contains:

None

Constructors:

```
iostream(streambuf *)
```
Associates a given **streambuf** object with a stream.

Destructors:

```
~iostream( )
```

Protected Data Members:

None

Protected Member Functions:

None

Public Data Members:

None

Public Member Functions:

None

DESCRIPTION iostream is a combination of the **istream** and **ostream** classes to allow both input and output on a stream.

Class Interface Specification:

```
iostream_withassign
```

Declared in:

```
<iostream.h>
```

Derived from:

```
iostream
```

Base for:

None

Contains:

None

Constructors:

```
iostream_withassign( )
```
Default constructor, calls **iostream**'s constructor.

Destructors:

~iostream_withassign

Protected Data Members:

None

Protected Member Functions:

None

Public Data Members:

None

Public Member Functions:

None

DESCRIPTION iostream_withassign adds an assignment operator.

Class Interface Specification:

strstream

Declared in:

<strstrea.h>

Derived from:

strstreambase
iostream

Base for:

None

Contains:

None

Constructors:

strstream( )
Creates a dynamic **strstream**.

Destructors:

```
~strstream( )
```

Protected Data Members:

None

Protected Member Functions:

None

Public Data Members:

None

Public Member Functions:

```
char *str( )
```
Returns and freezes the buffer. The user must deallocate if it was dynamic.

DESCRIPTION **strstream** provides for simultaneous input and output on a **strstreambuf.**

Class Interface Specification:

```
strstreambase
```

Declared in:

```
<strstrea.h>
```

Derived from:

```
ios
```

Base for:

```
strstream
istrstream
ostrstream
```

Contains:

```
strstreambuf
```

Constructors:

```
strstreambase( )
```
Creates an empty **strstreambase**.
```
strstreambase(char *, int, char *start)
```
Creates a **strstreambase** with a specified buffer and starting position.

Destructors:

```
~strstreambase
```

Protected Data Members:

None

Protected Member Functions:

None

Public Data Members:

None

Public Member Functions:

```
strstreambuf * rdbuf( )
```
Returns a pointer to the **strstreambuf** associated with this object.

DESCRIPTION **strstreambase** specializes **ios** to string streams.

APPENDIX D

Glossary

3GL (third-generation language interface) Provides a level of abstraction above assembly language. Pascal, Fortran, Basic, Cobol, Algo, C, and Modula2 are examples of 3GL languages.

4GL (fourth-generation language interface) Provides a complete development environment that includes screen management, windowing capabilities, and high-level debugging capabilities.

Abstraction In object-oriented programming, it is defined as a mental activity that allows one to conceptualize a problem with the detail that is necessary for the current context.

Active The window or the icon that is in current use or currently selected.

Aggregation A relationship between objects where objects represent the constituent components that are associated with an object representing the complete assembly.

Algorithm A series of well-defined, step-by-step instructions that produce a solution to a problem in a finite number of steps.

Architecture Refers to the manner in which a system is divided into subsystems, and how those subsystems interact with one another.

ANSI American National Standards Institute.

Array An indexed data structure used to store data elements of the same data type.

Base Class The class that a derived class inherits. The relationship between the base and derived class depends on the access of the base class. If the access is public, then public elements of the base class will be public in the derived class, and protected elements in the base class remain protected in the derived class. If the access is private, then public and protected elements of the base class become private in the derived class.

351

Bit   A binary digit, the smallest unit of information that is usable by a computer. A bit is represented by either a 0 or a 1, and designates either the ON or OFF state.

Blob (Binary large object)   A blob is a data structure. Usually, a blob contains multimedia data. The multimedia data may be digitized sound, digitized video, graphics bitmaps, graphics metafiles, or digitized music.

Blob Stream   An object-oriented stream that inserts or extracts binary large objects. Blob streams are used to encapsulate multimedia I/O.

Block Device   A device that is capable of reading and writing chunks of data at a time. A typical block of data is 512 bytes.

Buffer   A holding area or transit area for data coming from an input device or going to an output device. Buffers are used to increase the efficiency of I/O operations.

Calling program   A program that calls, or invokes, a function or procedure.

Character Device   A device that processes data one byte or nibble at a time. Character devices are usually serial in nature.

Child Class   The same as a derived class—a child class inherits another class called the parent class. Child describes the relationship between itself and the parent class.

Class   An encapsulation of characteristics, attributes, and functionality that models some person, place, thing, or idea. A class is the implementation of an abstract data type with a designated set of behaviors. A class describes a type of data with specific operations that can be performed on that data.

Class (abstract level)   An interface that defines the behavior of its objects.

Class (implementation)   A unit that describes a set of data and its related operations.

Class Attribute   An attribute for which every instance of that class has the same value.

Class Descriptor   A metaclass that describes the attributes and methods of the class. It is an object that describes the class itself. An instance of the class will need to refer only to the class descriptor instead of individual references to every behavior.

Class Relationship Diagram   Design and documentation tool used to describe the relationships between classes in a software system. The class relationship diagram consists of four basic components:

- Relationship symbol
- Flow lines
- Horizontal and vertical specification
- A class grouping symbol

Concurrent   Events or tasks that are concurring simultaneously.

Constraint   Used to restrict operations on objects that may violate certain conditions that must remain true.

Containment   A relationship that exists between classes. In the containment relationship, the containing class owns the contained class. The containment class does not express inheritance, but rather privileged access and component connectivity.

Constructor   A C++ function that initializes a newly created instance of a class.

Data Structure   A logical or physical organization and representation of computer-based information or data. The standard data structures are: files, arrays, linked lists, stacks, queues, trees, and graphs. The new data structures include audio blobs and visual blobs.

Data Type   A set of data elements with a range of applicable operations that can be performed on them.

Declaration   One or more instructions that specify a type, characteristic, or amount of data associated with the identifier. Storage is not allocated at time of declaration.

Definition   Specifies a name and a set of attributes of a variable and allocates storage.

Delete Operator   Used to deallocate memory. The memory is deallocated with the delete operator if the memory was dynamically created by the *new* operator.

Derived Class   A class that has inherited a base class. A derived class is also called a child class, or the descendant of the base class. The derived class may or may not have its own data members or member functions.

Device Dependency   A condition of software design and implementation. If the software execution depends on the particular structure or architecture of a device or devices, the software is device-dependent. Device dependency is incremental and can be measured on a continuum. Some software can be more device-dependent than others.

Device Independency   The measure of how little a software design or implementation relies on the hardware structure or architecture for its accurate execution.

Dynamic (or Late) Binding   The capability to bind the variables dynamically to objects at runtime.

Dynamic Encapsulation   Combines data and/or operations into a single, well-defined programming unit.

Enumerated Data Types   A set of data that are defined by a programmer in a particular program.

Event Driven   Refers to a model of I/O, or to programming that involves either hardware or software responding to signals or conditions in an asynchronous manner.

Extensibility   The ease with which software allows enhancements (adding of new objects and functionality due to changes in specifications) with little or no modification of existing design.

Field   An item of meaningful data.

FIFO (First-In-First-Out)   FIFO is normally associated with queues.

File   A data structure consisting of a sequence of components. It is usually associated with program I/O, a means by which the program communicates with the outside world. It can contain data, programs, or both.

File Stream   Provides a means for data to flow between the program and the outside world.

File Stream Buffer   The connection between a program and the file components.

Function   A subprogram that returns a single value or a set of values, or performs some specific task.

Index   An ordered data structure of a table that provides rapid optimized access to the data stored in the table. The data can be accessed rapidly by the system in which the index is used.

Information Hiding   Accomplished when there exists a relationship between the data and its related operations, such that performed operations outside the unit cannot affect the data inside the unit. This can be called *encapsulation*.

Inheritance   Provides the means for building new classes from existing classes. Instead of designing a completely new class, inheritance allows the characteristics of the parent class to be contained in the child class. The inheritance relationship is a set union between the classes under consideration.

Inline Function   A function whose implementation is coded following the function header.

Instance   An object that has been created from a class. The class describes the structure of the instance, while the current state of the instance is defined by the operations performed on the instance. The instance is also known as a *run-time class*.

Instantiation   The process of creating an object from a class.

IS-A   A relationship between a derived class and its base class. The derived class IS An instance of the base class. The IS-A relationship is accomplished through the inheritance mechanism.

ISO   International Standard Organization.

Logical I/O   Input and output operations performed without concern to the physical structure of the data.

Macro   A set of precoded source statements added to a source module by an assembler or compiler preprocessor in reply to a source reference.

Member   Any element in a structure or class.

Message   A call to a member function.

Metaclass   A base class for other classes. The metaclass contains operations that the derived classes can understand.

Method   A function or procedure that implements a unit of action or functionality for a class or instance of a class.

Methodology   The standard procedure for performing a task.

MIDI (Musical Instrument Digital Interface)   A standard for representing digitized music and commands to synthesized instruments.

Multimedia   A form of representation that can combine text, graphics, voice, sound, animation, full-motion video, and music in a single medium. The medium must contain at least two members from the aforementioned list to be classified as multimedia.

Multimedia Stream   The extension of **iostream** classes to encapsulate multimedia I/O operations and data.

Multiple Inheritance   Occurs when a derived class inherits more than one base class in a nonlinear fashion.

New Operator   Used to dynamically allocate memory.

NULL Class   The class that contains no data member or member functions. The NULL class is a member of every class.

Object   The instantiation of a class that models some person, place, thing, or idea. The object is the runtime version of a class. In object-oriented programming, the object represents the runtime unit of modularity.

Object Model   Defines the detailed structure and behavior of each object of the system.

Object-Oriented Database   An object-based database management system that provides ordered storage and retrieval of data in the form of encapsulated objects. A true object-oriented database management system provides object orientation at both the back and front end.

Object-Oriented Stream   The application of object-oriented design and programming techniques to the device I/O stream concept.

Object Programming Language   A language that supports the object paradigm. It provides support for programming of object classes, methods, inheritance, and so on. For a language to be considered object-oriented, it must support at least encapsulation, inheritance, and polymorphism.

Operation   As defined for object-oriented programming, *operation* is some kind of transformation that can be applied to the behavior of a class.

Operating System   A collection of programs that control the operation of the computer. The operating system provides the programming with a virtual machine. The operating system also insulates the programmer from the details of peripherals connected to the computer.

Overloaded Constructor   Performs different tasks, depending on argument type and the number of arguments that it receives.

Parameter   Data that is received by a function in order for it to perform.

Parent Class   The same as the base class; it is the relationship that exists between a class (child) that inherits another class (parent).

Pointer   Used to represent a memory address. It can point to the addresses of different data types. Another name for pointer is Address Variable.

Polling   The calling of a series of terminals, or checking a series of buffers, one by one, to see if they have data to transmit.

Polymorphism   The property that allows an operation to have a single message or interface and perform differently, depending upon the data type. The implementations are defined differently, but the function or procedure maintains the same interface for each implementation. The correct implementation is executed at runtime. Polymorphism allows for class telescoping. Using polymorphism, a class can be designed that models the behavior of all future classes that derive from it.

Private   Attributes of a class that can be accessed only by the methods defined within the class.

Protected   Attributes of a class accessible to both the base class and any derived class methods.

Protoclass   The set difference between *N* classes. Given a class *M* with the members {1,2,3,4,5}, and a class *P* with the members {1,2,3,4,5,6}, the protoclass of *P* will be {6}. Every class has a protoclass and a NULL class.

Pseudocode   An informal set of English-like statements accepted within the computer industry to represent common computer programming operations. Pseudocode can be used to describe the steps in an algorithm.

Public   Attributes of a class that can be accessed by any method in any other object.

Query   A request for action or for data. Queries are also database commands that return selected values. The database is not modified.

Queue   A memory storage structure composed of a list, or sequences, of data elements. Queues have a FIFO (first-in-first-out) structure. All insertions of elements into the queue are made at one end of the queue, and all deletions are made at the other end of the queue (the front of the queue).

Reading   Obtaining data from an input device or a data structure.

Redefinition   Used to redefine the features inherited by a derived class from its base class. The redefinition is intended to create a different implementation other than the one inherited from the base class. The redefined version of a feature has arguments that match those of the original in number. The method used to redefine the feature will determine whether the correct version is chosen during runtime or compile time.

Runtime Error   Occurs when a program attempts to perform an illegal operation, as defined by the laws of mathematics, logic, or the particular compiler in use.

Segment   A variable-length, independently addressed portion of a program that can be loaded into a noncontiguous memory.

Single Inheritance   Occurs when a derived class inherits from base class in a linear fashion.

Specialization   The process of modifying or extending the functionality of a class or set of classes through inheritance to handle new data representation or functionality.

Spooling   On input, *spooling* is the transferring of data to secondary storage, and holding them for processing. On output, spooling is the transferring of data to secondary storage for eventual output.

Stream   An input and output abstraction that represents data going to or from devices as generic sequences of bytes. Ideally, the device is some generic device, and the data can be streamed to the device without regard for specific or particular hardware structure. The stream concept promotes device-independence.

Structure   A collection of data members, or data fields, and function members. Also called *struct*.

Structural Model   Describes the structural properties of objects from a static perspective. These properties include the logical elements of the objects required for the application.

Structured Design   A methodology that requires software to be designed using a top/down modular approach. Structured design also uses the technique of stepwise refinement.

Structured Programming   Allows programs to be written using well-defined control structures and independent program modules, with well-defined interfaces.

Subclass   A derived version of another class. The derived version is redefined.

Superclass   A base class for derived classes. A superclass is an *ancestor* class.

Syntax Error   An error created by violating the required syntax, or grammar, of a programming language.

System Architecture   Describes the components of the system, the services provided by each component, and the manner in which these components interact.

System Design   Describes the planned intentions for the procedures performed by each component of the system; the role of each component in these procedures; the data elements used and saved for these procedures; and result of these procedures.

Table   An ordered set of information organized in rows and columns. Table is another name for *array* or *matrix*.

Virtual Function   Has the same name but different implementations for various classes within a class family. A virtual function is dynamically bound. Virtual functions are used to implement runtime polymorphism.

White Space   Blanks, tabs, new lines, formfeeds, and so on, are all forms of white space.

Writing   Often associated with the output of data to a display monitor, printer, or file. In addition, data can be *written* to such data structures as arrays, structs, or objects. A write operation is usually a destructive operation.

Windowing   One among many techniques employed in user-interface design and development. Windowing creates logical groups of input areas and output areas on a display unit. These logical groups are separated by frames, colors, location, size, and sometimes level. Designers and developers refer to these visual segregations of data as windows. The logical groupings can represent different functional parts within one application, or different applications sharing the same display unit, where each window represents a different application.

APPENDIX E

Bibliography and Reference

Abel, Peter. *IBM PC Assembly Language and Programming*, Second Edition. Englewood Cliffs, NJ: Prentice Hall, 1991.

Adams, Lee. *High-Performance Graphics in C Animation and Simulation*. Blue Ridge Summit, PA: Windcrest, 1988.

Andleigh, Prabhat K. and Michael R. Gretzinger. *Distributed Object-Oriented Data Systems Design*. Englewood Cliffs, NJ: Prentice Hall, 1992.

ANSI Committee Document, 1994. Doc. No. X3J16/94-0027 W621/NO414.

Asante, Molefi Kete. *Kemet, Afrocentricity, and Knowledge*. Trenton, NJ: Africa World Press, 1990.

Baker, Louis. *C Mathematical Function Handbook*. New York: McGraw-Hill, 1992.

Banks, Michael A. *The Modem Reference*, Second Edition. New York: Brady Books, 1991.

Barkakati, Nabajyoti. *The Waite Group's Turbo C++ Bible*. Carmel, IN: SAMS, 1990.

Berger, Marc. *Computer Graphics with Pascal*. Menlo Park, CA: Benjamin Cummings Publishing, 1986.

Benedikt, Michael, editor. *Cyberspace: First Steps*, Fourth Edition. Cambridge, MA: MIT Press, 1992.

Berkley, Edmund C. and Lawrence Wainwright. *Computers, Their Operations and Applications*. New York: Reinhold Publishing, 1956.

Berry, John. *The Waite Group's C++ Programming*. Indianapolis: Howard W. SAMS, 1988.

Blain, Derrel R., Kurt R. Delimon, and William J. English. *Real-World Programming for OS/2 2.11*, Second Edition. Indianapolis, IN: SAMS Publishing, 1994.

Campbell, Joe. *C Programmer's Guide to Serial Communications*. Carmel, IN: SAMS, 1987.

Christian, Kaare. *Borland C++ Techniques and Utilities*. Emeryville, CA: Ziff Davis Press, 1993.

Conger, James L. *Windows API Bible: The Definitive Programmer's Reference*. Mill Valley, CA: Waite Group Press, 1992.

Conger, Jim. *Windows API New Testament*. Corte Madera, CA: Waite Group Press, 1993.

Cox, Brad J. *Object-Oriented Programming: An Evolutionary Approach*. Reading, MA: Addison-Wesley, 1986.

Davis, Phillip J. and Reuben Hersh. *The Mathematical Experience.* Boston: Houghton Mifflin, 1981.

Davis, William S. *Operating Systems: A Systematic View,* Third Edition. Reading, MA: Addison-Wesley, 1987.

Eckel, Bruce. *C++ Inside and Out.* Berkeley, CA: Osborne McGraw-Hill, 1993.

Ellis, Margaret A. and Bjarne Stroustrup. *The Annotated C++ Reference Manual.* Reading, MA: Addison-Wesley, 1990.

Ezzell, Ben. *Graphics Programming in Turbo C++: An Object-Oriented Approach.* Reading, MA: Addison-Wesley, 1990.

Ferraro, Richard F. *Programmer's Guide to the EGA and VGA Cards,* Second Edition. Reading, MA: Addison-Wesley, 1990.

Harmon, Paul and David King. *Expert Systems.* New York: John Wiley & Sons, 1985.

Heimlich, Richard, David M. Golden, Ivan Luk, and Peter M. Ridge. *Sound Blaster: The Official Book.* Berkeley, CA: Osborne McGraw-Hill, 1993.

Jacobson, Ivar, Magnus Christerson, Patrik Jonsson, and Gunnar Övergaard. *Object-Oriented Software Engineering: A Use Case-Driven Approach.* Workingham, England: Addison-Wesley, 1992.

Kolatis, Maria Shopay. *Mathematics for Data Processing and Computing.* Reading, MA: Addison-Wesley, 1985.

Luse, Marv. *Bitmapped Graphics Programming in C++.* Reading, MA: Addison-Wesley, 1993.

McCracken, D.D. *Digital Computer Programming.* New York: John Wiley & Sons; London: Chapman & Hall, 1957.

Meyer, Bertrand. *Object-Oriented Software Construction.* New York: Prentice Hall, 1988.

Norton, Peter and Robert Jourdain. *The Hard Disk Companion.* New York: Brady Books, 1988.

Petzold, Charles. *OS/2 Presentation Manager Programming.* Emeryville, CA: Ziff Davis Press, 1994.

Petzold, Charles. *Programming Windows 3.1,* Third Edition. Redmond, WA: Microsoft Press, 1992.

Plauger, P.J. *The Standard C Library.* Englewood Cliffs, NJ: Prentice Hall, 1992.

Schildt, Herbert. *Using Turbo C++.* Berkeley, CA: Osborne McGraw-Hill, 1990.

Seyer, Martin D. *RS-232 Made Easy: Connecting Computers, Printers, Terminals, and Modems,* Second Edition. Englewood Cliffs, NJ: Prentice Hall, 1991.

Sippl, Charles J. *Computer Dictionary,* Fourth Edition. Indianapolis: Howard W. SAMS, 1985.

Tanenbaum, Andrew S. *Operating Systems Design and Implementation.* Englewood Cliffs, NJ: Prentice Hall, 1987.

Teale, Steve. *C++ IOSTREAMS Handbook.* Reading, MA: Addison-Wesley, 1993.

Watt, Alan. *Fundamentals of Three-Dimensional Computer Graphics.* Workingham, England: Addison-Wesley, 1989.

INDEX